RESEARCH METHODS FOR SPORT STUDIES

This comprehensive and accessible textbook is essential reading for those undertaking research into sport from a social science or management approach, either as part of an academic course, or for those employed within sport-related industries.

It provides a step-by-step guide to the research process, from the concept stage through to the presentation of results. Throughout the book, the research methodology is brought to life through the use of relevant case studies and examples. The book covers key topics such as:

- Conceptual methods
- Selecting the appropriate research design
- Undertaking a literature review
- Using a range of key research methods such as questionnaires, interviews, content analysis and ethnographic studies
- Interpreting your data, including guides to descriptive and inferential statistics
- Writing a research report

Designed exclusively for students in sport studies, this book is essential reading for students undertaking a research project or dissertation.

Chris Gratton is Professor of Sport Economics and Director of the Leisure Industries Research Centre at Sheffield Hallam University. He was chair of the sports-related subjects panel in RAE 2001 and has published extensively in the area.

Ian Jones is a senior lecturer in Sport and Leisure Studies at the University of Luton. He teaches research methods to sport and leisure students at undergraduate, masters and doctoral levels.

RESEARCH METHODS
FOR SPORT STUDIES

CHRIS GRATTON AND IAN JONES

Routledge
Taylor & Francis Group

LONDON AND NEW YORK

First published 2004
by Routledge
11 New Fetter Lane, London EC4P 4EE

Simultaneously published in the USA and Canada
by Routledge
29 West 35th Street, New York, NY 10001

Routledge is an imprint of the Taylor & Francis Group

Designed and typeset in Zapf Humanist and Eras by
Keystroke, Jacaranda Lodge, Wolverhampton, West Midlands
Printed and bound in Great Britain by MPG Books Ltd, Bodmin

British Library Cataloguing in Publication Data
A catalogue record for this book is available from the British Library

Library of Congress Cataloging in Publication Data
A catalog record for this book has been requested

ISBN 0–415–26877–x (hbk)
ISBN 0–415–26878–8 (pbk)

CONTENTS

3 THE RESEARCH PROCESS   31

4 RESEARCH QUESTIONS, AIMS AND OBJECTIVES   38

5 REVIEWING THE LITERATURE   50

6 THEORIES, CONCEPTS AND VARIABLES IN SPORT RESEARCH 71

7 RESEARCH DESIGNS FOR SPORTS STUDIES 91

13 ANALYSING DATA II: QUALITATIVE DATA ANALYSIS 217

14 WRITING THE RESEARCH REPORT 228

PREFACE

The growth in sport as an area of academic interest has stimulated much research in the many areas encompassed by the term 'sport studies', as can be seen by the growth in research-based books and journals over recent years. Yet still there is much to be learnt, and research has a significant part to play in the future of sport as an academic subject, especially if it is to gain the academic credibility accorded to other, longer established fields. Despite the rapid expansion of academic courses in sport-related studies, there are few specialist texts available for the sports researcher approaching the subject from the social sciences perspective. The sports scientist, for example, may use a text such as Thomas and Nelson (2001), but for those interested in the more social or management-based aspects of sport, there are few available resources. New or inexperienced researchers in these fields are required to utilise sources more focused on leisure studies, or more generic research methods texts. Whilst these texts are often excellent, we think that it is important to be able to ground some of the theoretical concepts involved in a sporting context, so that researchers may be able to contextualise what may otherwise seem to be highly abstract accounts of the research process.

This book has a number of objectives:

1   To stimulate interest in sports research, to inform the student as to the importance of research in developing knowledge, and to encourage the student to both read further research, and more importantly, carry out their own research into areas of sporting interest.
2   To act as a practical handbook for researchers. Rather than to be read in one go, the text acts as a resource that the researcher can refer to at different times during the research process.

3   To relate elements of the research process to actual examples of sports research, so that the theory introduced can be related to actual practice.

The text, although providing a full introduction to research methods in sport studies, is not exhaustive, and students are encouraged to read further into particular areas of interest or specialisation. We are, for reasons of space, unable to include a full description of different types of statistical analysis, for example. We have, however, provided an overview, which will be enough for some students. Others will require further or more advanced information, and for such students, we would recommend the use of one of the many available statistical textbooks (for example Vincent 1995). Alternatively, those focusing on qualitative data may wish to read Miles and Huberman (1994) for a much fuller account of the differing methods of qualitative analysis than we could provide here. In the same way, the chapter on using the Internet lists only selected resources, as a full list is beyond the scope of this volume.

This handbook will hopefully be of interest to a wide audience. Its primary audience will be students undertaking courses in sports-related studies, including sport management, the sociology of sport, sports marketing, sport-related tourism, physical education, recreation management and other similar degrees. It is not aimed, however, at those undertaking research into the natural sciences and sport, and for those whose interests lie more in the physiology or anatomy of sport, we would suggest an alternative text such as Thomas and Nelson's *Research Methods in Physical Activity* (2001). This text is also aimed at those working in the sport industry, where research may be a requirement of the position (a requirement, we would argue, that applies to the majority of jobs in the field).

One theme that is central to the text is that there is no one correct way of doing research. The 'best' way of undertaking research depends on several factors, for example the nature of the research question, the skills of the researcher, the intended outcomes of the research, the availability of time and resources and so on, so that each research question has its own unique characteristics that need to be taken into account. A good researcher will have the flexibility to adapt to such factors, rather than being constrained by a particular approach or doctrine. A second theme is the need to view research as integral to knowledge about sport, rather than as 'abstract', or removed (from our experience, it is sometimes the case that students cannot always see the relevance of a research methods course to their own personal interests or agenda). A number of examples are provided within the text to link knowledge about sport to research methods, and to demonstrate the links between the research process and our academic understanding of sport.

A number of more experienced researchers may be disappointed with the relative lack of attention given to some of the more complex philosophical debates underlying sports research. We have avoided a detailed discussion of this for two main reasons. First we feel that, especially among inexperienced researchers, spending time on such debates may well detract from the actual experience of research: a novice researcher should not be overly concerned as to whether their approach is post-positivist, postmodernist or somewhere between the two, or whether they should be considering issues related to a radical feminist epistemology. Secondly, for those interested in such matters, there are other, more specialist texts available that do more justice to the subject than we could here, and we would suggest the interested student will use such texts to develop their own interests in such matters.

THE STRUCTURE OF THE BOOK

This book is based upon the concept of the 'research process'. Whilst it could be argued that our conceptualisation of the research process is perhaps too neat and tidy, and that 'real life' research rarely follows such a structured approach, it is, nevertheless, a useful framework upon which to develop an understanding of sport research. The first chapters introduce the concepts and traditions of research, and are concerned with the underlying theory and philosophy of sports research. Chapter 1 introduces the concept of 'research', and its role within sport studies. Chapter 2 outlines some of the differing approaches to the nature and acquisition of knowledge. Chapter 3 then introduces the concept of the 'research process', around which the remainder of the book is based. The first stage of the research process is that of selecting an appropriate topic for investigation, and Chapter 4 outlines some of the strategies that can be used to identify and assess suitable research questions, aims and objectives. The next stage is to read around the subject, and Chapter 5 introduces the concept of the literature review, the actual processes of finding and reviewing the literature, and writing this review in an appropriate format. Chapter 6 then introduces the importance of identifying the appropriate theories, concepts and variables within a research project. Chapter 7 describes some of the different designs you can use to carry out your research. Together, these first seven chapters provide you with the 'background' information essential to understanding the nature of research itself, and the issues specific to the development of your own research project.

The second part of the text is concerned with the issues related to actually undertaking a research project. Chapters 8 to 11 look at some of the data collection methods that you can use to collect your own data. We examine the use of questionnaires, interviews and unobtrusive methods in these chapters, as well as introducing a particular methodological approach, that of sports ethnography, in Chapter 11.

The third part of the book is concerned with the analysis of the data that you will collect, and the reporting of the research. Chapter 12 outlines some of the techniques of analysing quantitative data, and introduces *SPSS for Windows* as a tool for the analysis of quantitative data. Chapter 13 describes how to analyse and make sense of the qualitative data that you may collect. Chapter 14 discusses putting it all together, in terms of writing up your research report. The Internet is becoming an increasingly important tool, and Chapter 15 outlines the use of the Internet in sport research. We have also included a further chapter – Chapter 16 – especially for those undertaking research as part of a taught course, for example those undertaking a final year dissertation as part of a degree course in Sport Studies, where some of the specific issues of student research are covered.

USING THE BOOK

It is likely that you will be using this book in one of two ways. First, you may be undertaking a research methods course as part of a wider programme in Sport Studies. If so, the content of the book is designed to be consistent with a typical teaching schedule (schedules will vary considerably, however the content tends to remain relatively constant). In this case, you may well find yourself reading the book sequentially. Secondly, you may be using it as a handbook to assist you with an actual research project, in which case you may be more selective in your approach. For example you may wish to read the chapter on student issues at an early stage.

Whatever your situation, we have provided a number of activities at the end of each chapter. The general activities will be suitable for those learning about research, and provide valuable experience of some of the elements of the research process. Other activities will be more appropriate to help you whilst you are actually carrying out the research, and will help you in assessing your own research.

Finally, it is important that you view research as an opportunity, whether it be an opportunity to engage with an area that attracts you, an opportunity to develop your own interests, an opportunity for personal development, or even as a personal challenge which will test your abilities to the full. Whichever it is, we hope that you will enjoy the research process and be successful in your research career.

Chris Gratton
Ian Jones
March 2003

CHAPTER ONE

WHAT IS RESEARCH?

In this chapter we will:

- Introduce the concept of 'research'.
- Discuss some of the reasons why we undertake research.
- Outline the different types of research.
- Describe how to approach the reading of research articles.

Research – 'Any honest attempt to study a problem systematically or to add to man's knowledge of a problem may be regarded as research.' (Theodorson and Theodorson 1969 cited in Reber 1995, p.663)

The aim, as far as I can see, is the same in all sciences. Put simply and cursorily, the aim is to make known something previously unknown to human beings. It is to advance human knowledge, to make it more certain or better fitting . . . the aim is, as I have said, discovery. (Elias 1986, p.20)

INTRODUCTION

Imagine that you are competing in a major sporting event. How are you going to approach this occasion? There will be two basic ways you can do so. First, you can simply not worry, and hope everything goes well on the day, and hope that whatever tactics you come up with are successful. Alternatively you can spend time training specifically for the event, by learning appropriate strategies and tactics, finding out the strengths and weaknesses of your opposition, finding out how others have fared against them in the past, and coming up with a detailed game plan based on the evidence that you collect. It is likely that the second method will give you the best chance of succeeding, and that the first option will leave you at best under prepared, leaving the result of the competition down to luck (at least on your side . . . it is likely that your opponents will have chosen the second alternative!).

Now consider the following questions about sport:

- Why do we participate in sport?
- What influences us in the types of sport that we choose to play or watch?
- How important is sport in social or economic terms?

These are just some of the questions that a student, sports manager, administrator, coach or sports enthusiast may be interested in. Again, these and other such questions about sport may be answered in two ways. The first way is through guesswork, personal opinion, anecdotal evidence and so on. Obviously this is not a satisfactory means to suggest answers upon which to base provision, policies, strategies, recommendations and so on. The second way they may be answered is through a logical, systematic approach, designed to maximise your chances of success, or, in other words, through undertaking *research*. Research implies 'a careful and systematic means of solving problems' (Thomas and Nelson 2001, p.3). It is the lifeblood of any academic discipline, and is the fundamental basis for our knowledge about sport. As Daniel Wann (1997) suggests: 'Quality research is the lifeblood of any scientific discipline. Without it, disciplines would stagnate, failing to advance past their current limits and understanding' (p.17).

In an area such as sport, which – despite its enormous social, economic, cultural and political significance – has emerged relatively recently as an area of academic interest, research is vital. As this book is being written, our knowledge about sport is substantial. We do know, for example, that most individuals are socialised into sport through their parents, schools, peers and the mass media. We know that sport performs a number of social functions, for example socio-emotional, political or integrative. We know that sport is big business, and that the money involved in both consumer and corporate spending on sport is increasing year on year. We know this because these are just some of the wide range of questions that have formed the basis for research projects in sport. Even a brief examination of some of the recent issues of research-based journals such as the *Sociology of Sport Journal*, or the *Journal of Sport Management* will provide an illustration of the variety and scale of sport research that has been, and is currently being, undertaken.

2

JOURNAL

Although the term 'journal' may describe a number of different types of publication, we will generally be referring to academic journals within this text. Academic journals are generally published several times a year and report the most up to date research on a particular area of interest, such as the economics of sport, or sports marketing. Most academic journal articles have undergone some form of refereeing process, whereby the quality and rigour of each article is assessed by a number of reviewers, each of whom will be an expert in their field. This ensures that the articles within such a journal are of an appropriate standard. Some sports-related journals include:

- *Sociology of Sport Journal*
- *Journal of Sport Management*
- *Journal of Sport Behavior*
- *Journal of Sport and Social Issues*
- *International Review for the Sociology of Sport*
- *European Journal of Sport Management*
- *European Sport Management Quarterly*
- *Culture, Sport and Society*

These journals are all published in paper form, however you can also access them, and many other journals, electronically through your library. Journals will index their content on a number of databases that your library will have access to. Thus, you can search journals for specific keywords related to your own research project.

Our understanding of sport is, however, far from complete. Changing social, political, technological and economic contexts all influence, and are influenced by, sport. Thus our knowledge is never absolute, and it is only through continual research that our understanding of sport is maintained and enhanced.

Research is not only for academia, however, and the skills associated with research are not just important for those wishing to publish in academic journals. The enormous growth in sports employment in recent years has led to countless professions where a knowledge of research methods is important. Those employed in the

3

sports marketing industry, for example, may need to be able to assess the effectiveness of a particular promotional strategy. Sport development officers may need to assess the reasons for non-participation in physical activity by members of a particular community. Governments may wish to measure the economic impacts of a particular sporting event, and so on. To be able to carry out such tasks, a wide range of research skills are required. The need for effective research is a continual one, and such skills are highly valued by a wide range of employers.

WHAT DO WE MEAN BY 'RESEARCH'?

Before embarking on the various methods and techniques of research, it is important to spend a bit more time considering what we actually mean by the term 'research'. A brief examination of different research methods textbooks will soon demonstrate the variety of different definitions of research, each definition correct in its own way.

Rather than spend time debating the merits of others' definitions, we shall use a relatively simple definition of our own at this stage, suggesting that:

> Research is a systematic process of discovery and advancement of human knowledge.

We are aware that this definition itself – like any other – is open to criticism. Through undertaking the process of research yourself, however, you will develop much more of an understanding of what research actually is than by reading and debating the validity of various textbook definitions. Even through simply reading research articles, you will soon develop an understanding of research, without necessarily being able to produce a clear, unambiguous definition yourself. It is this understanding, as well as a personal interest in research, that is more important to you as a researcher.

THE CHARACTERISTICS OF RESEARCH

Leedy (1985) and Walliman (2001) note a number of characteristics of research. These include the following:

1   Research is generated by a specific research question, hypothesis or problem.
2   Research follows a specific plan or procedure – the *research process*.

3 Research aims at increasing understanding by interpreting facts and reaching conclusions based on those facts.
4 Research requires reasoned argument to support conclusions.
5 Research is reiterative – it is based on previous knowledge, which it aims to advance, but it may also develop further research questions.

Research is, therefore, more than simply searching for facts. As we suggested earlier, research is a *systematic* investigation to answer a question. Many people associate research simply with methods of data collection such as interviews and questionnaire surveys. Data collection is just one part of a wider process, however, and other stages are equally important. Five important stages can be identified:

1 The stage before data collection, where the researcher decides upon the research question, the aim of the research, the research objectives and the theoretical framework that underlies the research.
2 The stage of designing how to collect the data to answer the question, or the *research design*.
3 The actual data collection stage, where the data is collected by one or more *research methods*.
4 The analysis of the data – with reference to the theoretical framework adopted – to answer the question.
5 The reporting of the research to communicate the findings to others.

These are all part of what can be termed the *research process*. The research process refers to the various parts of the overall process that guides a research project. This will be dealt with in more depth in Chapter 3.

WHY UNDERTAKE RESEARCH?

As we have already suggested, much of our knowledge about sport is based upon research carried out by others. By undertaking systematic investigation into certain areas, we have increased our knowledge about sport dramatically in recent years. The ways in which knowledge can be advanced by research are outlined by Hussey and Hussey (1997), who summarise the different purposes of research as follows:

- To investigate some existing situation or problem.
- To provide solutions to a problem.

- To explore and analyse more general issues.
- To construct or create a new procedure or system.
- To explain a new phenomenon.
- To generate new knowledge.
- A combination of two or more of any of the above.

Each of these can be fruitfully applied to many different aspects of sport. A further – and equally valid – purpose of research is to allow you to engage with some aspect of sport that interests you, so that you can add to existing knowledge as a personal achievement. Carrying out research into a specific area is one of the best ways to develop your own understanding of a particular area of interest. Finally, you may also wish to enhance your employment prospects in a particular area of sport. Undertaking a detailed piece of research, for example in the form of a student dissertation, is often a good way to convince an employer that you have both interest and competence in a certain area.

THE DIFFERENT TYPES OF RESEARCH

So far we have examined research as a single concept. There are, however, a number of different ways of classifying research, depending upon the purpose of the research, the data that is collected, and how such data is analysed. Four general types exist, these being referred to as *exploratory*, *descriptive*, *explanatory* and *predictive*.

- *Exploratory research*. Exploratory research takes place where there is little or no prior knowledge of a phenomenon. Thus, there is a need for an initial exploration before more specific research can be undertaken. This type of research looks for clues about the phenomenon, attempts to gain some familiarity with the appropriate concepts and looks for patterns or ideas emerging from the data without any preconceived ideas or explanation. A researcher undertaking an investigation into the effects of the Internet upon sports organisations, for example, may well be undertaking exploratory research, as there are unlikely to be any well-established theoretical models available. Exploratory research is generally followed up by further research that tests any ideas or hypotheses generated.
- *Descriptive research*. Descriptive research describes a particular phenom-enon, focusing upon the issue of what is happening, rather than why it is happening. Thus, research to find out how many people attended the 2002 Winter Olympics, and whether more males than females attended, would be

an example of descriptive research. There is no attempt to explain the results obtained.

- *Explanatory research.* This type of research is involved in explaining *why* something happens, and assessing causal relationships between variables. Thus, a researcher interested in why more males attended the 2002 Winter Olympics would be undertaking explanatory research. Explanatory research requires some sort of *theoretical framework* so that explanation may be deduced from the data (theoretical and conceptual frameworks are discussed in more depth in Chapter 6).
- *Predictive research.* Predictive research forecasts future phenomena, based on the interpretations suggested by explanatory research. Thus, the findings from the explanatory research cited above may be used to predict gender differences in attendance during the 2006 Winter Olympics.

PURE AND APPLIED RESEARCH

Each of the types of research we have identified above can also be placed on a continuum between *pure research* and *applied research* depending upon its context. At one end of the continuum, pure research takes place to explore a particular concept, or issue, without regard for a specific problem, and may be carried out to simply gain a better understanding of the overall concepts, for example the development of a model of coaching behaviour. Such research in itself has no immediate value beyond contributing to an area of intellectual inquiry. Applied research, on the other hand, is undertaken to solve a specific problem or provide a solution to a practical question. An example of this may be a particular sports organisation that wishes to explore potential markets, and commissions research to determine demand for a sports-related service or product, or research to explain why individuals drop out from a particular fitness programme after a short period of time.

Both Thomas and Nelson (2001) and Yiannakis (2000) suggest that researchers should – if they are interested in the 'worth' of their research – be prepared to test their findings 'beyond the boundaries of academe' (Yiannakis 2000, p.119). Thus research that tends towards the pure should be followed by further research that applies any findings to a 'real life situation'. In reality, however, research that leans towards the 'pure' tends to be more common in 'academic' circles. Even this research may, however, have future practical value in terms of its application by others provided it is not written in a way that alienates it from those who may find the results useful (Ingham and Donnelly 1992).

PRIMARY AND SECONDARY RESEARCH

There is also a distinction that can be made between primary and secondary research. Primary research generally refers to research that has involved the collection of original data specific to that particular research project, for example through using research methods such as questionnaires or interviews. Secondary research refers to research where no such original data is collected, but the research project uses existing (or secondary) sources of data, for example census data. Most research projects will contain an element of secondary research in establishing and evaluating the types of data that have been collected in previous research projects in the area as part of the literature review (see Chapter 5).

THEORETICAL AND EMPIRICAL RESEARCH

We can also distinguish between *theoretical* and *empirical* research. Theoretical research generally uses the findings from existing works to develop new ideas through analysing existing theory and explanations. These new ideas are not tested through collecting evidence in the form of primary data. Empirical research, on the other hand, supports the development of new ideas through the collection of data (empirical means based upon observation or measurement rather than theoretical reasoning). Thus, a researcher who develops a theory of sport fan violence through visiting a library and developing their own explanation through reading existing work will be undertaking theoretical research. The researcher who takes this one step further and collects data to test their explanation will be undertaking empirical research. Although theoretical research has its merits, we would suggest that you should – if at all possible – support your findings empirically through the collection of primary data.

SOME MISCONCEPTIONS ABOUT RESEARCH

As well as being able to define what is meant by research, it is also useful to describe some of the misconceptions often associated with research.

■ Research is not simply the gathering of existing information. Reading an article on the economic impacts of major sporting events and making notes is not research. Neither is collecting existing information to write an essay or paper on the economic impacts of the Summer Olympics.

8

- Neither is research simply the collection of new data. You may be interested in the reasons why individuals take up competitive tennis. Simply going to a tennis club and asking them is not research.
- Research is not setting out to prove an opinion, based on personal experience. For example you may not attend major sporting events because of ticket prices, and decide to set out to prove that ticket prices are the most important deterrent to attendance.
- Research is not necessarily the production of something completely original. Often students are daunted by the suggestion that they are required to produce some original findings, and often overestimate what is meant by 'original'. Research can, for example, involve the testing of existing theories on new situations, which would still produce original findings. As Veal (1997) notes, there are a number of different ways to make a piece of research original, such as testing an existing theory in a different geographical area, or replicating an existing study using a different methodology (see Chapter 4). The production of significant levels of original knowledge is generally a requirement only of postgraduate degrees such as MPhil or PhD.
- Research does not always involve a problem. Many textbooks – including this one – do use the term 'research problem' frequently. Although research often involves the solving of a problem, it can, as is often the case in theoretical research, simply be done to advance the scope of human knowledge.

UNDERSTANDING SPORTS RESEARCH

By far the best way to begin to develop your initial understanding is to read a variety of actual research. Whilst research textbooks will provide the necessary theoretical grounding, Worsley (1992, p.79) notes that they do tend to 'present an *unreal and idealised* account of research' (his italics). He goes on to suggest that:

> The best way to learn about research methods, apart from conducting research under supervision, is also, alas, the one requiring most effort. Most students . . . reading a book or article pay most attention to the theories or concepts used and the overall argument, some attention to the actual substantive findings, and very little heed to the methods used. This is particularly so if the results are statistical or presented in tabular form. Yet simply paying more attention to how a study was done, what the substantive results were, and assessing whether they support the conclusions, will teach more than reading a dozen texts.

The suggested activity at the end of this chapter involves you reading and assessing some sports research. This is an activity that should not just be done once you have read this particular chapter, but you should ensure that reading and evaluating research is done on a continual basis. You will find that, as your research knowledge increases, you will be able to become more critical of the research, and the methodologies and methods adopted, and be able to more clearly identify the strengths and weaknesses within a piece of research. At first, this may seem a difficult and daunting task, especially if you are reading research undertaken by experts in a particular field. You should persevere, however, as the benefits will be worthwhile. Try not to be put off by the complex statistical analyses employed, or by the – sometimes impenetrable! – academic writing that is often used (especially in some of the more sociologically based pieces of research). You should try initially to find some less complex articles, especially if the research is in an area with which you are not overly familiar.

HOW TO READ RESEARCH

As we suggested earlier, you may find reading research articles a difficult task at the beginning of your research career. Thomas and Nelson (2001) and Baker (1994) provide a few useful pointers to bear in mind whilst you are reading a piece of research.

- *Locate and read a few articles from within a field you are comfortable with.* By doing this, the concepts involved and the technical language often used may not be as big a stumbling block as otherwise may be the case. It is also more likely that you will be able to understand the overall aims of the research.
- *Read studies that are of interest to you.* Do not feel obliged to read through every article at first. Neither should you be afraid to stop reading after you have started if the article is not of interest to you – do not attempt to plough through it! Think of the areas that interest you, and focus on them at the beginning.
- *Read the abstract first.* The abstract will help you decide whether the article is relevant without having to read the entire report. If the article doesn't seem of interest after you have read the abstract, then move on to an article that is of interest.
- *Identify the research question and objectives.* Is the research question a clearly defined hypothesis, or a vague area for investigation? What is the overall aim of the research? What about the objectives?

10

- *Why did the researcher(s) choose a particular setting or sample?* Where was the data collected? Who from? What were the strengths and/or limitations of this choice?
- *What were the methods chosen to collect data?* How were the data collected? Why was this method or methods chosen?
- *What were the most important findings?* Identify the most important findings made by the author. How do these findings relate to the overall research question?
- *Do not be over-concerned with statistical analysis.* Do not pay too much attention to what tests were used, and the level of significance at first. Try simply to determine the general meaning of the results.
- *Be critical but objective.* You may find it difficult to evaluate the research critically, especially considering that it is likely that the reviewing process adopted by most journals would screen out most examples of questionable research. Try to assess, however, the strengths and limitations of the research.

KEY TERM

ABSTRACT

Research reports often commence with an abstract. The abstract is a short section, generally of about 100–200 words, outlining the aims of the research, the methods employed to collect data, the sample from which the data was collected and a summary of the main conclusions. Abstracts allow researchers to identify whether a piece of research will be valuable in their own studies without having to read the entire article.

The second way of learning about research is to undertake it yourself. This is especially useful if, for example, you are to undertake a one-off piece of important research, such as a final year undergraduate or postgraduate dissertation. Try to undertake a small research project beforehand, ideally during your training in research methods, so that you do not approach your research 'cold', but with some awareness of the research process, its potential pitfalls and the time and effort required to undertake a research project.

1   There are a number of definitions of research. Defining research is perhaps less important than understanding its nature.
2   Research is important for the advancement of any academic field or discipline.
3   Research can be classified as exploratory, descriptive, explanatory or predictive depending upon its purpose. It can also be classified as either theoretical or applied depending upon the level of application of the findings to 'real life' situations.
4   Research may involve the collection of new data (primary research) or the use of existing data (secondary research).
5   The best way to begin to develop your understanding of research, its role, and the types of research is to undertake some reading. Choose some appropriate articles, and begin to read!

ACTIVITIES

You should familiarise yourself with the key academic journals in your area of interest. If you are interested in sports management, for example, ensure that you locate and read at least one article from the *Journal of Sport Management* or other appropriate journal. When you have located an article that you are comfortable with, read it with the following questions in mind:

- What is the question being asked in the research?
- How has the author answered the question?
- What type of research is being undertaken – exploratory, descriptive, explanatory or predictive? Is it pure or applied?
- How has the research added to our knowledge about sport?

Once you have become more familiar with research methods, reread the article. Try to identify the particular strengths and weaknesses of the research.

You should also begin your *research diary*. In this diary you should be recording everything of importance to your research, from your ideas from initial brainstorming to contact details of potential informants. Such a diary can be an extremely useful resource, and you should ensure that it is as detailed as possible. Some of the things you may include in such a diary are:

- Summaries of your meetings with tutors/supervisors.
- Ideas relevant to the research, for example in terms of potential information sources, or possible directions for the research.
- Problems that have arisen, and ideas as to how to deal with such problems.
- Short and long term objectives.
- General thoughts about the research process.

FURTHER READING

Rather than suggest any particular reading for this chapter, the activity above should be sufficient. At this stage, however, you should also be reading around your own subject area and beginning to develop a few ideas about your own research!

CHAPTER TWO

RESEARCH TRADITIONS

In this chapter we will:

- Outline the general philosophical approaches underlying the research process.
- Describe the characteristics of qualitative and quantitative research.
- Describe the characteristics of deductive and inductive research.

INTRODUCTION

In Chapter 1 we suggested that one of the aims of sport-related research is to advance our knowledge about sport. Unfortunately, whilst the term 'knowledge' may seem relatively straightforward, there are a number of issues related to what 'knowledge' actually is, and the means by which knowledge can be acquired. Before introducing the practicalities of sports research, and some of the issues of research design and administration, it is important to introduce some of the underlying philosophical issues. The study of the philosophy of knowledge is referred to as *ontology*, and the philosophical study of how such knowledge is acquired is referred to as *epistemology*. The ontological and epistemological positions that researchers take have important implications for the way that research is approached, notably in the type of data that is collected, how such data is collected, the way that such data can be interpreted and the conclusions that can be drawn. Although you may consider that philosophical debates may lack immediate relevance to your research project, we would suggest that an awareness of the debates within these areas is important for two reasons.

1   The issues related to the differing approaches we discuss are implicit to some extent in all research. Thus a broad ontological and epistemological awareness is important so that you can understand the assumptions inherent in different types of research that you may read.

2   This understanding may help you to determine the most appropriate design to answer your research question. Thus, if you are interested in understanding why something happens, then an interpretative approach using an inductive methodology may be more suitable. If, however, you are interested in describing, comparing or measuring, then a positivistic, deductive approach will be more appropriate.

KEY TERMS

ONTOLOGY AND EPISTEMOLOGY

- Ontology refers to the philosophy of the existence and nature of phenomena.
- Epistemology is the branch of philosophy that deals with how knowledge of such phenomena is acquired.

It is important, however, to note that you should not become overly concerned with the issues contained within this chapter at the expense of other aspects of the research process, especially if you are relatively new to research. Unless you are undertaking research at a masters or doctoral level, then you shouldn't worry about these issues in too much depth. Rather you should have a general awareness and understanding of them, and it is worth revisiting this chapter after you have developed your research question, when some of the issues will be more relevant to you.

THE NATURE OF KNOWLEDGE

Two broad approaches to the nature of knowledge exist:

1   Positivism
2   Interpretivism

Each has differing epistemological and ontological assumptions, and each has differing implications for the methodology adopted by the researcher, the data that is collected, and the interpretation of such data.

15

Positivism

Positivism refers to the school of thought that the only 'true' or valid form of knowledge is that which is 'scientific', that is where the principles and methods of the natural sciences (such as chemistry or physics) are used to study human behaviour, which in itself is objective and tangible in nature. In the same way that a chemist can observe the effect of adding one chemical compound to another, make precise observations or measurements, and develop laws of nature, the social researcher can observe human behaviour and measure 'facts', and 'laws' of behaviour can be developed. These 'laws' could then be applied to other contexts to explain or predict future behaviour (one of the early goals of sociologists was to be able to develop a number of such laws that would one day be able to predict all aspects of human behaviour!). Concepts such as feelings, emotions, beliefs and so on have no place in research as they cannot be directly observed or measured, they are unreliable and they are not constant over time. Positivists would assume that the sports environment is relatively stable across different times or settings. Within such a stable context, the precise measurement and analysis of 'facts' allows the development of theories, which can then be tested through further measurement, and used to predict future behaviour. Measurements themselves should be objective and not subject to the influence of the researcher's values or interpretation; others could see the same evidence for themselves and reach the same conclusions based on the evidence. This approach to obtaining knowledge involves precise measurements, which can be controlled or manipulated by the researcher. Such exact measurement allows statistical analysis which provides an impartial and precise answer. Careful research designs can show causal relationships, for example X causes Y. Finally, the whole process of investigation is objective: the researcher has no influence on the findings, and has no personal influence on the results. Such an approach has a number of characteristics, including:

■   *Control*. The researcher is able to control one variable, and assess the influence that it has on another variable, for example the presence of a crowd upon shooting performance in a particular sport. The researcher can control the size of the crowd, measure both the crowd size and performance, and draw inferences from the data.
■   *Replication*. To explain a phenomenon, the same results would need to occur if the experiment was to be repeated, that is an increase in crowd size would always lead to a decrease in performance.
■   *Hypothesis testing*. Positivistic research involves the creation of a *hypothesis*, which can then be systematically tested.

16

HYPOTHESIS

A hypothesis is essentially a predicted result, based on existing knowledge. For example a hypothesis may be that *'Higher income is positively related to higher participation levels in outdoor sports'*. Hypotheses must be *testable,* so that the hypothesis can either be supported or refuted by the research.

Many research projects also present a *null hypothesis*. A null hypothesis suggests that there is no relationship between the variables under investigation. It is the null hypothesis that is tested by statistical analysis (Chapter 12 will examine this issue in more depth).

The positivist approach has its undoubted strengths, notably in terms of precision, control and objectivity. Through precise control and measurement, it is possible to suggest that A causes B, for example. Statistical analysis removes the need for more individualistic or intuitive interpretation, and generally the interpretation is clear cut. Positivist research is also generally more straightforward in terms of planning. Data is normally collected in one go, and analysis of all of the data takes place at one time, therefore it is often a lot easier to anticipate time schedules and plan accordingly, which has the great benefit – especially for student research – of being less risky.

A POSITIVIST STUDY – FACTORS AFFECTING SPECTATOR ATTENDANCE

Wakefield and Sloan (1995) wanted to find out the effect of six factors – team loyalty, parking, cleanliness, crowding, food service and fan behaviour – on sport spectators' desire to attend matches. They developed a number of hypotheses that positive experiences related to each of the factors would result in increased desire to attend future games. A sample of fans provided numerical (and thus precise and objective) data on each factor, and the numerical data was statistically analysed to investigate any apparent relationships (thus removing any ambiguity regarding the interpretation of

17

the data). The statistical analysis determined that fans who had positive experiences in respect of each of the factors were more inclined to attend matches on future occasions, rather than those with negative experiences, thus identifying causal relationships, or 'laws' of behaviour, which could then be applied to other populations. The strengths of the research were that it was carefully controlled, data was collected from a large sample and it was objectively analysed to produce precise results regarding the apparent relationships between experiences and desire to attend. The weaknesses of this approach, as with much positivist research, were that it could not explain the findings with any certainty. For example, crowding was identified as an important deterrent to future attendance. However, the design adopted could not explain *why* this was important (for example whether it was due to physical discomfort, fears about safety, etc.), only that – statistically – it was important!

In your reading you may notice that the early years of sports-related research were dominated by the positivist approach. The approach is still evident; however, for reasons which we will outline below, alternative approaches are becoming more widespread.

VERIFICATION AND FALSIFICATION OF HYPOTHESES

Ideally, if you are adopting a positivist approach, you would like to be able to demonstrate that your hypothesis is true, for example the hypothesis that 'all swans are white'. To test this, first you would have to observe the colour of every swan. This, in itself, is an impossible task. Secondly, you could not be sure that all swans born in the future would be white. Thus, it is almost impossible to completely verify a hypothesis. On the other hand, a sighting of just one black swan would clearly falsify the hypothesis. It is generally much easier to falsify a hypothesis than it is to confirm one, and you should be aware of this when you come to test your own hypotheses and suggest that you have 'proved' it!

Interpretivism

The limitations of the positivist approach are evident, and from these limitations an alternative perspective, or more accurately now a collection of related perspectives – those of interpretivism – have developed. Norbert Elias (1986, p.20), one of the founding figures of the sociology of sport, has argued that:

> Natural scientists, together with the type of philosophers of science who are deeply committed to the belief in the primacy of law-like natural sciences, have used all their intellectual strength and their social power in order to convince others that the 'method' of the natural sciences . . . is the only legitimate method of scientific discovery. The defenders of this view, as a rule, have very little experience in social science research . . . It needs to be said, therefore, clearly and unequivocally, that it is possible to advance knowledge and to make discoveries in the field of sociology with methods which can be very different from those of the natural sciences. The discovery, not the method, legitimises research as scientific.

The key argument of those rejecting the positivist approach is that sport is a social phenomenon, that is those who participate in, watch or manage sports are acted upon by a number of external social forces, but also have free will to respond to such forces in an active way, and are not inanimate objects, whose behaviour can be understood in terms of causal relationships. When examining sport we cannot predict whether X will always cause Y as – unlike the subject matter of the natural sciences – we all have, to differing extents, freedom to act in a number of different ways. Positivism does not take into account intangible concepts related to this freedom, such as feelings or emotions, and the role of such concepts in explaining our sporting behaviour. These concepts form the basis of the interpretative approach. They are not measured numerically – such an approach would argue that these concepts are too complex to be reduced to numbers. Rather, they are 'measured' using words, statements and other non-numerical measures, collecting data from the viewpoint of the participant. The data is then interpreted by the researcher, who attempts to uncover meanings, values, explanations and so on.

The interpretative approach also has its strengths and weaknesses. The strengths are that such an approach allows the researcher to gain an insider's perspective, to try and understand the subjects 'from within'. This may allow concepts that may otherwise be missed by a positivistic approach to be identified, or explained. Interpretive approaches also allow the researcher to explore and uncover explanations, rather than deduce them from measurements. Thus, whereas a positivist approach may suggest a relationship between X and Y, an interpretative approach may be able to describe and explain that relationship from the viewpoint of those being investigated. Although these are the strengths of the interpretative approach, positivists may argue that there are also weaknesses. The subjective nature of interpreting people's thoughts and feelings leads to questions over reliability and validity (we shall deal with these concepts later in the book). The findings are less likely to be generalisable to other settings, and the overall time and resources required to collect such information tends to be greater. This needs to be a consideration, especially within the context of a student project.

CASE STUDY

AN INTERPRETATIVE STUDY – THE CONSTRUCTION OF SPORT SUBCULTURES

Donnelly and Young (1988) were interested in how individuals became socialised into particular sporting subcultures, notably those involved with rugby and rock climbing. Rather than 'measure' the process numerically and identify causal relationships or 'laws' of socialisation as would be the case in a positivist approach, they were interested in the meanings and perceptions held by people as they became socialised into the group. They found that individuals joined groups on the basis of what they had read or learned about them from sources that portrayed stereotypical views, and thus made a number of mistakes when becoming socialised into the group, mistakes that were rectified through further socialisation. By interviewing members of the subcultures, they were able to gather 'rich', non-numerical data related to the complex interactional processes of becoming a member of a group, and highlight the individual's experiences of developing and confirming an identity. The rich description and interpretation of experiences was more informative than simply measuring and statistically analysing variables, and enabled the researchers to describe in depth some of the issues faced by such individuals, such as the stereotypical views of such groups, and the consequent mistakes made in trying to join the group.

Some authors have noted alternative paradigms within the rather broad paradigm of interpretivism. Thus, you may come across approaches labelled *critical theory*, *constructivism, realism* and *critical interpretivism* to name just four. Critical theory emphasises the relationship of social 'reality' within historically situated social structures. Constructivism suggests that multiple realities exist, formed within a particular context. The researcher studies how reality is 'constructed' by the individual within this context. Realism suggests that there is actually a 'real' truth to be discovered, albeit with limitations, and that this truth can be discovered using elements of both the positivist and interpretive approaches. Critical interpretivism is a blend of several overlapping elements, historiography, ethnography, comparison, investigation, critical sociology and 'gonzo' ('gonzo' refers to a particular type of approach that involves the researcher taking a position that is as close as possible to the subject without becoming part of it, and using that position to present a vivid and personalised account). In reality, unless you are researching at postgraduate level, for example as part of a piece of doctoral research, it is generally unlikely that an in-depth examination of these alternative paradigms will be necessary. If you do need further information, then we would suggest you read a more specialist text, such as Lincoln and Guba (1985) for information on the first three, or Sugden and Tomlinson (1999) for an account of critical interpretivism.

QUANTITATIVE AND QUALITATIVE RESEARCH

We have already alluded to the different types of measurement that are associated with positivist and interpretative approaches. This brings us to a second distinction that is often made in research. Rather than referring to the underlying philosophy of the nature of knowledge, this distinction – between qualitative and quantitative research – refers to the characteristics of the data collected by the researcher. In the preceding discussion, it was noted how differing assumptions could be made about the nature of knowledge. These differing assumptions are translated into the use of different types of data. Positivists assume that behaviours can be observed and numerically and objectively measured and analysed. The use of numerical measurement and analysis is referred to as a quantitative approach, that is research that involves measurable 'quantities'. Thus, you may be interested in the relationship between economic investment in sport and subsequent success. You may approach this by measuring how much money has been invested into a particular sport, and measuring performance in that sport in terms of medal counts at major events such as the Olympics. This would give you a set of numerical data, which could then be statistically analysed to determine whether a relationship existed between the two. This is quantitative research. Both variables are directly measurable, and easily converted into numerical form, which can then be statistically analysed (thus closely related to the positivist paradigm).

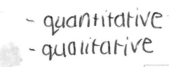
- quantitative
- qualitative

A QUANTITATIVE STUDY –
SKIERS' CONCERNS AND SOMATIC ANXIETY

Bray *et al.* (2000) wanted to investigate the relationship between somatic anxiety and the 'non-performance' aspects of competitive ski racing, for example friends' evaluations of general skiing ability. They measured the concerns of skiers regarding how they were to be evaluated, both performance and non-performance related, and competitive state anxiety. These measurements were all made using scales (see Chapter 8) that generated a numerical score for each aspect. Statistical analysis was then carried out on the numerical data to determine that non-performance-related concerns were significantly related to somatic anxiety, that is the more anxious the skier, the greater their concerns about how others saw them. This piece of research was both positivist and quantitative in nature. It measured variables by assigning them numerical values, which were then subject to statistical analysis, and causal relationships were inferred. The approach was appropriate in that it could identify a relationship between the relevant variables in a clear and objective manner.

Qualitative research, on the other hand, aims to capture qualities that are not quantifiable, that is reducable to numbers, such as feelings, thoughts, experiences and so on, that is those concepts associated with interpretive approaches to knowledge. Qualitative research uses non-numerical data and analysis to describe and understand such concepts. Thus the researcher may take an alternative approach to understanding spectators' intentions to attend matches, by asking them to identify some of the reasons why they would not go to future matches. Such thoughts are difficult to meaningfully convert into numbers, and thus it is data in the form of words that have to be interpreted by the researcher that is relevant. Unlike quantitative research, the issue of 'how many' is not relevant, as Krane *et al.* (1997, p.214) suggest:

> placing a frequency count after a category of experiences is tantamount to saying how important it is; thus value is derived by number. In many cases, rare experiences are no less meaningful, useful, or important than common ones. In some cases, the rare experience may be the most enlightening one.

A QUALITATIVE STUDY – SOURCES OF STRESS IN ELITE FIGURE SKATERS

Scanlan *et al.* (1991) wanted to identify sources of stress amongst top level figure skaters. Rather than simply measure factors causing stress, they wanted to identify the factors suggested by the skaters themselves. Through interviewing 26 elite skaters, they were able to collect rich, non-numerical data. This data was then analysed to suggest that there were five main sources of stress, these being the negative aspects of competing, the negative aspects upon relationships with others, the demands of elite participation, personal struggles, and traumatic events such as failure or injury. The quantitative issues of 'how many' were not important, rather the qualitative issues of the source of stress were considered more important, explaining, rather than describing, thus allowing strategies to be formulated to deal with such stress.

The characteristics of quantitative and qualitative research are summarised in Table 2.1.

THE GROWTH OF QUALITATIVE RESEARCH IN SPORT STUDIES

In certain research areas, for example sports psychology, early research was dominated by positivist, quantitative approaches. Controlled experiments were undertaken in laboratory settings to measure behaviour, and develop 'laws' of human behaviour. Much of this research did provide useful information; however the need to understand the underlying experiences, feelings and emotions related to behaviour has been acknowledged in recent years, and as a consequence qualitative research is taking on increasing importance within sport studies, to the extent now that it is no longer seen as 'inferior' to quantitative research.

Table 2.1 Characteristics of quantitative and qualitative research

Quantitative research	Qualitative research
■ Uses numerical analysis to measure social phenomena to provide 'facts'	■ Relies on non-numerical analysis to provide understanding
■ Assumes a single, objective social reality	■ Assumes social reality is a subjective experience
■ Assumes social reality is constant across different times and settings	■ Assumes social reality is continuously constructed and related to the immediate social context
■ Uses statistical analysis to determine causal relationships	■ Objectives are description, understanding and meaning
■ Studies samples with the intention of generalising to populations	■ Uses smaller samples, or 'cases'
■ Researcher is objective, and 'detached' from the subjects under investigation	■ Data is rich and subjective
	■ The location of the research is often natural
■ The setting is often contrived	■ Flexible approach to data collection
■ Data is collected using inanimate objects, for example pen and paper	■ Often non-traditional approaches, e.g. content analysis
■ Associated with the positivist approach	■ The researcher is the data collection instrument
■ Generally deductive	■ Associated with the interpretative approach
	■ Generally inductive

APPLYING QUALITATIVE TECHNIQUES IN SPORT MARKETING

Smith and Stewart (2001) have noted that qualitative research is under-utilised in the field of sport marketing, suggesting that this may be due to uncertainties about the methods by which qualitative data is collected and analysed, compared with the transparency, conciseness and clarity of quantitative data. Whereas sports managers may be more comfortable with the charts, tables and statistics generated by quantitative research, Smith and Stewart suggest that such research rarely generates hidden, deep or elusive information that may be useful to the sports marketer. Because of its nature, qualitative research is appropriate to develop information about the values, beliefs and behaviours of sport consumers, and uncover much richer information regarding the underlying (and thus harder to measure quantitatively) motivations and needs of the sports customer. By using qualitative techniques, the researcher is able to determine the views and perceptions of the consumer, rather than simply measure behaviours. Qualitative methods also have the advantage of being able to generate data that is unexpected, and have a degree of flexibility that can be extremely useful to the sports manager.

CHOOSING QUANTITATIVE OR QUALITATIVE APPROACHES

The decision to collect either quantitative or qualitative data depends upon the nature of the research question and the objectives of your research. Obviously if you are interested in the measurement of a particular phenomenon then you will need to collect quantitative data. If you are more interested in the thoughts or feelings of people, then these are difficult to quantify, and qualitative data will be more appropriate. There is no one 'better' approach, rather the approach should be dictated by the research question. Do not, for example, decide to collect qualitative data simply because you are uncomfortable with statistical analysis. Always ensure that your approach is appropriate to the research question, rather than to your skills and/or preferences. We will deal with this in Chapter 7, when we consider the different research designs that you may adopt.

MIXING QUANTITATIVE AND QUALITATIVE DATA

You may also decide to mix quantitative and qualitative data. There are differing views regarding this, and some academics suggest that the two forms are incompatible, as they rely on differing epistemological assumptions. Others suggest that often time constraints, the need to limit the scope of a study, and the difficulty of publishing such findings are also factors against mixing qualitative and quantitative data (Creswell 1994). On the other hand, Nau (1995, p.1) suggests that 'blending qualitative and quantitative methods of research can produce a final product which can highlight the significant contributions of both'. For example qualitative data can be used to 'support and explicate the meaning of quantitative research' (Jayaratne 1993, p.117) in terms of providing some explanation to quantitative measurements. Henderson et al. (1999, p.253) noted with reference to their study of physical activity and culture that:

Linking types of data provides a way to use statistics, the traditional language of research, along with anecdotes and narratives for further clarity in understanding physical activity involvement. Descriptive statistics do not tell the meanings of physical activity. In-depth interviews alone are not necessarily representative of the sample. Together, however, linking the data gives a bigger picture of some of the issues that described and mitigated the physical activity of these women of colour.

As we have already suggested, however, it is important that your approach is suited to the research question, rather than your own particular preferences. You can mix quantitative and qualitative methods in the following ways:

1   One may facilitate the other – thus a piece of quantitative research may identify the existence of a particular occurrence that could then be explained through the collection of qualitative data.
2   Both approaches investigate the same phenomenon. Quantitative methods may be used to collect relatively simple, or 'shallow' numerical data from a large sample, whereas qualitative methods may collect 'rich' data from a smaller sample.

One thing you should consider at the outset is whether you have the time and resources to carry out a multiple methods (the use of different methods to address different research questions regarding the same phenomenon) or mixed methods (where two methods are used to address the same research question) study. Often, such approaches require more in the way of time and money and this can be an important consideration, especially if you have constraints related to time and resources!

DEDUCTIVE AND INDUCTIVE RESEARCH

We can make one final distinction between different approaches to research in terms of *deductive* and *inductive* research. Deductive research is more generally associated with positivist and quantitative research. It involves the development of an idea, or hypothesis, from existing theory which can then be tested through the collection of data. A hypothesis is a statement of the relationship between two variables that can be tested empirically, for example a hypothesis could be that 'children with parents who participate regularly in sport are more likely to have positive attitudes towards sports participation themselves'.

Deductive research progresses through the following stages:

1   A statement regarding the theory used to underpin the research.
2   A statement deduced from that theory that would suggest, if the theory is true, the relationship between two or more variables – your hypothesis.
3   Collecting data to test this hypothesis.
4   Using the results to confirm, modify or refute the theory used to develop the hypothesis.

Inductive research is more often associated with interpretative, qualitative studies. Here, the pattern is to collect data, and analyse that data to develop a theory, model or explanation. For example, you may be interested as to the sports participation patterns of immigrant groups. You may find that there is not enough existing evidence to develop a hypothesis. You could interview a sample of immigrant sport participants to collect data about their participation, which could then be used to develop an explanation. This theory can then be tested and refined if necessary through further data collection.

TWO BROAD RESEARCH TRADITIONS

We can summarise two general research traditions in Table 2.2. It is important to realise that these summaries are not concrete, and that it is entirely possible to carry out inductive research using quantitative methods, or vice versa.

Table 2.2 Two broad research traditions

Approach A	Approach B
■ Positivist	■ Interpretative
■ Quantitative	■ Qualitative
■ Deductive	■ Inductive
■ Questions such as 'what', 'when' and 'how many'	■ Questions such as 'why' and how'
■ Follows a predetermined design	■ Follows a flexible research design, that may be continually adapted
■ Establishes causality	■ Explains causality
■ Confirms theory	■ Develops theory

WHAT APPROACHES ARE SUITABLE FOR MY RESEARCH?

Although it is important to have an awareness of the research traditions and approaches described above, it is important not to be too constrained by them when undertaking your research. You should not consider any approach as necessarily better than any other, and choose the approach that best suits the objectives of the research. For example, if you are interested in describing what is happening in an area where there is a considerable amount of existing theory, then a deductive approach may be appropriate. If you are interested in explaining why something is happening, and the area is relatively new, or under-researched, then an inductive approach may be better. It is relatively easy to become immersed within the complex issues of ontology and epistemology. In reality, the key question to ask is what approach will best suit my research? Secondly, time and resources can be a major issue. Inductive research tends to take longer and takes more resources than deductive research, as theories have to gradually emerge from the data, rather than be tested by data collected in one go. A third consideration is that deductive research is often lower risk than inductive research, where it can be possible for many hours of data collection to prove fruitless. A final – and often overlooked – consideration is that of your own stance. You may – as many experienced researchers do – develop your own preferences towards a particular approach. Some of the questions that you may want to consider are:

1   Can I measure the phenomenon I am interested in numerically?
2   Am I concerned only with measurable 'facts'?
3   Am I concerned with the individual's views or explanations of what is happening?
4   Do I think that the 'truth' is different for each individual, and I cannot develop scientific 'laws' of behaviour?

If you answer 'yes' to the first two and 'no' to the last two questions, then you are likely to follow a positivist, quantitative approach. If you responded 'no' to the first two and 'yes' to the final two, then you are likely to follow an inductive, qualitative approach.

1   Two broad approaches to the nature of knowledge exist – positivism and interpretivism.

2   Positivists adhere to the tenets of the natural sciences and view behaviour as directly measurable and explainable via laws.

3   Interpretivists suggest that individuals have freedom to act in particular ways, and that they experience things differently. Thus, the researcher has to interpret 'reality' from each individual's experiences.

4   Distinctions can also be made between quantitative and qualitative research. Quantitative research is based upon numerical measurement and analysis. Qualitative research is based upon non-numerical analysis of words, feelings, emotions and so on.

5   Research may follow a deductive or an inductive process. Deductive research involves the testing of a predetermined theory, explanation or hypothesis. Inductive research generates the explanation from the data collected.

ACTIVITIES

Reread some of the research articles that you used at the end of Chapter 1. For each article, try to identify:

1   Is the research positivist or interpretative in nature? What are the key factors that lead you to this decision?

2   What type of data is collected? Quantitative, qualitative or a combination of both?

3   Does the research follow an inductive or a deductive approach? If the research is deductive in nature, try to identify (a) what is the underlying theory used by the researcher(s), and (b) what is the hypothesis?

- Is your research positivist or interpretative in nature? Can you justify your approach in terms of its appropriateness to the research objectives?
- Are you collecting quantitative or qualitative data? Can this be reconciled with your choice of a positivist or interpretative approach?
- Are you following a deductive or an inductive design? Can this be reconciled with your answers to the above questions?

CHAPTER THREE

THE RESEARCH PROCESS

In this chapter we will:

- Introduce the concept of the 'research process'.
- Outline the different stages of this process.
- Describe how the different stages interrelate as part of one overall process.

INTRODUCTION

When people think of research, many will think immediately of the collection of quantitative or qualitative data through interviewing, questionnaires or other methods. Whilst such primary data collection is an important part of many research projects, there is much more involved, and it is generally more appropriate to consider data collection as part of a wider process involving important stages both before and after those of data collection. This chapter introduces this concept of the 'research process', describes the elements within the process, and the relationships between the elements. It is important that you have an understanding of all elements of the research process before commencing your research project so that you have an idea of the 'big picture'.

THE RESEARCH PROCESS

The research process described in the following section is a very generalised model of carrying out research. In reality, the process is much less 'neat', and you will generally find that you will not usually follow the process stage by stage, but will often move continually back and forth between the elements, or carry out two or more of the elements concurrently, especially if you are undertaking a more interpretative or qualitative study. Although different models of the research process exist, each containing different numbers of stages, most include the same general elements. The research process that we will refer to consists of eight elements (Figure 3.1).

It is important to remember that these are not isolated, discrete stages, but are actually part of one overall process. As we said earlier, it may also be the case that for certain methodological approaches the order of the stages may be somewhat different; for example a qualitative research project may involve a continual integration of reviewing the literature and data collection. Alternatively, a grounded approach (see Chapter 7) will generally involve data collection at a

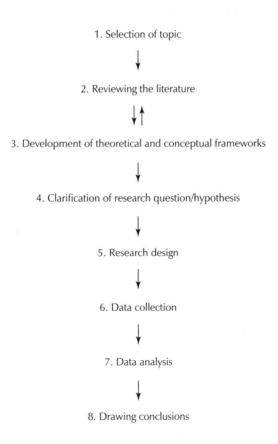

1. Selection of topic

2. Reviewing the literature

3. Development of theoretical and conceptual frameworks

4. Clarification of research question/hypothesis

5. Research design

6. Data collection

7. Data analysis

8. Drawing conclusions

Figure 3.1 The research process

much earlier stage, before the theoretical and conceptual frameworks have been fully developed. Thus, you should be prepared to be flexible, depending upon the nature of the research being undertaken. Whatever approach you take, however, it is important that you maintain a sense of coherence within the overall research project, or what some refer to as a 'golden thread', or 'vertical thread'. This thread should be the research question, and everything within the research process should be related to answering that question. This chapter will briefly outline the stages of the research process. Each of the areas will be covered in more depth in later chapters of the book.

Stage 1. Selection of topic

The stage that will take up most, if not all of your time at the beginning is that of selecting a topic, and developing a preliminary research question and set of objectives. The selection of your research question is a crucial stage, as an inappropriate topic or question will often lead to irretrievable difficulties later in the research, so it is worth dealing with this stage carefully. It is unlikely that you will develop a final question and set of objectives at this stage of the research process, and the following two stages are important in developing and assessing your question more fully. We will discuss some of the issues related to coming up with a research question in more depth in Chapter 4.

Stage 2. Reviewing the literature

This stage is covered in more depth in Chapter 5. A literature review essentially consists of critically reading, evaluating and organising existing literature on the topic to assess the state of knowledge in the area. During this stage you should aim to become an 'expert' in your field of research. The literature review is generally done alongside the development of the theoretical and conceptual frameworks (stage 3 of the research process). Reading widely may also alert you to other helpful factors, such as whether similar research has already been carried out, show you the types of findings that you could expect, or provide descriptions of the theoretical frameworks and previous methodologies adopted by others doing similar research.

Stage 3. Development of theoretical and conceptual frameworks

As you read the literature, you should be continually developing and refining your theoretical and conceptual frameworks. This is a stage that can often be overlooked in the haste to collect data. It is, however, a vital part of the research process, and is important in alerting you to potential problems before they occur. Your theoretical framework refers to the underlying theoretical approach that you adopt to underpin your study, for example social learning theory, or theories of self-efficacy. The conceptual framework defines and organises the concepts important within the study. These issues are covered in more depth in Chapter 6.

Stage 4. Clarification of the research question

Stages 1, 2 and 3 of the research process will initially, in many cases, become a circular process, whereby initial research questions are chosen, investigated and often rejected for a number of reasons, for example:

- The question lacks sufficient focus.
- The conceptual framework has identified problems in either defining and/or measuring the appropriate concepts.
- There are too many moderating or intervening variables.
- The project is unfeasible in terms of complexity, access, facilities or resources.

Stages 1 to 3 can take longer than initially anticipated, and you may well become discouraged by a lack of success in identifying a good research question or hypothesis. There are no easy methods to come up with an appropriate question, and it can be very much a case of perseverance. Once you have developed a good, focused research question, then the rest of the research process is based upon answering that specific question. The importance of developing a clearly focused question and set of research objectives at this stage cannot be overstated. A common fault is the lack of clarity over the overall aim of the research. Without this, it is difficult to maintain your vertical thread.

Stage 5. Research design

Once the focused research question has been ascertained, the next stage is to consider two questions:

1   What data do I need to collect to answer this question?
2   What is the best way to collect this data?

Breaking this down into more detail, the issues faced by the researcher are:

■   What overall research design should I use? Will I, for example, use a cross-sectional, experimental or longitudinal design?
■   Will I need to collect primary data, or will there be suitable secondary data to use?
■   What methods, for example interviews, questionnaire surveys and so on, will be the best ones to collect the primary data?
■   Who should participate in the research, and how will I gain access to them?
■   What are the exact procedures that I should adopt in my data collection to ensure reliability and validity?

These issues are covered in depth in Chapter 7, as well as throughout much of the rest of the text.

Stage 6. Data collection

Once the issues identified in stages 4 and 5 of the research process have been addressed, then you should have a clear idea of what data to collect, and how to collect it. You have to consider which methodology to choose, and which methods to utilise within the methodology. The background to this is dealt with in more depth in the next chapter, and the actual practical issues of collecting data are dealt with in Chapters 8 to 11.

Stage 7. Data analysis and discussion of the findings

The data you collect in stage 6 needs to be analysed to provide answers to your research question. Methods of data analysis should always be related to the objectives of the research, that is your analysis should answer the research question or hypothesis. In your discussion of the results, reference should also be made back to the literature reviewed in stage 2; for example, how do the findings add to this literature? Do they support the literature? If not, what are the possible reasons why? A common fault is to discuss the findings with no reference back to the literature reviewed as part of stage 2 of the development of the conceptual framework. Chapter 12 deals with issues of quantitative analysis, and Chapter 13 discusses some of the methods of qualitative data analysis that you may use.

Stage 8. Drawing conclusions

This should relate back to the focused research question. Here, the answer to the research question(s) should be clearly stated. You can evaluate how successful you have been in achieving your research objectives, and highlight the strengths and weaknesses of the research. You may also want to make recommendations for further research.

SUMMARY

1 Research is not just about the collection of data. Data collection is important, but it is simply part of a wider process – the *research process*.
2 The research process follows 8 steps: selection of topic, reviewing the literature, developing your theoretical and conceptual frameworks, clarifying your research question, developing a research design, collecting data, analysing data, and drawing conclusions.
3 Relating your project to the research process will allow you to develop and answer your research question in a logical and systematic manner.

ACTIVITIES

■ Reread one of the pieces of research from the activity suggested at the end of Chapter 1. Can you relate this research to the research process? Does the research follow this process? Are the steps easily recognisable?

You should be thinking about your project in terms of the entire research process at an early stage, rather than simply thinking about one stage in particular, for example the data collection stage. You should also ensure that whilst your research project may consist of different stages, it is important that the final written submission reads as a single coherent piece of work.

FURTHER READING

At this stage it can be a good idea to catch up on your reading! Try to locate some of the key textbooks and journals in your particular field and try to get a feel for the range of topics that are covered in that field, and some of the key theories and ideas that exist within those topics. The following are two texts that you may want to browse through:

Coakley, J. (1997) *Sport in Society: Issues and Controversies*, Boston: McGraw-Hill.
Coakley, J. and Dunning, E. (eds) (2000) *Handbook of Sport Studies*, London: Sage.

Alternatively you may want to browse through some journals. Try the *Sociology of Sport Journal* or the *Journal of Sport Management*, for example, or any journals publishing in your particular areas of interest.

CHAPTER FOUR

RESEARCH QUESTIONS, AIMS AND OBJECTIVES

> ### In this chapter we will:
>
> ■ Describe some of the ways by which you can identify and develop a potential research question.
> ■ Outline some ways by which you can focus your research question.
> ■ Discuss some of the means by which you can assess the strengths and weaknesses of your research question.
> ■ Describe the content of a research proposal, and identify some of the common weaknesses in research proposals.

INTRODUCTION

The starting point for any research project, and the first stage of the research process, is to decide upon your initial research topic. This is an important stage – a poorly thought out research question can lead to irretrievable difficulties in your research project later on. It can also be a difficult task, and one that can be extremely time consuming! In this chapter we will describe some of the strategies that you can use to develop your research question, and focus the aims and objectives of your research, and also outline some of the means by which you can assess your research question.

Before you start considering your research question, it is worth revisiting the concept of research outlined in Chapter 1. As we noted, a feature of research is that it adds to knowledge. Often, however, students overestimate the extent of originality required in a research project, and feel that they have to produce something completely new. In reality, this is unrealistic in almost all cases. Nearly all research builds upon work done by others, and uses existing knowledge. It is highly unlikely that you will come up with a completely original piece of research, and building upon the work of others through using existing knowledge provides the framework for a more realistic research proposal. Thus, you should not be concerned if your research topic does not seem as original as it could be. It should have some degree of originality, but often this can be achieved in a number of ways, as we will discuss later in the chapter.

COMING UP WITH A RESEARCH TOPIC

It is extremely unlikely that you will identify a clearly focused research question straight away, and before you even begin to develop and focus your research question, you will generally need to identify a broad topic. You may find that coming up with this initial topic proves difficult. Veal (1997) and Saunders *et al*. (2000) provide a number of possible sources to help you:

- *Existing Literature*. Past research projects are a useful source of ideas. By looking at past research, for example reading journal articles, you may develop an idea of the types of questions researched in your field of interest. Reading current journals is also a useful means to assess the types of subjects that are at the forefront of research. From such reading you may encounter a certain idea, argument or theory that interests you, and that you would be interested in developing further.
- *Social concerns*. You may wish to explore certain contemporary social concerns and problems related to sport; for example you may be interested in sports provision in deprived inner-city areas, or the sports experiences of minority groups. Other social concerns such as violence or cheating in sport may also interest you.
- *Popular issues*. There may be certain popular issues that are worthy of investigation. An examination of newspapers or Internet sites may indicate such issues. Choose a quality newspaper or magazine and identify the relevant sporting issues of the moment, and brainstorm, using those issues as a basis for your research. Often you may be able to explore such issues from an academic perspective.
- *Your own personal characteristics*. What are your own strengths and interests? In what subjects are you both knowledgeable and interested? What about your own career aspirations? If you are interested in a career in sports marketing then it would be a logical idea to undertake research in this area. If you would like to become a coach or teacher, then undertaking a related

piece of research will not only give you valuable experience, but will also look good on your CV.

- *Brainstorming.* Brainstorming with others is a good way to develop topics. Discuss potential ideas with others, and use this interaction to develop, critique and refine possible questions. Write down as many words as you can think of related to the areas of sport that interest you. Then write words such as 'why', and 'how', and see if any questions emerge.
- *Your tutors.* Your tutors will have their own research areas and areas of expertise, and they will generally be extremely happy to supervise in these areas. Talk to your tutors, and see if they can guide you in the right direction (although it is not necessarily their role to provide you with a question!).

When you have identified a topic and have undertaken some preliminary investigation, it may well seem that your topic has already been explored in some depth, and there may be little scope for original research. If this is the case – and it is very likely that it is – you should not be discouraged. As we noted earlier, almost all research builds upon, and uses existing theories and ideas. Often, your originality comes not from generating new ideas and theories, but in using existing ones in an original way. Veal (1997) provides a number of examples of how you could do this:

- *Geographically.* Certain theories may have been developed and empirically tested in one area but have not received the same attention elsewhere. Thus, you may find research focused on sport in the USA. Undertaking similar research in the UK would provide you with the basis for an original study. Alternatively, existing research may have examined sports provision in an urban context. You may wish to carry out similar research in a rural setting, which again would form the basis for an original study.
- *Socially.* You may find that certain social groups have not received as much attention as others. Existing work may focus exclusively upon men, and exclude women, or you may find a certain theory that has not been applied to the elderly, or to the physically disabled for example.
- *Temporally.* A theory may have been developed a number of years ago, thus its relevance in contemporary society could be investigated. Comparing the findings would be an original study in itself. You may also come across a study that took place some years ago. Collecting more up to date data may also form the basis for an original project.
- *Contextually.* You may find existing theories from outside the field of sport studies that have yet to be applied to the sport context. Alternatively, you

40

could revisit existing research using new theories and assess whether such theories have greater explanatory power.

■ *Methodologically*. You could collect different data to explore a phenomenon. An example may be if you find a theory that has been tested quantitatively, and apply a qualitative research design, or if you collect data using in-depth interviews rather than questionnaire surveys.

Thus the issue of originality should not be a major stumbling block to your choice of topic. What you should be careful of, however, is undertaking research where the theories are so well established that you are certain as to your findings before you even start the research!

The next stage, after deciding upon the initial topic, is to begin developing a focused research question. One of the continual complaints of examiners of research projects is that the research question chosen is too broad. Stating that 'I would like to research the growth of Western sports in China' for example is too broad and lacks direction. Which sport are you interested in? All sports, or just one of them? What exactly is it about the growth that you are interested in? Are you interested in the whole of China, or a particular region? What is the timescale of the research? The research question is vital for a good piece of research. Without a good, focused question, it is almost impossible to carry out research successfully. De Vaus (2001) suggests some guidelines to focus your question that can be applied to sports research and are outlined in the following section.

FOCUSING YOUR RESEARCH QUESTION

1   Define your core concepts. If you are discussing participation in sport, what exactly do you mean by participation? Do you mean participation in all sport? Or just organised sport? Does it mean regular or sporadic participation? Unless you can clearly define or specify your core concepts, you cannot develop your research question. Any ambiguity over your key concepts needs to be removed.
2   What is your time frame? Are you interested in the contemporary picture, or do you want to measure changes? If so, over what time period?
3   What is the geographical location? One community, facility or sports team? Are you going to compare one or more locations?
4   What aspect of the topic are you interested in? If you are researching the commercialisation of the Olympics, for example, are you interested in

the economics, the experiences of the athletes or the impact of commercialisation upon spectators?

5   What is your unit of analysis (i.e. the 'thing' that you collect data about and from which you draw conclusions)? Is this a person (e.g. sports participant or fan), an organisation (e.g. a sports team) or an event?

The following is an alternative process that you may find useful in focusing your question. It is not a widely recognised process, but can be remarkably effective in helping you to focus your research question:

1   Write out your provisional research question. For example, 'What is the effect of injury upon the self-efficacy of tennis players?'
2   Identify the key terms (or 'concepts' – more about them in Chapter 6) in the research question, for example 'injury', 'self-efficacy' and 'tennis players'.
3   Try to identify whether you can break down each of your key terms into more focused categories; for example 'injury' could be broken down into 'upper body' and 'lower body'. 'Upper body' could be broken down into 'preferred arm' and 'non-preferred arm'. 'Tennis player' could be broken down into 'competitive' and 'non-competitive'. 'Competitive' could be broken down into 'elite' and 'non-elite' and so on.
4   You can then identify a number of alternative research questions (see Figure 4.1).

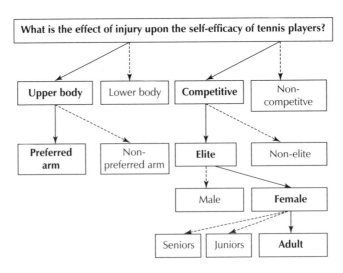

Figure 4.1 Focusing a research question

Thus, by identifying alternative categories, and making choices between categories, the question has been focused from:

What is the effect of injury upon the self-efficacy of tennis players?

To:

What is the effect of injury to the preferred arm on the self-efficacy of adult, female, elite competitive tennis players?

Even when you have decided upon a research question that you think is appropriate, it is not always possible to undertake the research to answer that question. You will also need to consider the 'CAFE' acronym (Clarke *et al.* 1998) to ensure that it is feasible. CAFE refers to four considerations, these being complexity, access, facilities and resources, and expertise.

- *Complexity*. A particular topic may involve several competing theories, or just one complex theory. Could you do the topic justice within your research if this is the case? This may be the case if you are limited by time or resources, or in terms of your own personal background. Do you have the ability to undertake a research project in the chosen area?
- *Access*. How easy will it be for you to collect the data? How realistic is it, for example, to send questionnaires to professional sports club owners, or elite athletes and expect a response? There is often a tendency to be over-optimistic in terms of response rates and so on, and you need to consider this carefully.
- *Facilities and resources*. Consider the demands of your research. Will you require extensive travel to carry out interviews? Will you be able to afford to send out a large number of questionnaires, each containing a pre-paid reply envelope? You need to identify any specialist resources at this stage.
- *Expertise*. Consider your expertise. Would you be happy undertaking a research project that necessitated the use of complex multivariate analysis? Would you have the relevant sociological or psychological expertise to examine group behaviour in sport? If you are undertaking a dissertation as part of a taught programme, it may well also be wise to consider the expertise of your tutors, especially if they are particularly renowned in a certain field.

When you are developing your research question, you should continually refer to the following list:

✓ You must have a focused research question. Vague statements of intent such as 'I would like to investigate violence in sport' are inappropriate. If you cannot clearly state your research question, then you will need to revisit your intended research.

✓ The research question must be of interest to you. Research projects take a considerable length of time and effort, and you should ensure that you have sufficient interest in the research to be able to read extensively around the topic, spend time, effort and resources collecting data, and write a substantial research report at the end. If you lack sufficient interest, then your chances of completing the research project are correspondingly reduced.

✓ The research question must be feasible – especially in terms of time and resources. Most projects have a limited time allocation, and you should ensure that yours in achievable within the time.

✓ The data must be obtainable – you should not assume that by sending questionnaires you will get a response. Sport governing bodies, for example, are often inundated with requests from researchers, and may be unlikely to respond.

✓ You must have the appropriate skills to undertake the research. How confident are you in interviewing senior managers of sports organisations, or carrying out complex statistical analysis?

✓ You must be able to cope with the relevant theoretical and conceptual issues related to the research. If you are undertaking a sport psychology piece of research, have you appropriate psychological expertise?

Gill and Johnson (1997) note that your topic should have, if possible, a *symmetry of potential outcomes*. What this means is that your research will have value no matter what your findings are. You may be interested to find out whether there is a relationship between the anxiety of umpires before a game and how many years they have been umpiring. If there is no such relationship, then the findings may have little interest or relevance. One solution is to amend the research question, for example to investigate the causes of stress amongst umpires. In this way, the findings will have relevance and interest whatever they are. In this

44

instance, you need also to confirm any assumptions, for example you are assuming that umpires actually experience stress!

You will also need to develop a number of *research objectives*. These are the objectives that you will need to achieve to answer the overall research question. They are essential in guiding your approach. Your research question may be something like

> *How successful was the marketing policy of my local sports team last season?*

Your objectives may be as follows:

- To determine the marketing policy of the team, and to identify any objectives set by that policy.
- To determine and apply a suitable operationalisation of (or a way to measure) 'success' based on such objectives.
- To compare the findings with secondary data to allow a more detailed evaluation of the marketing policy.
- To produce recommendations on policy for subsequent seasons.

The objectives thus set the scene for the project, and identify the key tasks that need to be undertaken. They are also useful in providing a measurable set of targets for the researcher. When setting your objectives, remember the 'SMART' acronym. Thus, your objectives need to be:

- *Specific*. You must be clear about what is to be achieved.
- *Measurable*. You must be able to identify when such objectives have been achieved.
- *Achievable*. You must have a likelihood of success in achieving your objectives.
- *Realistic*. The objectives must be realistic in light of any constraints that you may face, such as time, money or access.
- *Time bound*. You should be able to set specific targets for when each objective is to be accomplished.

Thus, if you are interested in the cultural impacts of professional sport, you may set yourself an objective 'to review the literature on the cultural impacts of hosting a mega-event'. Whilst the review of literature is a necessary process, by relating it to the above list, we can see that it is, in fact, not an objective.

45

SETTING AIMS AND OBJECTIVES –
SPORT ENGLAND AND ECONOMIC ANALYSIS

Sport England (2002) wanted to evaluate the economic impact of sport in a number of regions. To achieve this, they set a number of clear aims:

- To develop a standard economic model that can be applied to all of Sport England's regions to enable comparability between regions and providing a relatively easy mechanism whereby the assessments can be updated to enable us to measure change over time.
- To conduct economic impact of sport assessments in all nine Sport England regions.
- To report the economic value of sport in these regions.

To achieve these aims, a number of clear research objectives were developed. These included:

- To identify the regional sources of relevant economic data.
- To identify where relevant economic data is not available at the regional level.
- To collect relevant regional economic data.
- To apply an appropriate model to the regional economic data, initially from three pilot regions, in order to ascertain the overall economic impact of sport in each region.
- To modify the model, as necessary, based on its application to the three pilot regions.
- To apply the modified model (if modifications are required) to the regional economic data from the remaining six Sport England regions.

These objectives can all be related to the SMART concept, and, as such, provide a clear, focused and measurable set of objectives that together allow the aims of the research to be achieved.

46

WRITING A RESEARCH PROPOSAL

An important part of many research projects, and a key element for anyone wishing to secure funding for research is that of writing a *research proposal*, or a plan of the intended research programme. Even if it is not a formal requirement, it is still a useful exercise to undertake during the early stages of your research. You should try to produce your own research proposal as soon as you have determined your research question. This proposal can be very effective in clarifying in your own mind the overall aim of the project, and how you intend to achieve that aim, and to identify potential problems with the study. Requirements for a research proposal will depend upon its purpose. However, there is certain information related to the research process that will generally be required:

- A clear statement of the overall aim and associated objectives of the research.
- A statement outlining the originality, relevance and importance of the research.
- A brief description of existing work in the area.
- How the research is to be conducted, the research design to be adopted, anticipated methods, and an indication of the likely sample group.
- How the data collected are to be analysed.
- The anticipated time scale for the research.
- The anticipated outcomes of the research.
- Any specific requirements in terms of access, financial requirements, etc.

WEAKNESSES IN RESEARCH PROPOSALS

In many cases, your research proposal will be assessed, by either your institution or funding body. If it is not, then you need to assess it yourself, which can be a difficult task. One way to do this is to compare your proposal against a set of criteria or headings. Leedy (1985) has listed the weaknesses commonly found in research proposals, and by comparing your proposal with his list, you may be able to identify weaknesses in your own proposal. The most relevant weaknesses identified are as follows:

1. *The research problem:*

    - The problem is of insufficient importance or unlikely to produce any new or useful information.

- The hypothesis upon which the research is based is unsound, or is not based on any existing evidence.
- The problem is more complex than the investigator appears to realise.
- The research is overly complex, with too many elements.

2   *The approach:*

- The proposed methods are not suitable to achieve the research objectives.
- The description of the approach lacks specificity and clarity.
- The research design has not been carefully considered.
- The statistical aspects have not received sufficient attention.

3   *Personal characteristics:*

- The researcher does not have adequate experience or ability to undertake such a project.
- The researcher seems unfamiliar with recent or important work in the area.

Even if you are not required to produce a research proposal for assessment, it is essential that you consider the points raised above, and critically assess your own research proposal. Even better, get a colleague to play 'devil's advocate' and critically question your proposal. It is much better that problems are identified at this stage, when you can change your approach, than after you have begun to carry out the research!

SUMMARY

1   The first stage of the research process is to identify a research topic for investigation. This can be a difficult task, but it is important to the success of the subsequent research project.
2   There are a number of sources of ideas for research topics, the main ones being existing literature, social concerns and popular issues, personal characteristics and preferences, brainstorming, and debate with your tutor.
3   Although some degree of originality is desirable, the extent of this originality is often overestimated. There are a number of ways by which research can be seen to be original, for example through applying existing theory to new situations, or using different approaches.

48

4   The topic should lead to a focused question, which forms the 'vertical thread' of the research.
5   Answering the research question must be achievable, in terms of the personal abilities of the researcher, access to an appropriate sample, and the availability of any specialist resources or equipment.

ACTIVITIES

You should come up with two or three possible research questions. Assess each question, and for each:

■   Identify whether you feel that it is a good research question. Try to identify the limitations of each of the questions and rewrite accordingly if necessary.
■   Identify a series of objectives that would need to be met to answer each question.
■   Assess those objectives in terms of SMART, that is are they specific, measurable, achievable, realistic and time bound? Again, rewrite if necessary.

ABOUT YOUR RESEARCH PROJECT

The activities above are all important to your research project as well, and you should carry them out with reference to your proposed question. You should also undertake the following tasks:

■   Refer to the criteria mentioned earlier in the chapter (see the checklist 'Choosing your research question'), and assess whether your research question fulfils these criteria.
■   Can you relate your question to the four elements of CAFE outlined in this chapter?
■   Is your question sufficiently focused, or can you focus your question further in any way?

49

CHAPTER FIVE

REVIEWING THE LITERATURE

In this chapter we will:

- Introduce the role of the literature review, and outline why it is an important part of any research project.
- Describe some of the sources of literature available to you.
- Describe some guidance for assessing the quality of the literature that you identify.
- Provide guidance on writing and presenting the literature review.

INTRODUCTION

Before commencing data collection, and before you have even considered your research design, it is important that you become knowledgeable in your chosen subject, understanding not only the appropriate concepts, but also the work that has been done on the subject previously. As Jankowicz (1995, pp.128–9) notes:

> Knowledge does not exist in a vacuum, and your work only has value in relation to other people's. Your work and your findings will be significant only to the extent that they are the same as, or different from, other people's work.

Reviewing the literature is an essential task in all research. No matter how original you think the research question may be, it is almost certain that your work will be building on the work of others. It is here that the review of such existing work is important. A literature review is the background to the research, where it is important to demonstrate a clear understanding of the relevant theories and concepts, the results of past research into the area, the types of methodologies and research designs employed in such research, and areas where the literature is deficient. This reading will then form the basis for a significant element of your research report, where your understanding of this literature is presented in a written form. Thus, the literature review can be seen to consist of two different aspects:

1   The actual process of locating, reading and organising the appropriate academic literature; and
2   The presentation of the information collected above as part of the research report.

Thus you will need to read and report the literature critically, demonstrating an awareness of the state of knowledge on the subject, both in terms of the strengths of existing literature, and any weaknesses, or omissions. You also need to place your own research objectives within this context. The reader of your research needs to understand and appreciate your research in the light of existing work. The understanding will come from your definitions and explanations of key terms and concepts. Appreciation of your research will come from your identification of weaknesses in existing research, and how your study will contribute to the body of knowledge in the area.

PURPOSES OF THE LITERATURE REVIEW

You should consider the purposes of the review of the literature before you start, as this will make it easier for you to identify the things that you should be looking to do. These are as follows:

■   *To demonstrate your familiarity with, and knowledge of the subject.* A good review will inform the reader that the researcher is competent to undertake research in that particular area.
■   *To provide an outline of the relevant theories and concepts important within your research project.* Using an appropriate theory is important to allow you to have a framework within which to explain your findings. Concepts are important so that others may share and understand your findings in the knowledge that the often rather abstract phenomena under investigation are clearly outlined. The literature will be able to help you gain a clear understanding and definition of appropriate concepts, as well as provide an indication of how they have been used in past studies.

- *To focus the research question.* One of the biggest problems faced by researchers is that they are unable to complete the research because they have not sufficiently focused or delimited their research question. By reading how others have focused their research, and gaining an understanding of the types of questions that have been tackled in the past, you will be able to gain ideas on focusing your own research question, and get an indication of the sorts of research questions that have been successfully answered in the past.
- *To determine the extent of past research into the subject matter.* It is important to determine at an early stage whether you have identified an original research question, or whether you are simply repeating past research. The review of literature will enable you to identify gaps in existing research, which can be filled through new research.
- *To develop a hypothesis.* Your hypothesis is the predicted outcome of the research based upon logical reason or existing evidence. The literature will help you to develop this hypothesis. Otherwise your hypothesis is likely to be no more than educated guesswork!
- *To identify methodologies and methods that have been successfully utilised in the past.* You may be able to gain valuable insights into how others have approached similar questions, for example in terms of sampling methods, data collection instruments, methods of analysis and so on (although you should avoid simply replicating existing methodologies without careful consideration).
- *To help ensure all relevant variables are identified.* A thorough search of the literature should identify all the moderating variables that may have an influence upon the research programme.
- *To allow comparison of your findings with the findings of others.* You may wish to compare your findings with the findings of other researchers, thus you will need to identify these. You will also need to identify how your work builds on the work and adds to knowledge.

SOURCES OF LITERATURE

One worry that researchers beginning a project often have is that there will be insufficient literature available, especially if the question is tightly focused. In practice, this is rarely the case. A search through library databases will soon demonstrate the large amounts of information available to you. The problem tends to lie in where to find the appropriate information, and what to do with the information when you have found it. There are a number of varied information sources, of which the main ones available to you are as follows:

- *Books*. Books are an obvious source of information, and often are the first information resource to be utilised. Books are good for providing a broad overview of the topic, and describing the key research that has been undertaken. However, they are unlikely to be sufficient, as they will often lack sufficient depth or focus upon the topic being researched, especially if they are general textbooks. Another potential problem is that books may become outdated, especially in a rapidly developing field such as sport studies. Thus you should ensure that you are looking at the most recent texts available. Books will often provide you with a list of further useful sources in their reference section or bibliography.
- *Peer-reviewed journals*. These will be an important source of information to you. You should be using contemporary articles from peer-reviewed journals wherever possible. Peer reviewing is a process whereby the work submitted for such journals is assessed by independent, expert reviewers, who ensure that the publication is of the appropriate standard. Such journals will show the up to date research being carried out in the area, and you should ensure that you have identified relevant articles within them.
- *Conference papers*. These are often more difficult to obtain, and the quality may not always be as high as with journal articles. However, conference papers do often provide useful insights into the type of research being carried out in the field, especially in terms of work in progress, or developing fields of study. If you can actually attend conferences in your subject area, then this is an excellent method of identifying the most up to date research being carried out.
- *The Internet*. The Internet is a potentially useful resource. However, this usefulness must be tempered with an awareness of its limitations. As noted above, peer-reviewed publications effectively undergo a rigorous quality control procedure, which is generally absent from the Internet. Whilst there are a number of extremely high quality peer-reviewed sources on the Internet,[1] there is also literature that has not undergone any such procedure, and thus the quality of such information may be debatable. It is important that the quality of any sources from the Internet is carefully evaluated. The Internet does, however, provide a wide range of secondary data that may be useful to you (see Chapter 15 for a more in-depth analysis of the use of the Internet in sports research).

1 For example *Sociology of Sport Online* is an online journal available at http://www.brunel.ac.uk/depts/sps/sosol/index.htm.

- *Past theses*. These can provide large quantities of detailed information. However, at masters and Ph.D. level, they are generally very specific. You can search relevant indexes, such as the *Index to Theses* (www.theses.co.uk). Once you have identified relevant theses, they can be obtained using inter-library loans. Often they will be provided in microfiche form, so you will need access to a suitable reader. Undergraduate dissertations may also be useful to you, however they can be more difficult to trace, and you will generally have to approach each individual institution rather than a centralised record.
- *Newspapers/magazines*. Newspapers and magazines can provide useful and up to date data. Back issues of quality newspapers are also widely accessible as they are stored on CD-ROM. Care needs to be taken with such sources, however, as reports may be distorted in some way, and such sources generally do not provide a bias-free perspective.
- *Trade journals*. Trade journals will provide useful data on current trends and developments in the area; however they are not aimed at an academic audience. They may not be available as widely as academic journals in libraries, and you may need to contact the relevant association directly if you require particular issues.

FINDING THE LITERATURE

Faced with this seemingly enormous range of literature in a number of different formats, beginning the literature review will seem a daunting task. Unfortunately there is no one best way of finding the literature. The important advice to be aware of before you start is as follows:

- Start as soon as you possibly can. If, for example, you are undertaking a final year undergraduate dissertation, then you should be looking to begin your literature search towards the end of the preceding year if at all possible.
- Be systematic as far as possible, but always be on the lookout for relevant literature that you may uncover by accident.
- Keep careful records of your searches, and of any literature that you uncover from the beginning of the search. Do not imagine that you will be able to locate relevant details later.

You will need to conduct a systematic and detailed search as soon as you begin the research project. There are a number of different ways of locating literature, and you will probably need to use all of these methods.

- *Databases*. You will find these at your library. Journal articles (or more commonly the abstracts of journal articles) will be indexed within a specific field on a database, which can then be searched electronically using one or more keywords. The search will provide information about articles containing that keyword – again, normally an abstract – so you can decide whether the article is relevant to your research, and enough detail will be given for you either to locate the article in your library, or to obtain it from other sources. You may also be able to use a citation index, which will identify which other works have cited a particular article themselves. Previously, indexes were published in paper format, but most are now available on CD-ROM. Occasionally such indexes may also be 'online', that is they will allow you access to the full text of the article, which can then be printed. However, searching using electronic databases is not a guarantee of being able to find all of the relevant literature. It requires careful planning. You should, beforehand, write down *all* of the key terms that may be appropriate to your research project, including variations. Identify alternative words for each key term (for example 'coach' and 'instructor', or 'fan' and 'spectator'), and note variations in spelling (for example 'behaviour' and 'behavior', 'organisation' and 'organization').

RELEVANT DATABASES FOR SPORT RESEARCH

There are a number of databases that you can use to search for relevant literature. This is not an exhaustive list, so check with your librarian for any other sources of information. Some of the databases will be freely accessible; others will require you to log on using a username and password. If this is the case, see your librarian to find out how to get these details.

- *Sport Discus*. This is your first database to investigate in most instances. Sport Discus contains references to journal articles, books and conference papers from a variety of disciplinary approaches, such as sociology, psychology, physical education and so on, from 1975 onwards.
- *ASSIA*. This is a general database focusing on the social sciences; however it does contain a number of useful sports-related articles.
- *PsychInfo*. If you are undertaking research into the psychological aspects of sport, then you should access this database. It contains psychological abstracts from key journals from as early as 1887!

- *Sociological Abstracts*. This will help you locate articles that have approached sport research from a sociological perspective.
- *Pro Quest*. This will enable you to locate articles in the areas of business, management, economics and finance.
- *British Humanities Index* – This is a general index covering a variety of newspapers and journals. It will be of interest to those studying sport from a humanities perspective, such as those researching sports history.
- *Zetoc*. This provides access to the British Library's Electronic Table of Contents (ETOC), and provides details of a range of journal articles and conference proceedings.

- *Library catalogues*. You can search for items on library catalogues. However, such searches are less detailed. They are generally a good means to locate appropriate books, but generally less useful to locate journal articles.
- *Internet searches*. There is a wealth of information on the Internet. However, searching the Internet can be a difficult and time consuming task. As we suggested earlier, there is also less 'quality control' of sources, and you need to be extremely cautious in your use of the Internet. See Chapter 15 for a more detailed discussion of the Internet as a research resource.
- *Publishers' web pages*. These can be a valuable resource, and will often list journal contents pages as well as relevant books. For example, www.leisurestudiesarena.com/leisurestudiesarena/homepage.htm will provide up to date information on the sports-related books and journals produced by Routledge.
- *Research articles*. One method to quickly develop your bibliography is to locate a relevant, up to date book or article. Read the list of references at the end of the work, and identify important sources from the references. Obtain those references, and repeat the process looking for new sources. Using this method, you can build up a substantial bibliography in a relatively short period of time. Be aware, however, that this is unlikely to identify very recently published sources.

FOCUSING YOUR LITERATURE SEARCH

A common error, especially in student research, is to focus too early in the initial review of literature, and become discouraged at the apparent lack of available sources. Thus, the student who is interested in why women begin to play rugby union, may – quite correctly – identify theories of socialisation as a possible theoretical framework. The student may then carry out a search for literature on women's socialisation into rugby, find relatively little of it, and become discouraged by the apparent lack of material. An alternative, and more appropriate, approach would be to avoid becoming too focused in the initial search for related literature, for example:

- *Theories of socialisation in general.* These will not be found in the sports section of the library, but in the sociology or social psychology sections. You may find research into the socialisation of women into many social groups seemingly unrelated to sport. You must remember, however, that both the underlying theoretical frameworks used by these authors, and the methodologies that have been used in such research, may provide important background information to you.
- *Socialisation into sport.* There is a wide range of literature based upon socialisation into sport; for example you may find the work of Donnelly and Young (1988) of interest. They investigated the processes by which males were socialised into two sport subcultures, those being rugby and rock climbing. They provide a useful symbolic interactionist perspective of socialisation that you may find helpful.
- *Socialisation of women into sport.* You may now focus further by investigating the research carried out on the socialisation of women into sport, to identify any particular gender issues that may be appropriate.

By the end of this search, even if no literature has been found specifically on the socialisation of women into rugby, you should have achieved the following:

- To have gained a clear understanding of the theoretical concept of socialisation.
- To have an overview of the nature of existing research into the socialisation of women into groups, research into the area of socialisation into sport, and the socialisation of women into sport.
- To have identified gaps in the research, which will be used to develop your research question. You will then attempt to fill a gap in the literature with your own research.
- To have developed ideas about the likely, or suggested findings of your own research.
- To have developed ideas on possible methodologies that could be used based on past research.

ASSESSING THE LITERATURE

Once you have identified the literature, then the next stage is to read, digest and fully record the literature that you have found. Whilst you read each article, you should consider both the content of the article, and the implications for your own research project. You should make notes whilst you are reading each article with this in mind. You should also carefully record the full reference for your bibliography. Once you have read and made notes on several articles, then you should consider organising them into a structured form, with articles taking a similar approach being placed together.

It is important that you don't assume that each piece of literature you find is of the same standard. You will need to critically assess the quality of the literature that you obtain, and ensure that you pay more attention to works that are more relevant, or of higher quality, than to works that are only partially related, or of lower quality. There are a number of criteria that you can use to assess these factors, including:

■ What is the source of the literature? Is it from an international, peer-reviewed journal or a trade magazine for example? A peer-reviewed article should carry more weight than the trade journal, yet the trade journal may be more useful in identifying areas of study that are of immediate relevance and practical interest. A trade journal will, however, generally lack any sort of academic or theoretical framework.

■ Who are the authors? Are they recognised experts in the field? What other work have they published in a similar area? What are their qualifications for writing such a book or article?

■ Is that piece of literature referenced elsewhere in other articles on the subject area? If so, are such references positive or critical?

■ When was the article published? Is it a recent article or has it been superseded by other research?

■ Using your own knowledge, how good do *you* think the article is?

Be prepared to be critical of the research both in your reading and the write-up of the literature review if you can support your criticisms. This may especially be the case if the work is several years old, and theories and methods have since developed, or if your source has not been subject to an academic review process.

HOW DO I KNOW WHEN I HAVE COLLECTED ENOUGH LITERATURE?

The question of when you have sufficient literature is a difficult one to answer. There is no set amount of literature that you should include, and some research projects will contain much more literature than others. You should aim to reach what could be referred to as 'saturation', that is when reading new articles, you are coming across the same references again and again. If you have all of these references, then this suggests that you have covered the main literature sufficiently. Do make sure, however, that you keep an eye on the key journals in your field throughout the remainder of the research programme to ensure you don't miss anything relevant that is published after you have completed your literature search (although you would not be penalised for not including an article that was published close to your submission date).

HOW SHOULD I WRITE UP THE LITERATURE REVIEW?

You will need to communicate your review to readers of the research report, so that they also can judge how your research fits in with existing work. A common error is to produce an annotated bibliography, rather than a review of the literature. An annotated bibliography is an organised list of sources, each of which is followed by a brief note or 'annotation', stating and evaluating the content of the research, and its usefulness to your research. Instead, your review should demonstrate to the reader the underlying state of knowledge in the area, highlight the gaps in existing research, and demonstrate how your research fits in to the state of existing knowledge. This will involve much more of a synthesis of the literature into a coherent review rather than a list of sources.

The literature review should start with an introduction, identifying the topic under investigation and providing a context for the review. This should be followed by the main body, where the literature is reviewed. Often it is useful to begin the review with a broad overview of the relevant ideas, concepts and definitions, before narrowing down to more relevant works. Past research should be grouped together under appropriate categories, for example:

- Studies involving similar research problems.
- Studies involving similar methodologies.
- Studies coming to similar conclusions.

Those studies that are seen as more significant to your research should be dealt with in more depth than those that are less relevant.

It is important that the literature review is not just a generic review of the subject matter. It should, instead, be a review of the state of knowledge of the subject area of your research project, and the implications of such knowledge for your own programme of research. At the end of each section, you should summarise such implications for your research. Finally, you should conclude the literature review with an evaluation of the current state of knowledge in the area, and summarise the relationship of your study to the literature, suggesting your anticipated findings – if appropriate – in the form of a hypothesis. You should ensure when you write up your literature review that you make it clear how the work of others is related to your study. It is also important to assess where the literature may be deficient. If your study is filling a gap in existing literature, for example, you should aim to clearly demonstrate that such a gap exists in your review, and relate your research question to this gap.

CASE STUDY

EXTRACT FROM A LITERATURE REVIEW

The following is an extract from a literature review (Wann 1994), investigating how fans of unsuccessful sports teams felt their team had performed in the past, and would perform in the future. Note how the review highlights the past research into the subject area, and develops an appropriate hypothesis for the study based on the literature.

Wann and Dolan (1994) described a bias among highly identified fans as these persons believed the team had and would win more games than low identification fans. Hirt and Ryalls (1994) stated that the Wann and Dolan results should be understood in terms of effects of self-esteem. Hirt *et al.* had found that, although highly identified fans were positive about the team's future immediately after a victory, they were negative about the team's future after watching a defeat (Hirt, Zillman, Erickson and Kennedy, 1992). Hirt and Ryalls argued that the bias found by Wann and Dolan (1994) may be related to the past success of the target team. They stated that, had the team been unsuccessful, highly identified fans would have felt that the team had won fewer games the past season and would win fewer games next season. However this prediction contradicts the behaviour of many fans, those who seem to display an undying optimism. Therefore, in contrast to Hirt and Ryalls (1994), it was hypothesised that highly identified fans of an unsuccessful team would report a bias in their evaluations of past and future performance. This prediction was based on their wish to maintain a positive social identity, a desire only relevant to those for whom the group was meaningful (Tajfel and Turner, 1979).

Note how the author has summarised past research, and identified a gap in knowledge, that of whether the biased views of fans may be related to the need to maintain self-esteem. There is enough evidence within existing literature to suggest a hypothesis in terms of fans' evaluations of past and future performances which was then tested in the research project.

Note that a literature review is not simply a *list* of relevant literature, but an organisation of past work into a logical structure under common themes or ideas. A literature review where each paragraph begins with the name of a different author is usually a sign that the researcher has produced an annotated bibliography rather than a literature review. We recommend that you select a highly regarded journal publishing sport-related research, such as the *Sociology of Sport Journal* or the *European Journal of Sport Management*, and read as many literature reviews as possible to get a 'feel' for what a well-written review is like.

HOW NOT TO WRITE A LITERATURE REVIEW

The following is a hypothetical example of a poorly written literature review:

There are a number of authors whose work is important in this respect. Birrell and Loy (1979) have described four functions of the media with regard to sport: providing information, integrating society, arousal, and escape. Gruneau (1989) found that entertainment was a key element in mediated sport, with the focus upon spectacle, drama and risk. These factors were emphasised by the producers of televised sport. Nixon and Frey (1996) suggested that television has affected sport in a number of ways, such as improving its popularity, increasing salaries, and enforcing rule changes to make the sport more viewer-friendly. Coakley (1998) has also described the effects of the media upon sport. This research will look at the effects of television on one particular sport, that of tennis, to determine how the sport has been affected by the media, and assess the findings in light of the works mentioned above.

Note how the review is simply a list of works, with no effort by the author to relate the works to his or her own research question, or to identify themes or patterns within the literature. Additionally the author devotes exactly the same amount of space in the review to less important sources as is given to important, or 'classic' sources.

HOW DO I REFERENCE OTHER AUTHORS?

You will need to reference the work of others throughout your literature review (as well as the rest of the report). A reference consists of three elements:

1   The text that has come from the original author, whether quoted directly, paraphrased or summarised. For example, the following extract from Coakley's text *Sport in Society: Issues and Controversies* may be included within a literature review (inside quotation marks, as it is a direct quote): 'Today, international sports are less likely to be scenes for nationalistic displays than to be scenes for commercial displays by large transnational corporations.'

2   The abbreviated reference within the text to show where the statement originated. Normally (although not always) this is placed at the end of the statement, for example: '. . . by large transnational corporations' (Coakley 1998, p.417). This shows that the author of the quote was Coakley, the source was his text published in 1998, and the quotation was taken from page 417. If you had simply taken Coakley's ideas and rewritten them in your own words, then the page number is not necessary. If you had referred to different works by Coakley, both published in the same year, then you should differentiate between them using 1998a, 1998b, and so on.

3   The full reference in the reference list or bibliography at the end of the research report. Identifying the text published by Coakley in 1998 allows the reader to identify the full source of the quotation or idea, for example:

> Coakley, J. (1998) *Sport in Society: Issues and Controversies*, Boston: McGraw-Hill.

The full references are then placed in alphabetical order in either a reference or bibliography section at the end of the research report. Thus, the reader can, simply by looking at the reference within the text, locate the full details of the source material.

There are a number of purposes of referencing. Jankowicz (2000) provides a useful list, from which we can see the key purposes:

- *To attribute a quotation*. If you use the words of other authors, you must enclose them using inverted commas, and provide a reference, rather than claim them as your own. As we noted above, for such direct quotations you should also provide the page number, as is shown in the following example: 'until fairly recently, most sociologists, and social historians, and many anthropologists have neglected sport as a potentially fruitful object of study' (MacClancy 1996, p.1).
- *To justify an important statement*. If you are making an important claim, then you should support your claim with a reference. An example of this may be that you want to make the point that sport has, for a long period of time, been overlooked by many as an area of academic study, and therefore write a statement to this effect. At the end of the statement you should support your claim through providing a reference to other authors who agree, i.e. 'Sport has been overlooked for many years as a legitimate area of academic study' (MacClancy 1996). This shows that you have not simply made up the statement, but that it is a statement based on a source. This source can then be checked by the reader. Note that a page number is not required, as you are not directly quoting the author.
- *To justify your approach*. You may wish to justify your approach to your research by referring to similar authors who have taken the same approach or used similar theories or models with successful results.
- *To demonstrate breadth of reading*. A further advantage of consistently referencing your sources is that you can demonstrate the breadth of your reading (although you should resist the temptation to throw in references at every available opportunity). It is tempting to include references that you

have not actually read or used as a strategy to boost your bibliography, and demonstrate more reading than you have actually done. This practice should be avoided at all costs!

KEY TERM

HARVARD SYSTEM OF REFERENCING

There are a number of different methods you can use to reference the work of others. We would suggest that the *Harvard system* is an appropriate method, and will refer to its use throughout this text. The Harvard system involves citing in the text the surname of the author, the year of publication you refer to, and the page number for a direct quote, for example '. . . as Smith (1997) suggests', or '. . . (Johnson 2001, p.265)'. The reader can then refer to the alphabetical list of references at the end of your research report to see the full citation of the work. Most journals and textbooks will use this particular system, and it is worth paying particular attention to how authors have referenced their work when you are reading these sources.

Wherever possible, you should use the original text or article rather than use what is referred to as secondary referencing. If in your reading (for example of Coakley 1998) you find a reference to Hoffman (1992), then it's important that you don't give the impression that you've directly accessed and read Hoffman's text yourself, which would be misleading. To avoid such potential problems, you should acknowledge in the text that what you're citing or quoting has come from another source (which you have actually read). Thus, rather than write: '*As Hoffman (1992) notes, a number of works have identified the strong apparent relationship between sport and religion. . .*', which would suggest that you have read Hoffman's work yourself, you should acknowledge the true source of your information. For example, '*As Hoffman (1992, cited in Coakley 1998) notes, a number of works have identified the relationship between sport and religion.*' Thus it is clear that you have got your information from Coakley, rather than Hoffman. You should then only include Coakley (1998) in your list of references or bibliography.

MAINTAINING YOUR REFERENCES

It is important to keep a record of all material at the time you use it. Whatever you do, don't think that you will be easily able to locate your references in a couple of hours at the end just before the deadline! The best way is to store the full reference on computer (remember to keep a backup!) or on a card index system, together with a brief summary of the content of the reference, including any important methodological points. You should also state the source of the reference.

STRUCTURING YOUR LITERATURE REVIEW

When you write a literature review, you should follow the same guidelines as with any piece of academic writing. Always begin the review with an introduction, and complete it with a summary – you should also introduce and summarise any major subsections of the review. If you feel that it is appropriate, you don't have to have just one literature review chapter – break it up into two if necessary. Remember to cite all sources, and make sure that all such sources are included in your bibliography or reference list. Avoid statements such as 'it is a well-known fact that . . .', or 'it is widely believed that . . .' unless you can provide evidence to support such claims. You should also avoid the use of jargon or technical terms, and attempt to make the review as readable as possible. As with any piece of work, ensure that you check your grammar and spelling carefully, as mistakes will detract from the quality of the review.

A further point concerns the inclusion of direct quotations. It is all too easy to insert large numbers of direct quotations into a review, and this can seem a quick and easy method to boost word counts. However, it can be a debatable practice. We would recommend that you keep the use of direct quotes to a minimum, and only use them when the original author has stated a point in such a clear and concise manner that you are unlikely to be able to state the point as well. Otherwise, use your own words as far as is possible. In terms of the actual structure, then it is often a good idea to follow the same sort of approach as we suggested with finding the literature. Start with a broad perspective, and introduce your key concepts and theories. Gradually focus your review so that it becomes more specific to your particular research question.

- Gain familiarity with the subject before writing.
- Construct your bibliography as quickly as possible – identify and access the key sources that you will need at the earliest possible stage.
- Allow yourself much more time than you initially think you need to write the review. It is rare to complete the review in one go, and generally a number of rewrites are necessary. You should be prepared for this.
- Work from an initial plan, but be prepared to continually refine and develop your structure.
- Include subheadings where necessary to guide the reader.
- Summarise your key findings regularly in longer literature reviews.
- Be selective – include literature that is relevant to your research, and spend more time on higher quality or important articles.
- Extract the relevant information from each study you use. Do not spend an inordinate amount of time describing each study in depth.
- Be up to date. Look at the dates from your bibliography. Are the key works recent, or are they several years old? If the latter, are they still 'cutting edge' or have they been superseded by more recent works? Do include, however, 'classic' works in your field wherever appropriate.

RELATING YOUR LITERATURE REVIEW TO YOUR RESEARCH QUESTION

The literature review should relate to your research project, that is it should not be just a review of the literature per se, rather it should be a review of the literature in terms of how it relates to your research project. By reading the literature review, the reader should get a sense of how the research question has 'emerged' from the literature, and even an idea of what the research question actually is without your explicitly stating it. By the end of the literature review, there should be a clear indication of what you are doing, how it is adding to existing literature, and, if appropriate, what you could expect to find.

Many inexperienced (as well as more experienced) researchers find writing the literature review a difficult part of the research process. Unfortunately there are no easy answers, and it is the case in most instances that you will have to rewrite and restructure the literature review a number of times. Even well-known authors

66

publishing in top journals will have rewritten their literature reviews a number of times. For this reason, we recommend that you commence the writing of the review as soon as possible, rather than leaving it to the last minute!

MISTAKES OFTEN MADE IN THE LITERATURE REVIEW

Many students find writing the literature review a difficult part of the research process, and it can often be a relatively weak section. The common mistakes made in such reviews include the following:

- Making the review simply a list of past studies, or producing an annotated bibliography.
- Not relating the literature review to the study, and making it simply a general review of the subject matter.
- Not taking time to identify the best sources, and give such sources due emphasis, while at the same time overemphasising weaker or less important sources.
- Failing to appreciate the relevant wider (i.e. beyond just that which is sports-related) literature.
- Relying on secondary rather than primary sources of literature (textbooks rather than journal articles for example).
- Uncritically accepting the findings of existing literature rather than critically evaluating them.
- Not considering contrary findings and alternative interpretations.
- Raising problematic issues but not addressing them.

IDENTIFYING SECONDARY DATA

Using existing literature can help you not only in terms of providing the background to your own data collection, but can sometimes provide you with the actual data to answer your research question. Data can be separated into two forms: *primary data* – data that you have collected yourself, through your own questionnaires, interviews, observations and so on – and *secondary data*, which has already been collected by others. Secondary data comes in a wide range of forms, such as research articles, annual reports, government publications and so on. When searching through the literature you may find secondary data which will help you answer your research question. This may be either raw data, or data that has been previously analysed. Using secondary data can save a significant

You will reach a stage where you think you are approaching the end of your literature review. If so, you need to ask yourself the following questions:

- ✓ Have I covered the key literature? If I read recent journal articles in the field, are there any sources used by the authors of those journals that I should have used?
- ✓ Is the literature review up to date? Have I covered recent sources? Have I included any outdated material?
- ✓ Do I relate that literature to my research question?
- ✓ Have I included literature that contradicts, as well as supports my viewpoint?
- ✓ Have I produced a critical assessment rather than a descriptive review?
- ✓ Have I organised the review into a logical and coherent structure rather than simply producing a list of literature?
- ✓ Have I identified the gaps/weaknesses in existing literature?
- ✓ Does my research question emerge clearly from the literature?

amount of time and effort, and may even produce higher quality data than if you had collected it yourself. There are potential problems with using secondary data however. First, you need to ensure that the data collected was valid and reliable, and not subject to any serious methodological errors. Second, you need to be aware of when the data was collected, and whether it is still appropriate, or is dated. Remember that secondary data was collected with a different purpose from the one that you are to put it to, and you should always be aware that the original author of the data may have been subject to particular constraints, had a particular agenda and so on. You need to be aware of any issues, and state them clearly in the final written report (it is no good being aware of the limitations if you don't make this awareness clear to whoever will assess your report!). Things you may wish to consider when using secondary data are:

- ■ Who collected the data? What were their qualifications for doing so?
- ■ What was the purpose of the data collection? Were there any factors that may have influenced the collection and presentation of the data (was the data collection sponsored by an outside organisation for example?).
- ■ How was the data used or analysed by the original author?

■ Has the data been used as secondary data in any other research project of which you are aware?

CASE STUDY

USING SECONDARY DATA

Malcolm *et al.* (2000) wanted to test the assertion that there had been considerable change in the demographic characteristics of football crowds over recent years. To do this, carrying out primary research would obviously be impractical. Therefore they used secondary data in the form of a number of past football crowd surveys. Whilst each of the existing surveys provided descriptive data on the composition of football crowds, on their own, none of the surveys provided any information as to the changing nature of the crowd. Yet, by collecting each survey, and by using the data as if it were a longitudinal study, the authors were able to determine that, despite the claims of some writers, the composition of crowds had remained consistent over a number of years.

SUMMARY

1   It is important that you develop your own expertise in the subject matter at an early stage in the research process. This is done through locating, reading and reviewing relevant literature.
2   The written review of this literature also forms an important part of your written report.
3   In your search for literature, you should not restrict yourself. Broaden your search at the beginning, and be prepared to seek out different sources. You should then gradually focus your review towards your particular research objectives.
4   Always relate your review to your own research question, rather than simply making it a review of the state of knowledge in the area per se.
5   Existing literature may, in certain cases, provide you with existing data with which you can achieve your research objectives.

The best way to get a 'feel' for what a literature review involves is to read as many reviews as possible.

- Choose a subject area of interest to you. Locate a number of sources pertaining to the topic using each of the search methods discussed in this chapter, including the use of a CD-ROM such as Sport Discus. Ensure that at least two articles that you locate are recent pieces of research from peer-reviewed journals.
- Read the articles, and pay special attention to the literature reviews. You should note how the author has structured the review, what has been included, and how the review is focused towards the overall research question.

ABOUT YOUR RESEARCH PROJECT

Once the first draft has been completed, you should critically assess your own literature review. Consider the following points:

- Have you included all the key works or are there any omissions that you are aware of?
- Have you used a range of sources, including journal articles, or have you relied upon a few textbooks?
- Have you synthesised your reading into a comprehensive review of the literature, or have you just listed descriptions of past research?
- Have you related the review to your research question, and considered the implications of the literature review for your research question?
- Have you correctly referenced all of your sources, paying particular attention to secondary referencing?

70

CHAPTER SIX

THEORIES, CONCEPTS AND VARIABLES IN SPORT RESEARCH

In this chapter we will:

- Introduce the role and importance of theory within your research project.
- Describe how you should be able to relate your question to existing disciplines in sport.
- Describe how to develop a conceptual framework for your study.
- Introduce and define the concepts of reliability and validity, describe the relationship between the two, and outline their importance within your research project.

INTRODUCTION

For many sport students, the importance of theory within a research project can be a difficult issue, yet it is one of the most important considerations, and in many cases underpins the entire research project. Unfortunately there is a tendency for many students, once they have identified a research question, to get carried away and go straight into the data collection stage of the research, arguing that the data alone is key to answering the question. What is required, however, is an appropriate theoretical framework within which such data can be analysed, interpreted and explained. This chapter introduces some of the issues related to choosing your theoretical framework, and relating this theoretical framework to your study. Theories are constructed from *concepts*, and a key process here is to identify exactly what concepts are involved, their relationships to each other, and how they are to be investigated, so that your data can be related to your choice of theoretical framework. This is the process of developing your conceptual framework, and this will also be outlined. Finally the issues related to the reliability and validity of your study will be described, that is the extent to which your research actually measures the concepts under investigation.

THEORIES AND THEORETICAL FRAMEWORKS

Theories are, simply, explanations of why things occur. If you drop a basketball, it will fall to the ground at a particular speed. If you repeat the experiment, the result will be the same. All your results show is that a basketball will fall to the ground at the same rate each time, and no more. This is, therefore, an example of very basic descriptive research. To explain why this is the case an appropriate *theory* is required. In this instance, the theory of gravity can explain your findings, that is to say *why* the basketballs all dropped at the same rate. The same theory could also be used to predict that any further basketballs dropped would also fall at the same rate. Thus the data itself is of limited value (other than to confirm the theory). Only when the data is related to existing theory can we explain the findings, and take our understanding beyond the basic descriptive level. It is therefore important that your research has a theoretical grounding if you want your research to be more than simply descriptive, and this will come from the theory that you choose to underpin your research project. At an early stage, you should be thinking carefully about your theoretical underpinning. As Yiannakis (1992, p.8) suggests:

> Research that is not theoretically informed, not grounded in the existing body of knowledge, or of the 'shotgun' variety that fails to raise and investigate conceptually grounded questions, is likely to generate findings of a narrow and ungeneralisable value.

This importance of theory is significant to your research, and it can be demonstrated using a relatively simple example. Imagine that you have come up with the following research question: '*Do sports fans identify more strongly with their favourite team when the team are winning?*' It would be relatively easy to make the appropriate measurements (whether the team are winning and how strongly a sports fan identifies with his or her team) and collect data accordingly. The answer to the research question is likely to be 'yes', in that a sports fan is likely to identify strongly with their team when they are winning (we shall assume for the sake of simplicity that there are no other factors affecting this relationship). That, however, is the only conclusion that can be drawn from such research without a theoretical framework. You would be unable to explain this finding, that is to say *why* it had happened. Neither would you be able to predict the same finding in the future with any confidence. Thus, you would need to place your findings within an appropriate theoretical framework. In this instance it would be appropriate to use a theory such as social identity theory to make sense of the findings. One of the tenets of this theory is that we prefer to identify with groups that positively enhance our self-esteem, that is groups that are seen positively by others. With this theory, we could reasonably hypothesise that people would identify with their team (i.e. be a member of that particular group) if they are seen positively (i.e. by being successful). Using an appropriate theory, therefore, has allowed us to explain the findings. We could also use this theory to try and predict future behaviour in this context. Unfortunately, many research projects are examples of what Phillips and Pugh (1994) refer to as 'intelligence gathering'. This refers to the gathering and presentation of data, with no reference to any such theoretical framework. Essentially this is descriptive research, and simply describes data. For example, it would be relatively easy to collect data to answer the question 'what was the proportion of male to female participants at the 2000 Olympics?' By using an appropriate theory, you may be able to propose a plausible explanation of *why* there were such differences. As we noted in Chapter 2, this use of theory may be through a deductive approach, that is where you select your theory beforehand, create a hypothesis, and test this hypothesis through the collection of data. Alternatively you may consider an inductive approach, whereby theory is developed from the data that is collected, and used to explain your findings.

CONSIDERING YOUR APPROACH

Sport, as a whole, can be seen to be an interdisciplinary subject. This means that there is no single academic subject that we can refer to as 'sport studies', but rather that there are a number of different ways of approaching sport academically. Thus sport can be studied from a sociological perspective, a psychological perspective, a geographical perspective, an economic perspective and so on (the United Kingdom Quality Assurance Agency (QAA), for example, notes twenty-nine different subject areas related to the study of sport).

Within each of these broad disciplines, there are a number of more specific fields, or more specific components of the overall area. Thus sociologists may be interested in the field of socialisation into sport, or the relationship between sport and religion, for example. Each field itself will consist of a number of theories, for example the field of socialisation into sport will include theories such as Donnelly and Young's (1988) model of group socialisation. Thus, in this particular instance we can see our broad disciplinary framework as follows:

73

DISCIPLINE

A discipline refers to a particular approach to the study of an aspect of sport, and the approaches, techniques and theories used to study and explain that particular aspect. Thus, sociologists are interested in the relationship between sport and society, and have developed particular sociological theories to explain sports behaviour. The discipline of psychology, however, is more interested in intrinsic influences upon sports behaviour.

Discipline	Field	Theory
Sociology	Socialisation into sport	Donnelly and Young's (1988) model of group socialisation

At this stage, you need to start thinking about your theoretical orientation, and try to locate your ideas within this type of framework. Although this is something that you may develop as you read around your topic, it is important to be aware at an early stage whether you intend to approach your research sociologically, or using an economic approach, for example. If you are a keen hockey player then you may consider a proposal along the lines of 'I want to research whether the size of the crowd has an effect on the outcome of hockey matches'. If this is the case then you need to identify your disciplinary approach, in this case sport psychology. Through reading around the sport psychology literature you can then identify your field. You can also, if possible at this stage, identify your specific theory. For example, in the above case the researcher may adopt social facilitation theory (Zajonc 1965). From our experience, a lack of theoretical awareness is a major cause of poor research. You should identify your theoretical orientation, and then apply it to the situation, for example:

Discipline	Field	Theory	Application
Psychology	Crowd effects on performance	Zajonc's (1965) theory of social facilitation	Crowd effect on the outcome of hockey matches

It is important to clarify the role of theory in your research. Thus, rather than undertaking a piece of research into football, start thinking about the theory that you will be using in your research project. This can then be applied to the appropriate context. When you are developing this table (what Jankowicz (2000) calls a 'provenance table') you can work either left to right or right to left, or a combination of both at the same time using this approach. Thus you can start off intending to undertake a piece of research based on your own sport preferences, such as hockey. This is perfectly acceptable provided that you can complete the rest of the provenance table. You may consider that you would like to do a piece of research from a psychological perspective, as you may feel you have the appropriate interest and expertise. All that then remains is to identify – most probably after you have begun reading around the subject – your theoretical grounding, such as social facilitation theory. Alternatively, start with a theory that you are interested in, and then try to complete the rest of the provenance table.

The above approach leans very strongly towards a deductive (and thus positivistic) approach to research. It can still be a good idea to consider your theoretical approach if you are considering an inductive study. Alternatively, you may wish not to choose your theoretical approach beforehand, and adopt a strictly inductive approach (for example if you are undertaking an exploratory study). In this case, you should develop your use of theory throughout, as well as at the end of the data collection phase. It is important, however, that you ensure that you do provide some theoretical grounding to your research even if this is the case.

HOW DO I KNOW WHICH THEORY TO USE?

At an early stage, it is likely that you may find it difficult finding appropriate theories, or deciding which theory is best for you. If you are undertaking a deductive study, you will need to have a clear idea of your theoretical framework at the outset. Even if you are undertaking an inductive approach, it is useful to have an idea of some of the appropriate theories that may be able to inform your study, without necessarily restricting yourself to any specific theories. There is no easy answer at this stage. It is generally a case of reading around the subject, and trying to identify which theories have been used in past studies. Your review of literature should alert you to the theoretical approaches adopted by other researchers in the past. Alternatively, you may want to read around some of the broader, non-sports-related literature and identify theories from these sources. As always, don't restrict yourself if possible, and be prepared to search through the wider sociological, geographical, management-based literature and so on. Alternatively, you can always discuss this issue with your research supervisor or tutor, who may be able to put you on the right track.

CONCEPTS AND CONCEPTUAL FRAMEWORKS

As we suggested earlier, theories are explanations with which we make sense of our findings. These explanations are built up using *concepts*. A concept is often easier to identify than it is to define. We would suggest that a concept is a representation of an object, a property, or behaviour. Examples of concepts are age, intelligence, anxiety, self-confidence and so on. Having a shared understanding of what concepts actually are is important so that researchers may be able to understand or replicate others' work. Thus, when one researcher discusses a particular concept, such as 'intelligence', others will know exactly what he or she is referring to. The conceptual framework describes and explains the concepts to be used in the study, their relationships with each other, and how they are to be measured. By having a shared understanding of the appropriate concepts and conceptual framework this is possible. As Miles and Huberman (1994, p.18) describe:

> Categories such as 'sociocultural climate', 'cultural scene', and 'role conflict' are the labels we put on 'intellectual bins' containing many discrete events and behaviours. Any researcher, no matter how inductive in approach, knows which bins are likely to be in play in the study, and what is likely to be in them. Bins come from theory and experience and (often) from the general objectives of the study envisioned. Setting out the bins, naming them and getting clearer about their interrelationships lead you to a conceptual framework.

Developing your conceptual framework requires five main steps:

1   Identifying the relevant concepts.
2   Defining these concepts.
3   Operationalising the concepts.
4   Identifying any moderating or intervening variables.
5   Identifying the relationship between variables.

We can illustrate the process with reference to a hypothetical research proposal based upon Chelladurai's (1990) work on leadership styles in sport. Say, for example, that you are interested in whether there is any relationship between the leadership style of sports coaches, and the consequent success of the teams that they coach. Thus, the research proposal was based on the following question: *'How does the leadership style of a sports coach affect the performance of their team?'*

The first step is to identify your concepts, or 'building blocks' within the statement. In this instance, these are:

- Leadership style
- Sports coach
- Performance
- Team

Secondly, you must be able to define these concepts. This will help you clarify exactly what you are investigating. These definitions should, if at all possible, come from existing literature, and use commonly accepted definitions, so that your research can easily be compared to both existing theory and the findings of others. Here, *leadership style* could refer to whether the coach displays autocratic or democratic leadership behaviour. *Sports coach* could be defined as the individual with overall responsibility for the strategy, tactics and training of the team. *Performance* could be defined as the team's win/loss record. The concept of 'team' would not have to be defined in this instance. Instead, it would be important, and more useful to the researcher, to identify the specific criteria under which teams would be included, for example professional rather than amateur teams and so on.

At this stage, if there is sufficient evidence within the existing literature, you may want to suggest a *hypothesis* rather than a research question. As we noted in Chapter 2, a hypothesis is a suggested relationship between concepts to be tested empirically. A hypothesis generally requires four things:

1 It must be adequate. A hypothesis must be able to explain findings or relationships that are determined by subsequent data collection.
2 It must be testable. Unless a hypothesis can actually be tested empirically, then it has little value.
3 It should require relatively few assumptions, for example a hypothesis should not only be valid if a considerable number of conditions have to be met.
4 A good hypothesis must be better than other possible or rival hypotheses, that is it should have better explanatory power than alternative hypotheses that could be considered.

Whether you decide upon a hypothesis or a research question, the next step in developing your conceptual framework is that of operationalising your concepts. Operationalising a concept means deciding how that concept is to be measured. Being able to produce an outstanding piece of theoretical work as the background to your research is of little use if you are unable to subsequently test your theories empirically, or if your measurements of the concepts do not actually reflect what you think they do!

EMPIRICAL

Often you will see reference to good research as being 'empirical' in nature. This simply means that the conclusions drawn are based upon evidence (or data) rather than simply conjecture or speculation.

The term 'measurement' may suggest a purely quantitative approach. Even if you are undertaking a qualitative study, however, it is important to have a clear idea as to how you are going to 'measure' your concepts. If you were going to undertake a qualitative approach on the effects of leadership style, trying to explain why the coaching style had a certain effect on performance, then how would you identify and evaluate the qualitative data provided by the players of that sports team? Often, within a qualitative study, this is a more emergent process, and you will develop your understanding of the appropriate concepts throughout the data collection and analysis process (see Chapter 13 for a more in-depth account of qualitative analysis).

As is the case with defining your concepts, try to use generally accepted measures of a concept (you should be able to identify these when you are reviewing the literature). There are two reasons for this. First, it will allow you to compare your findings with existing literature more effectively, and second, it will give you confidence that your measures are actually valid and reliable (we will explain these terms later on in this chapter). Using the above example, leadership styles can be operationalised by using Chelladurai and Saleh's (1980) Leadership Scale for Sport, a forty-item scale that can assess the coach's leadership style. Operationalising the concepts of *sports coach* and *team* is not appropriate here, as the clear definitions provided at the first step should be sufficient. We simply need to know whether they are a coach, and of which team they are a coach. Operationalising 'performance', however, leads us into a problem of how such a concept can be accurately measured. We defined performance earlier in terms of win/loss record. This is an obvious way of measuring performance, yet is it a valid measure of performance? There are a number of factors that are of concern here, for example the obvious point that a team may perform well and yet still lose. Conversely, a team may play badly and defeat inferior opposition. Thus, the concept of performance is likely to be a problematic one in this research project and will need to be reconsidered.

DIFFICULT TERMS TO OPERATIONALISE

Within sport studies, there are a number of terms that are difficult to operationalise accurately, and you should critically assess your own oper-ationalisation of your concepts. Such terms include 'performance', as noted above. Another common concept used rather vaguely is that of 'effect', such as in *'what has been the effect of commercialisation on the Olympic Games?'* There are so many ways that 'effect' could be operationalised, that until you can clarify exactly what is meant by effect, and how it will be measured, the question is almost meaningless. In the same way terms such as 'change' or 'influence' are also difficult to define unambiguously. Thus, you should ensure that throughout stages 2 and 3 of the conceptual frame-work development, you always ensure that you have clear, unambiguous and valid definitions and operationalisations.

Quantitative data collection tends to involve the collection of factual or directly measurable data, yet, as we have just shown, this is not always straightforward. Although the data itself may be clear, the operationalisation of the data has important implications for the validity of the research (we shall discuss this concept in more depth later in this chapter), and also for how your data is to be analysed. Take the following example. You may be interested in the relationship between income and interest in sport. To determine income, a number of different ques-tions could be asked:

1   What is your gross annual income?
2   Is your gross annual income: under £10,000   £10,001–£15,000
    £15,001–£20,000   above £20,000
3   Do you earn more than £20,000 per year? Yes   No

These questions are asking roughly the same thing, but in a different way, and each will give you a different response. These responses will all provide accurate data, yet they may all result in different types of conclusion to your question. The questions above show respectively an example of interval level data, ordinal data and finally nominal data. Each of these types of data can be analysed differently, and may give you differing results to your research question. This will be dealt with in more depth in Chapter 12. At this stage, however, it is important for you to consider exactly what you will be measuring, and why such measurement is being adopted.

TYPES OF MEASUREMENT

Variables can be quantitatively measured in four different ways: nominal, ordinal, interval and ratio.

- *Nominal scales* group subjects into different categories, for example grouping football players on the basis of the team they play for is an example of a nominal scale. A nominal scale does not suggest any relationships between the groups, for example grouping together those playing for team X under the label '1' and those playing for team Y under the label '2' does not suggest that those in team Y are somehow different, or 'better' in any way.
- *Ordinal scales* have a rank order, but do not indicate the difference between scores. Think, for example, of placement on a squash ladder. The person on top has performed better than the person second, and so on. Thus data is ordered, but there is no indication of how much difference there is between players. The player assigned a score of '1' is not necessarily twice as good as the player assigned '2'.
- *Interval scales* have equal intervals of measurement, for example a gymnastics scoring scale. There are equal intervals between each score, i.e. there is the same difference between an 8.00 and a 9.00 as there is between a 9.00 and a 10.00. It is not the case, necessarily, however, that a 10.00 is worth twice as much as a 5.00.
- *Ratio scales* are also based on order, with equal units of measurement, but they are proportional. For example, if a basketball team scores 50 points, then that is worth twice as much as a team that scored 25 points. Ratio scales range from zero upwards and cannot have negative scores.

Once a concept has been operationalised, it becomes a *variable*. The two most important types of variables are *independent* and *dependent* variables. Independent variables are the presumed cause of the effect being researched, for example if gender influences attitudes towards violent sports, then it is gender that has the presumed effect upon the attitudes, therefore it is the independent variable. Dependent variables are those that can be explained by the effect of the independent variable, which in the above instance is the attitude towards violent sport. In the example we have already discussed, leadership style is predicted to influence performance. Therefore leadership style is the independent variable and performance is the dependent variable. You need to ensure that you correctly identify your independent and dependent variables, otherwise you run the risk of your conclusions becoming meaningless! One extreme example is that of the relationship between height and basketball players. You may be interested in why basketball players are taller than average. You may make the assumption that participation in basketball is the independent variable, and height is the dependent variable. It would be highly possible that you find data to support a relationship between the two variables, only by confusing the independent and dependent variables, your conclusion would be that playing basketball causes an individual to become taller! Although this is an extreme example, it highlights the dangers of incorrectly identifying your variables. Going back to our hypothetical research question, we are confident through carefully examining our variables that we have correctly identified them as independent and dependent variables.

- *Independent* variable affects *dependent* variable.
- *Leadership style* affects *performance*.

Therefore, superficially at least, it would seem that by measuring leadership style and performance, we could identify whether there is a relationship between the two. Unfortunately, research is rarely this straightforward. Leadership style will not be the only influence upon performance. Other variables may also have an effect on the relationship, and we will need to identify them. These are called *moderating*, or *extraneous* variables. Thus, the next stage of developing your conceptual framework is to identify these variables. This is important as too many unaccounted moderating variables will affect the validity of the research. Moderating variables for our hypothetical example may include:

- Different opposition
- Type of competition
- Team factors – injuries, etc.
- Weather

- Influence of the crowd
- Performance of the referee

With so many moderating variables, it may be difficult to conclude that the performance has been affected as a consequence of leadership style. One option for the researcher is to systematically identify and remove as many moderating variables as possible, for example researching teams involved in only one type of competition, using data collected from performances against one opposition team only. Often, however, there may be too many such variables. Therefore a further option is to measure such variables, and attempt to account for them in your analysis. However, this can often involve some very complicated statistics, and you need to consider your expertise in being able to undertake and evaluate such analyses. Generally, the more focused your research question, the fewer moderating variables you can anticipate, and this is a good reason for focusing your study as much as possible!

In some cases you will also encounter *intervening* variables. As the name suggests, these are variables that intervene between the independent and dependent variables. For example, rather than a direct relationship between leadership style (independent variable) and performance (dependent variable), it may be the case that there is another relationship involving a different variable:

Leadership style (independent variable)	affects	self-efficacy (intervening variable)	affects	performance (dependent variable)

You need to be able to control such intervening variables if you are to determine the true influence of the independent variable upon the dependent. Alternatively you need to assess the influence of the independent variable upon the intervening variable, and then the influence of the intervening variable upon the dependent variable. By ignoring intervening variables, you may well end up with an apparent relationship that does not actually exist, for example there may be a strong correlation between leadership style and team performance, yet it is not necessarily the case that leadership style does affect performance. Instead, it may be that self-efficacy is actually influenced by leadership style. Self-efficacy may also influence performance, with the consequence that the researcher makes a link between leadership style and performance that doesn't actually exist.

A similar, though slightly different, hypothetical case can also be provided to demonstrate some of the potential dangers in not assessing the relationships between variables carefully. You may be interested in the relationship between education and attitudes to competitive sport, i.e.

| Education | affects | attitudes to competitive sport |
| (independent variable) | | (dependent variable) |

You may well find a relationship between the two, and conclude that our attitudes towards competitive sport are shaped by our education. There may be an alternative explanation, however. Our education is often dependent upon the socio-economic class of our parents. What if our attitudes to competitive sport were also shaped by our socio-economic background? We would then have the following situation:

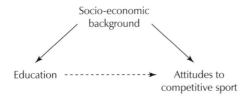

There may be no connection between education and attitudes towards competitive sport, yet your measurements would suggest there is (you may get a significant correlation between the two). This is an example of a *spurious relationship*, and you need to ensure that you are measuring relationships that actually exist.

Once you have identified your variables, you can graphically represent the relationships between them. This can be useful in clarifying the objectives of your research, and also to provide you with a framework for the interpretation of your data. Thus, using our hypothetical example, we could represent the relationships between our concepts as in Figure 6.1.

We can see that through developing our conceptual framework, our initial research question raises a number of potential problems, these being the difficulties in defining and operationalising performance, and also the issue of having too many moderating or intervening variables. By undertaking this process you can be made aware of these problems before the research commences, and can refocus your research topic to an area less problematic. As well as identifying such issues, the process is also invaluable in clarifying your research objectives, and helping you to develop a suitable research design to achieve such objectives.

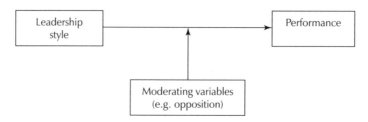

Figure 6.1

A CONCEPTUAL FRAMEWORK FOR SPORTS FAN SATISFACTION

Madrigal (1995) was interested in fan satisfaction in attending a particular sporting event. Rather than a single independent variable affecting satisfaction, he identified a number of relevant variables from the literature that could have an effect, for example:

- *Expectancy disconfirmation,* or the difference between the expected and actual outcome.
- *Team identification* – or the extent of the involvement of the fan with their team.
- *Quality of the opponent.*
- *BIRGing* – or the tendency to 'bask in reflected glory' of the team. Madrigal suggested that this was influenced by the three factors cited above.
- *Enjoyment.* This was also influenced by the same three factors.

Madrigal's conceptual framework is graphically represented in Figure 6.2.

theories, concepts and variables

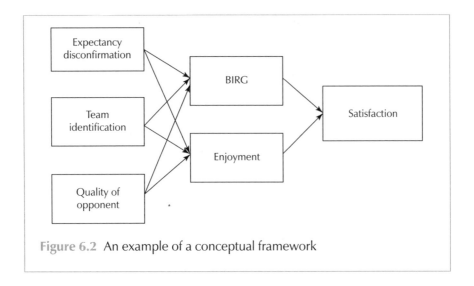

Figure 6.2 An example of a conceptual framework

RELIABILITY AND VALIDITY

It is also important to consider how 'truthful' your conceptual framework is, that is will your definition and operationalisation of your concepts actually provide a true answer to your research question. Two key concepts by which the quality of research is assessed are those of *reliability* and *validity*, and these are often used to assess how 'truthful' a piece of research actually is.

Reliability

Suppose that you are researching brand usage of products of sports sponsors. You ask your sample whether they have used a particular brand and the affirmative response is 75 per cent. You ask the same sample the following day, and the positive response is 51 per cent. Which is the correct answer? Obviously, to be sure that you had the correct answer, you would have hoped for approximately the same answer on both occasions. Reliability generally refers to the consistency of the results obtained. A number of forms of reliability are important to the researcher, three in particular:

- Inter-observer reliability
- Test–retest reliability
- Internal consistency reliability

Inter-observer reliability assesses the extent to which different observers would give similar scores to the same phenomenon, that is would two researchers measuring the same behaviour at the same time give such a behaviour equal scores? This is especially important if there are a number of people involved in collecting data for a research project.

Test–retest reliability is the extent to which the research would provide the same measurements if repeated at a different time, thus the test would give the same score over and over again (provided what was being measured wasn't actually changing!). If a measurement was taken of an athlete's ability at a particular sporting task in week one, and then the same measurement was taken in week two resulting in a different score, then what is the athletes true score on the task? Such a measure would be considered unreliable. One of your tasks as a researcher is to identify reliable measurements of the phenomenon under investigation.

Internal consistency reliability refers to the extent to which each question within a measure is actually measuring the same phenomenon. Thus, if you are assessing an individual's commitment to sport using a five-item scale, that is five questions that are analysed together to give an overall measure, then all five questions should be assessing commitment. This is more important when you use scales as a measurement technique (we will discuss the use of scales in Chapter 8).

Threats to reliability

Reliability is a prerequisite for any successful research project. A number of potential threats to reliability exist. These include:

- *Subject error*. The subject may respond differently depending upon when they are asked to supply data. If you question sports participants as to their predictions of future performance you may find that your results are different if you ask them directly before rather than directly after a match. This can be overcome by choosing a 'neutral' time to question them, for example in between matches.
- *Researcher error*. Two researchers may take slightly differing approaches to collecting the same data, which may result in different responses. If multiple researchers are to be used, then it is vital that the same procedures are followed by each. In some cases, the effects of the researcher cannot be overcome, for example if a male researcher and a female researcher both carry out interviews on a sensitive subject such as drug abuse in sport, or exploitation of child athletes, then this may lead to reduced reliability.

- *Subject bias.* Participants may give the response they think the researcher wants, or try and give the 'correct' answers. Anonymity should be stressed by the researcher if possible, as well as reminding the participant that there are no 'right' or 'best' answers.

Validity

A second important research issue is that of 'how do I know that the method I am using is really measuring what I want it to measure, and are my conclusions drawn from these measurements therefore valid conclusions?' This is the concept of *validity*. Validity has several different components. You should consider all of these components before rather than after you carry out your data collection!

- *Face validity.* Does your method appear appropriate to measure what you want it to measure at first glance? Ask a sample from the population that you are going to research. Do they think it measures adequately the concept you intend to measure? Although establishing face validity on its own is normally not sufficient, you should not overlook this stage, as without face validity it is impossible to achieve the other components of validity. Face validity is also important to prevent participants becoming frustrated by having to answer questions that they may feel are irrelevant or unrelated to the subject under investigation.
- *Content validity.* This is similar to face validity, except that it refers to the initial assessment from an expert's point of view. The expert should be aware of some of the more subtle issues and nuances of the concept, and be able to critically assess whether you have accounted for these.
- *Predictive validity.* Can your measures predict future behaviour? If someone scores highly on a test of positive attitudes to sport participation, will it predict their future sporting behaviour?
- *Construct validity.* Does your data correlate with other measures? If you have measured people's attitudes towards their own health and fitness, do the scores you obtained correlate with other scores such as attendance at health/fitness facilities, weight, diet, sports participation, etc.? This is the most rigorous form of validity, and you should aim to ensure this as far as possible.

VALIDITY AND RELIABILITY

Consider the following example. You are interested to know whether there is a link between how strongly a sports fan identifies with their favourite team, and how much they spend on merchandise in the stadium. The researcher may consider that the best measure of how committed a fan is to their team may be that of how many times a season they attend a match, and by using this as the independent variable then any relationship with spend (the dependent variable) could be determined. This, however, would not be a *valid* measure of sports fan identification. Fans on lower incomes may be just as committed but unable to afford to attend regularly. Time commitments with work or family may also reduce the frequency of attendance. Parents may attend regularly in order to take children to the game, but with no real interest themselves. Validity is thus likely to be low.

Reliability is also an important issue here. If a different measure of identification is used, for example simply asking fans how strongly they identify with the team, then it is likely that fans would give differing responses depending whether the team had just won, just lost, or not played recently. Thus the research would lack *reliability*.

It is, therefore, important to find a method that is both valid and reliable. One solution to this is to use methods that have been found to be both reliable and valid by other researchers. In the above instance, it would have been appropriate to measure fan identification using the sports spectator identification scale, a scale that has been found to be both reliable and valid (Wann and Branscombe 1993).

THE RELATIONSHIP BETWEEN RELIABILITY AND VALIDITY

Although we have looked at reliability and validity as separate concepts, they are related. A number of possible relationships exist between the two:

1   *The measure is neither reliable nor valid.* The lack of reliability means that sometimes the correct measurement is taken (and therefore is valid) but at other times a different (and thus invalid) score is achieved. You may be interested in an individual's perceived competence at sport. You may wish to measure this by asking them to rate their competence on a scale of 1 to

10. If you ask them after a heavy defeat, you are likely to get a different score than if you were to ask them after a good performance. Thus the measure is unreliable. On rare occasions valid measures may occur, although by chance. On most other occasions, however, a different, invalid score will be obtained.

2 *The measure is reliable but not valid.* The measure may be consistently measuring the concept incorrectly, thus reliability is achieved, but the scores are invalid. Using the example above, individuals may consistently report the same level of perceived competence in their sport after a number of separate heavy defeats, for example, using the 1–10 scale. Thus the measure is reliable as the measure results is a consistent score each time it is used. Different individuals, however, may interpret the scale differently. For example, one individual may view 7 as a high score, and another individual of the same perceived competence may view 10 as a high score. Thus the measure is not valid.

3 *The measure is valid but not reliable.* Although unlikely, it is possible that the spread of unreliable scores averages out to give an overall valid score for the population. The scores for each participant may vary from test to test, but the overall mean may remain constant. Thus a respondent with an actual perceived competence of 7 may respond 5 after one performance, and 9 after another, giving a valid mean of 7.

4 *The measure is valid and reliable.* This is what you must strive for in your research. Thus you need to identify a measure that accurately reflects the phenomenon, and results in the same score at different times.

SUMMARY

1 Theory plays a crucial role in most research projects. Having an understanding of the importance of theory, and of the particular theories to be used in your research is an important element of the research process.

2 Developing your conceptual framework is also an important stage of the research process. Undertaking this process will allow you to clarify the important concepts within your study, their relationships to each other, and their measurement.

3 You also need to consider issues of validity (the extent to which what you are measuring actually reflects the phenomenon under investigation) and reliability (the extent to which the findings would be the same if the research was repeated). Validity and reliability are two of the key areas upon which your research will be assessed.

Go back to some of the research articles that you have already read. Try and answer the following questions:

- Can you identify the theoretical framework used by the author(s)?
- What are the important concepts within the study?
- How have they been defined?
- How have the concepts been operationalised? Have the authors used their own measures or have they used existing measures from the literature?
- Are there any moderating or intervening variables within the study? How have they been accounted for?
- Can you identify any threats to reliability and validity within the study?

ABOUT YOUR RESEARCH PROJECT

- Can you identify the theory that underpins your project? Is it the most appropriate theory? Now is the time to start reading past studies that have also used the same theoretical approach. Reading such studies may help you with the next activity.
- Develop your conceptual framework paying particular attention to the operationalisation of your concepts. How will you measure (either quantitatively or qualitatively) the necessary concepts?
- Can you identify any moderating or intervening variables? If so, how do you plan to account for these?
- What are the threats to reliability and validity in your research project? What steps can be taken to minimise these threats?

CHAPTER SEVEN

RESEARCH DESIGNS FOR SPORT STUDIES

- Describe the different types of research design that you may adopt within your research project – experimental, cross-sectional, time series, longitudinal, case study, grounded theory and ethnography.
- Introduce the concept of sampling, and describe some of the sampling techniques that you may use.
- Describe some of the methods you may use within your research design to collect data from your sample.
- Introduce the concept of triangulation as a means of strengthening the validity of your research.
- Outline some of the ethical considerations to be made when considering your research design.

INTRODUCTION

Once you have developed your research objectives, clarified the role of theory within your research, and developed your conceptual framework, two questions need to be considered. These are:

- What data do I need to provide me with the information to answer my research question?
- What is the best way to collect this data?

You can approach your data collection in two ways. The first way is to collect your data from whatever sources are available, at whatever time you can. Hopefully this will give you the data to answer your question. In reality, however, this is extremely unlikely! The second, and preferable, approach is to develop a carefully considered research design that will allow you to systematically collect the data you need, whilst at the same time maximising the reliability and validity of your findings. The research design is the overall 'blueprint' that guides the researcher in the data collection stages. In later chapters we will deal with the specifics of data collection – questionnaire design, interviewing and so on – but in this chapter we will focus upon the wider context within which such data collection occurs. Seven research designs will be outlined, these being:

- Experimental
- Cross-sectional
- Time series
- Longitudinal
- Case study
- Grounded theory
- Ethnography

EXPERIMENTAL DESIGNS

Experimental designs are generally used to identify whether an independent variable has an effect upon a chosen dependent variable. The simplest form of experimental design involves the measuring of a variable (X1) from a single group (dependent variable), exposure of the group to a particular treatment (independent variable), followed by measuring the initial variable again (X2). The effect of the treatment is thus assumed to be the difference between the two measures.

$$X1 \rightarrow \text{treatment} \rightarrow X2$$
$$\text{Effect of treatment} = (X2 - X1)$$

You may be interested in the effect of mental rehearsal upon shooting performance in basketball. The above design would involve you perhaps asking your sample to shoot twenty free throws. This would give you a success score of between zero and twenty (X1). You would then ask them to visualise a successful shot a number of times (treatment) before asking them to repeat the shooting task, again giving you a score (X2). The effect of the treatment would then be calculated by working out the difference between the mean score after the visualisation and the mean score before, for example:

Mean score before visualisation   = 11.25
Mean score after visualisation   = 13.00
Effect of visualisation   = (13.00–11.25) = 1.75

You may already have spotted the limitations in the above design, however. Whilst it may be possible that any improvement may have been down to visualising the task, it may also be that simply by learning, the participants' performance on the task improved, and you have identified an apparent effect of visualisation that doesn't exist in reality. Alternatively, it may be that participants tired during the second set of shots, and the improvement caused by mentally rehearsing the shots was lost due to fatigue. One way to account for these moderating variables is to use a *control group*. This design compares two groups, which have been assigned on a random basis. One group is exposed to the treatment (for example being asked to mentally rehearse the shots). The other group (the control group) are not exposed to the treatment (they are not asked to rehearse the shots). The other moderating variables (such as learning, fatigue, etc.) should cancel each other out, as they are equivalent for each group. Measurements of the dependent variable are taken from each group before the treatment (pre-test), and again from each group after the treatment has been administered to the non-control group (post-test). The overall effect of the treatment is thus the overall difference in scores between each group:

Group 1
$X1 \rightarrow$ treatment $\rightarrow X2$
Effect of treatment $= (X2 - X1)$

Group 2 (control group)
$X3 \rightarrow$ no treatment $\rightarrow X4$ – effect of non-treatment $= (X4 - X3)$
Net effect of treatment $= (X2 - X1) - (X4 - X3)$.

Thus, repeating our earlier experimental design, we could more accurately assess the effect of visualisation:

Mean score before visualisation (treatment group) $= 11.25$
Mean score after visualisation (treatment group) $= 13.00$
Mean score before visualisation (control group) $= 11.00$
Mean score after visualisation (control group) $= 11.90$
Effect of visualisation $= (13.0 - 11.25) - (11.9 - 11.0) = 0.85$

You could then test the results from the two groups to see if there were any significant differences (such issues of quantitative analysis are dealt with in Chapter 12).

Experimental designs may be carried out in either a controlled (laboratory) setting, or in the natural environment. The main disadvantage with laboratory-based designs is the possibility that participants will behave differently if they are aware they are part of a research project. This may be overcome by undertaking the data collection in the natural environment. However, it may then be more difficult for you to control your variables. Experimental research designs are perhaps more closely associated with natural, rather than social science approaches to sport, and are generally associated with the positivist paradigm.

DEMONSTRATING CAUSALITY USING EXPERIMENTAL DESIGNS

Experimental designs are used to demonstrate causality, that is that the independent variable actually causes the effect upon the dependent variable. To achieve this, three conditions need to be met:

1   *Covariation*. This simply means that as the independent variable changes, then so does the dependent variable. Thus, if we ask individuals to mentally rehearse a basketball shot, then their performance should change as a consequence if causality is to be demonstrated.
2   *Time order*. It is important to ensure that the independent variable (i.e. the cause) actually happens before the effect upon the dependent variable, for example that performance does not start to improve before the mental rehearsal.
3   *Non-spuriousness*. As we explained in Chapter 5, some relationships may be due to the existence of an additional variable. Thus, all variables need to be accounted for. In the case of shooting basketballs, it may be that learning the task has led to the improved performance.

CROSS-SECTIONAL/SURVEY DESIGNS

Cross-sectional or survey research designs are perhaps the most common design within the social sciences, especially within sport-related research. As the name suggests, this design takes a cross-sectional sample from the overall population, for example taking a sample from a telephone directory. Data is collected, most commonly through interviews or questionnaires. Relationships are then identified from this data, and causal relationships may be suggested, which can then be

Table 7.1 An example of a cross-tabulation

	Preference for team sports (%)	Preference for individual sports (%)
Male	51	49
Female	87	13

generalised back to the population. You may also see cross-sectional designs referred to as *survey designs* in some of the textbooks.

An example of a cross-sectional design may be that of investigating gender differences in sport participation. The independent variable (gender) cannot be manipulated by the researcher, thus an experimental research design is inappropriate. A cross-sectional design therefore has to be used. A cross-section of the population is sampled and relationships assessed by statistical analysis, for example the findings may be cross-tabulated as in Table 7.1.

It may therefore be suggested, for example, that female athletes prefer team sports, whereas male demonstrate much less of a preference for either. The strengths of such a research design are that it is convenient to the researcher with limited resources. Obtaining a cross-sectional sample is often easier than obtaining an experimental sample, attrition rates will be lower, and random samples may be taken from the population to allow the findings to be generalised to the wider population.

TIME SERIES DESIGNS

A time series design involves measuring the dependent variable over an extended period both before and after the effect of the independent variable. It may be that you are interested in participation rates in golf after a major championship. You may hypothesise that, due to Bandura's theory of social learning (1977), more people will play golf after a major tournament has been televised. Thus you measure participation before the event, and after the event. The findings are shown in Figure 7.1.

Thus, you may consider that you have evidence to support your hypothesis that television coverage of the sport has led to increased participation. It may be, however, that had you taken extended measures before and after the event, your findings may have been as shown in Figure 7.2.

By taking extended measures both before and after, it now seems that participation just after the event is actually lower than could be expected! The

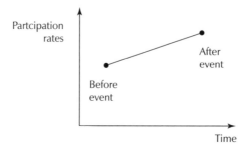

Figure 7.1 Participation rates before and after event

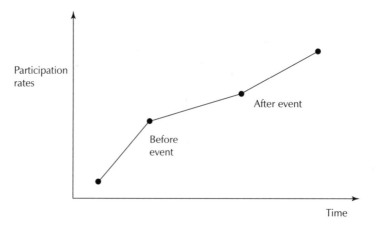

Figure 7.2 Extended measures of participation rates

time series design is useful in identifying such issues, however the time needed to undertake such a study makes this approach generally unsuitable for student research projects unless secondary data is used.

LONGITUDINAL DESIGNS

A longitudinal study is one that uses the same sample group and measures particular variables over an extended period of time. For example you may wish to examine the behaviour of employees of a sports organisation after a change in managerial policy to assess the effects of such a change, or you may wish to track the sport-related skills of a cohort of students throughout their education.

$$X1 \rightarrow X2 \rightarrow X3 \rightarrow X4 \rightarrow X5$$

time

You would take a measure of behaviour at X1, X2 and so on. The period of time involved could range from just a few weeks to several years. Longitudinal research needs to be approached with caution. It can take more time and resources than cross-sectional research, and there is always the issue of attrition, or dropout from participants. One alternative, although not totally desirable, is to approximate a longitudinal study using a cross-sectional research design. This is done by asking the sample to recall past attitudes and behaviours, describe their present attitudes and behaviours, and predict their future attitudes and behaviours. This is obviously a questionable research design, but it may prove useful where issues of time constraints and attrition are important. Another alternative to the traditional longitudinal approach is to choose groups at different stages in their development. For example, you may be interested in how attitudes towards competitive sport are developed during adolescence. Rather than take measurements with a single cohort over an extended period of time, a sample could be selected from different age ranges at the same time, and these could be compared, which would essentially be a cross-sectional research design.

CASE STUDY RESEARCH

Case study research involves the intensive study of a specific case. A case refers to a specific instance, for example you could undertake case study research on:

- An organisation
- A sports team
- A school
- An individual

The use of case study research is based upon the argument that understanding human activity requires analysis of both its development over time, and the environment and context within which the activity occurs. Case study designs are used to gain this holistic understanding of a set of issues, and how they relate to a particular group, organisation, sports team, or even a single individual. These issues are often researched using a variety of methods, over an extended period of time.

AN INDIVIDUAL ATHLETE

Sparkes (2000) was interested in the experiences of elite athletes whose career had been prematurely terminated by injury or illness. To do this, he undertook a biographical study of a single athlete, using the symbolic interactionist approach of interpretative biography. This approach involved 'The studied use and collection of life documents that describe turning points in an individual's life' (Denzin 1989, p.69 cited in Sparkes 2000, p.16), studying the individual in depth from a variety of disciplinary perspectives, involving extended contact with the participant. Through extended interactive interviews, Sparkes was able to collect extensive data about the subject, allowing him to conclude that the subject's strong athletic identity actually acted as an 'Achilles heel' in terms of reactions to injury. Thus, although not directly generalisable to the wider population, the findings were able to suggest that by understanding this 'Achilles heel', health care and physical activity professionals would be better able to deal with athletic injury or illness, enhancing the recovery and experiences of the athlete. The case study of a single athlete was able to provide such findings as it allowed the researcher a sense of the 'complete' experiences of the athlete, a depth of study often only available with the case study method. Had a larger sample been taken, then it would have been entirely possible that some of the depth, and thus understanding, would have been lost to the researcher.

Gall *et al.* (1996) note four characteristics of case study research:

1   Phenomena are studied through focusing on specific cases.
2   Each case is studied in depth.
3   Phenomena are studied in their natural context.
4   Case study research takes the perspective of those within the case, rather than the researcher's perspective.

You may consider the use of a case study design in three instances according to Yin (1994):

1   Your theory suggests particular outcomes in a particular context. Thus, you would need to choose a case that provided such an appropriate context.

2   To be able to describe and explain a unique or rare situation.
3   To describe and explain a case that has yet to be studied in any detail.

GROUNDED THEORY DESIGNS

Grounded theory is strongly associated with the inductive approach to research (see Chapter 2). Rather than enter the field or setting with any predetermined theories or ideas, the researcher will usually have no more than a generalised idea of the intended outcomes of the research. Theory is still an important part of the research, but is developed from the initial data collection, rather than testing predetermined hypotheses. These theories can then be tested, and the theory modified. More data can then be collected, and the theory continually modified through a combination of inductive and deductive approaches. This ensures that the theory is *grounded* within the data. Whilst this approach has its undoubted strengths, it can be time consuming, and the continual process of data collection and analysis can mean it is beyond the scope of many research projects. It can also be a risky strategy for student research!

ETHNOGRAPHIC DESIGNS

Ethnographic research is becoming increasingly accepted as a research design in social research into sport. We will deal with ethnography in some depth in Chapter 11, however we shall briefly outline the main concepts here. Essentially, an ethnography involves the in-depth study of a group through immersion into the culture of that group, often for an extended period of time, using multiple methods of data collection. The aim is to understand the behaviour or culture of that group by seeing it through the perspective of members of the group themselves. This involves the researcher becoming part of the group under investigation. Data collection is much more flexible, and data is collected as and when appropriate from available sources.

SAMPLING ISSUES

Once you have decided what information you need, and the design with which to collect data to yield this information, you need to identify from where the data is to be collected. In most cases the population under investigation will be too large to collect data from each member. Thus a *sample* must be taken. A sample refs to a subset of a specific population. Its purpose is, in most cases, to gain information about the overall population by selecting a smaller number of individual cases from the population. The responses of the sample, if it has *external validity*, can then be applied to the overall population. An example of this would be if you were researching the reasons why NBA basketball fans attended their first game. It would be impossible to question every NBA fan. Thus a smaller number of fans, who are representative of the population, are chosen. If, from this sample, it was determined that 50 per cent were taken to the game by their fathers, then it can be suggested that this is likely to be the case for the entire population of NBA fans.

Not all sampling has this particular purpose, however, especially in the more interpretative research designs. Sampling may also be done to select a group that demonstrates a certain theory or model particularly well, or simply to investigate a single group that is of particular interest to the researcher. In such cases, the results cannot be generalised to the overall population. In such cases you should aim to generalise to theory, that is your findings could be used to develop, refine or simply confirm an existing theory, which could then be applied to different samples.

SELECTING A SAMPLE

The first stage in selecting a sample is to define the *population*. The population consists of every individual case that possesses the characteristic that is of interest to the researcher. Thus, in the above case, the population may be defined as everyone that has attended an NBA game in the current season. Populations can be varied in size and location, and often you may have to delimit your population, or define your sample more narrowly. Thus you may have to define your population as fans of a particular basketball team. The disadvantage of this, of course, is that you may also – although not necessarily – lose generalisability, that is the extent to which findings from your chosen team could be applied to the other teams in the NBA.

The second stage is to determine your sampling method. In most cases, your aim is to produce a sample that is representative of the population. A high profile piece of research carried out for a number of years was the FA Carling Premiership survey. These surveys were designed to investigate the profiles, attitudes and behaviour of fans of teams in the English premier football league. Given the size of the population, a smaller sample obviously had to be taken. One serious criticism of the FA Carling Premiership surveys was that a number of questionnaires

were distributed in match day programmes. The achieved sample, that is the sample that completed and returned their questionnaires, was likely, in this case, to be unrepresentative of the population. The sample would, very possibly, under-represent less affluent fans who may not be able to afford the match day programme, less well-educated fans, who may not want to read the programme, and also younger fans, whose parents would perhaps be more likely to buy the programme and complete the questionnaire themselves, in all likelihood leading to misleading data regarding the composition of the crowd. In this example, it seems unlikely that the results from the sample could have been generalised to the population with confidence. This demonstrates the importance of appropriate sampling, and it is worth spending some time considering your sampling method. As we have seen, questionable sampling methods can seriously affect the external validity of the research.

A number of sampling techniques can be used. The most common are:

1   Random sampling
2   Stratified random sampling
3   Cluster sampling
4   Systematic sampling

1   *Random sampling.* A random sample is where every member of the popu-
    lation has an equal probability of being selected. This is considered the
    best technique to obtain a representative sample, and produce findings that
    will be generalisable to the overall population. The first stage is to define your
    population. The next stage is to ensure that each member of this population
    has an equal chance of being selected. The easiest way to do this is simply
    to place the names of all the population in a container, and pick names until
    the desired sample size has been achieved. Alternatively, each name can be
    assigned a number, and a random number table (available in most statistical
    textbooks and some research methods textbooks) or computer software can
    be used to select the sample.
2   *Stratified random sampling.* If there are certain subgroups within the popu-
    lation, for example based on age, sex and so on, then it may be necessary
    to ensure that they are adequately represented in the final sample. In this
    case, the population is divided into subgroups. Random samples are then
    taken from within these groups. Thus, you may divide your population into
    'male' and 'female', and randomly select 50 per cent of your sample from
    the list of your male participants, and the remaining 50 per cent from the list
    of your female participants. This will ensure your initial sample reflects the
    appropriate subgroups that are present within the population.

3 *Cluster sampling.* Cluster sampling is where groups are randomly selected, rather than individuals. Thus, if the researcher was interested in the attitudes towards intimidatory behaviour in little league baseball, then rather than select a random sample from the population of little league baseball players, a number of teams could be selected at random, and all players within those teams questioned. It is important to select a number of clusters to ensure generalisability with this method.

4 *Systematic sampling.* Sampling using this method involves selecting every *K*th case, for example taking every fourth name from a list, or every seventh person to enter a sports facility. Systematic sampling is best recommended when the list from which the names are taken is randomly ordered, otherwise some bias is likely to occur.

NON-RESPONSE BIAS

It is extremely unlikely that you will get responses from your entire sample, especially if you are using methods such as a postal questionnaire. Respondents may not have sufficient time, motivation or expertise to respond, they may fill in the questionnaire incorrectly, or they may simply not be reachable. As a result, the data you eventually collect may not always be representative of your population. You need to assess whether this is the case before you can generalise your findings, and this can be done in a number of ways:

■ Initially you should examine the characteristics of the achieved sample to try to identify any features that may suggest non-response bias, such as looking at the age and gender profiles, as well as any other variables that you may feel are important. Using a computer package such as *SPSS for Windows* (see Chapter 12) you could always display the response for certain variables graphically to examine response patterns.

■ If the information is available, compare the characteristics of your respondents with those of the population under investigation. Thus, for example, at the very simplest level you should be able to compare the gender distribution of your achieved sample with that of the population. If the gender balance of your population is equal, yet either males or females are under-represented in your achieved sample, then your sample is likely to be biased in this respect.

■ Send a follow-up letter to those who have not responded. If any further responses are obtained, then you can compare the characteristics of those who didn't initially respond with the original respondents to see if they differ in any way from your original respondents.

NON-PROBABILITY SAMPLING METHODS

In addition, you may also consider other non-probability methods of sampling, especially if you are undertaking research from an interpretative standpoint. You should be aware that you cannot generalise to the population using these methods, however you may be able to generalise to theory, that is theories and models can still be developed and refined from non-probability samples. The range of non-probability sampling methods includes the following:

1   *Snowball sampling.* You locate your initial participants, and these initial participants identify further potential participants themselves. Thus, you may find access to a 'gatekeeper', or influential member of your population. They can then introduce you to other participants, who themselves will be able to give you access to further participants. One potential advantage of this is that by being introduced by a known member of the population, you may be able to engender greater trust between researcher and subject.
2   *Theoretical sampling.* You identify cases that demonstrate a particular theory particularly well. You may be interested in the influence of the influx of foreign expertise upon the managerial culture of sports organisations, for example. You would therefore sample organisations that had experienced such expertise. This is more likely to be productive than a random selection from the entire population of sports organisations.
3   *Typical cases.* Your sample is chosen on the basis that they are 'typical' of a particular theory. For example you may wish to assess the impact of changing legislation affecting those using sports stadia with reference to a particular stadium that you consider 'typical'. The findings can then be generalised to those using other 'typical' stadia.
4   *Extreme cases.* You choose cases that are extreme cases of a theory. An example of this would be an investigation into the personality characteristics of elite athletes. You may wish to sample Olympic medal winners as extreme cases (remember that this is a hypothetical example . . . in reality your chances of getting access to such a sample is minimal at best!).
5   *Opportunistic.* You select samples as they arise, taking advantage of unexpected opportunities. For example you may be introduced to a particular key informant at an unexpected time.
6   *Convenience.* The sample is chosen as it is convenient in terms of location, accessibility, etc. Try to avoid convenience samples as far as you can – it is always tempting to hand out questionnaires to those you are in day to day contact with, or interview people that you know, but try to consider this as a last resort!

7 *Key informant technique.* Individuals are chosen on the basis of specific knowledge that they possess, for example they may have a particular role or responsibility within an organisation.

These methods are likely to have some form of sampling bias, and often this may be unavoidable. What you must do in this case is make an informed assessment of the sources of bias in your sample, and report these within the final write-up, and assess how such bias may influence your findings.

MISTAKES MADE IN SELECTING A SAMPLE

Your choice of sampling technique can be an important one for the success of your research project, so it is worth spending time considering your approach. Some of the common errors made in sampling – especially at undergraduate level – include:

■ Selecting individuals who are convenient, or readily available, for example individuals that are already known to the researcher.
■ Selecting individuals who volunteer to take part as well as those who are more randomly selected without reference to the potential differences between these.
■ Introducing bias through selecting a non-random sample.
■ Using a random sample when other sampling methods would be more appropriate.
■ Not obtaining a large enough sample for the purposes of the project.

DETERMINING THE SAMPLE SIZE

A frequently asked question is 'how big should my sample be?' Unfortunately there is no simple answer to this question, other than to say 'make sure it is big enough'! For the type of quantitative analysis typically collected as part of a quantitative study, you will need to balance the need for as large a sample size as possible with constraints based upon the issues of cost and time required for analysis. For basic descriptive statistics, an absolute minimum sample size of thirty would normally be required, with a larger sample more desirable. For more detailed inferential statistics thirty subjects per group would again be a suggested absolute minimum. The advice is to obtain the largest sample you can within the constraints mentioned above. A common error is to assume that the sample

Table 7.2 Sample size and confidence in your findings

Sample size	Results from sample		
	10 or 90%	30 or 70%	50%
50	8.3	12.7	13.9
100	5.9	9.0	9.8

Note: All figures assume 95% confidence level.
Source: Adapted from Veal 1997.

should be a certain percentage of the population, for example 10 per cent. In reality, there is no such relationship, and it is only the size of the sample that is important. Thus a sample of 100 is likely to provide equally accurate results whether the population consists of 5,000 or 50,000!

A second error is to assume that the finding from your sample will also be the true figure for the overall population. A sample can never provide a precise answer for the overall population. What it can do, provided it has been randomly taken, is to suggest the likely range within which the value for the wider population is likely to be. Table 7.2 demonstrates the relationship between sample size and the different ranges (or confidence intervals) within which the true value is likely to lie.

At the lower end of the sample size, problems can be illustrated with reference to some hypothetical findings. Imagine you are researching whether residents in a city took an active interest in the fortunes of their local sports team. From your achieved sample size of 50, you find that 50 per cent appear to take an interest. Table 7.2, however, shows that at the 95 per cent confidence level, the confidence interval for such a response is plus or minus 13.9. This tells you that it is likely that the actual percentage of residents taking an interest could range between 36.1 per cent and 63.9 per cent, a range of almost 30 per cent, which is clearly unacceptable if any firm conclusions are to be drawn. Increasing the sample size to 100 reduces the range to between 40.2 per cent and 59.8 per cent plus or minus 9.8. If you had the resources to sample 1,000 residents, then the range would drop still further to between 46.9 per cent and 53.1 per cent. Thus the importance of achieving as large a sample size as possible can be clearly demonstrated.

If you are looking at a number of subgroups, then you will also need to ensure adequate representation of each of these groups. For example, you may want to compare your findings above by gender. If your response is equally divided in terms of gender, then fifty responses will give you a sample size of twenty-five for each, which will not be enough to give you a sufficient degree of confidence in your findings. Thus the more subgroups you intend to involve in your analysis, the larger the sample has to be.

CASE STUDY OR ETHNOGRAPHIC SAMPLING

There are a number of issues of sampling that are specific to case study or ethnographic research. Your choice of case should rarely be random, rather it is more likely to be purposive, that is chosen to illustrate a particular situation. Often it may be a choice of convenience or access, for example you may have access to a particular organisation or sports-related body. When you are undertaking such research, the questions that you need to consider are:

- How many cases are required? Am I looking to provide a detailed analysis of the factors affecting one particular case, or would I like to be able to compare two or more cases to be able to assess the relative importance of such variables?
- Am I looking for a typical case, with which the results I obtain can be generalised to other cases? In which case, how will I identify what is 'typical'?
- Am I looking for an extreme or important case which will demonstrate a particular theory or model well?
- Am I likely to get access to my sample?

CASE STUDY

SAMPLING

Hardin (1999) was interested in the role conflict within expert coaches in their dual roles of teacher and coach. He wanted to discover the attributes of successful teacher/coaches to find out more about the requirements for successful sport instruction, which could then be used to inform the behaviour of other teacher/coaches. A random sample taken from the overall population of teacher/coaches would not have provided valid information, which needed to come from experts. Using past studies on expertise, Hardin was able to identify a number of criteria that could be used to inform his sample. Thus, coaches were selected if they fulfilled the following:

▼

106

- A minimum of five years' experience.
- A greater than 70 per cent win/loss record, or two or more playoff titles.
- Recognition of coaching (such as coaching awards).
- Proven leadership in coaching.
- Accessibility to the researcher.

Hardin was able to identify five coaches for an in-depth study based on these criteria, allowing him to conclude that expert teacher/coaches showed differing characteristics in each role, and that each environment was different, and thus needed to be accounted for by the teacher/coach, depending upon their role at the time.

WHAT METHODS SHOULD I USE TO COLLECT DATA FROM MY SAMPLE?

So far in this chapter we have covered the issue of research design, whereby you consider the overall framework of your data collection. We have also covered the issue of sampling, that is from whom this data is collected. The final issue within this chapter is that of how such data is to be collected. Thus the choice of appropriate methods becomes the final consideration of this part of the research process. Methods are, simply, the techniques by which you collect your data. The key methods that you may encounter are:

- Questionnaires
- Interviews
- Observation and participant observation
- Content analysis
- Ethnography

The choice of method is obviously important to the success of your project. Chapters 8 to 11 of this text examine each of the methods in turn, so we will only provide a brief outline here.

By this stage of the research process, you should be able to identify your own epistemological stance, tending towards either the positivist or interpretative. You should also have an idea of the type of data you need to collect, this being qualitative, quantitative or a combination of the two. Finally, you should also have an idea of your likely sample in terms of who you would like to collect data from, and the desired sample size. You can now begin to approach the issue of choosing your methods. There is no one set way to do this, however the following questions can guide your approach:

1   *Am I looking to collect quantitative data?* If so, then if that data can be directly observed, consider the use of observation as your data collection method (Chapter 10). If not, then consider the use of a questionnaire (Chapter 8). Alternatively, if you are intending to analyse texts, such as newspapers, television programmes, letters, speeches, etc. then use content analysis (Chapter 10).
2   *Am I looking to collect qualitative data?* If you are looking to explore the thoughts, feelings, emotions and perceptions of others, then consider the use of in-depth interviews (Chapter 9). If you are looking to explore such concepts yourself, then use participant observation (Chapter 10).
3   *Am I looking to carry out an in-depth investigation of a particular group or culture?* Consider the use of an ethnographic approach (Chapter 11).
4   *Am I looking to strengthen the validity of the findings through triangulation?* If so, consider using more than one method. We outline the concept of triangulation below.

You should also consider your own personal skills and preferences in making your choice. If you are not happy talking to others, then interviewing may not be the method for you! Or, if you lack confidence in dealing with numbers, then consider alternatives to a strongly quantitative questionnaire, requiring detailed statistical analysis. The most important thing to ensure, however, is that your choice of method is appropriate to meet your research objectives.

TRIANGULATION OF DATA

Whilst you are considering your research design, you may wish to consider the appropriateness of *triangulation*. Triangulation in its most common form refers to the use of multiple means of data collection to explore a single phenomenon. Consider the following example. You may be interested in how pupils on a physical education course react to a change in the nature of their course of study. You may collect data using a questionnaire, which suggests that pupils are not overly concerned provided they can comprehend the rationale behind the change. If you have designed and piloted your questionnaire carefully, you may have some degree of confidence in these findings. Now imagine that you have followed up this initial data collection by using an additional method, for example by interviewing a sample of pupils. These pupils also suggest they are not overly concerned, again provided the rationale behind the change is clear to them. Now, your confidence in the findings should be increased, as you have data from different methods which allows you to draw the same conclusions. This is the basis of triangulation, which refers simply to the use of more than a single source of data (although poorly thought out triangulation can also have the effect of increasing error rather than reducing it!). A number of types of triangulation can be identified:

- *Data.* This may refer to the use of different data sources, for example interviews and questionnaires. Alternatively it may involve using different informants, such as interviews with pupils and teachers, or informants with the same sample, but at different times.
- *Investigator.* Different researchers may collect, and draw their own conclusions from the same data.
- *Theoretical.* The same situation may be examined using different theoretical viewpoints. Generally, this form of triangulation will be beyond the scope of most student research projects.

As we have said, it is possible for triangulation to increase the error in your conclusions. In our example, pupils may have felt that the data from the questionnaires may have been made available to their tutors, and not wishing to be seen to be causing trouble, may have responded positively towards changes in their course. They may have been even more concerned about this during their interview, and again respond positively towards the changes. The researcher, meanwhile, writes up the report under the impression that the data triangulation has strengthened the validity of their findings! Thus you need to be cautious in triangulating your data, and identify any potential problems that may arise.

COMBINING QUANTITATIVE AND QUALITATIVE APPROACHES

So far in this chapter we have suggested that your design will lead to the collection of either quantitative or qualitative data. In many cases this is advisable, for example in terms of the expertise required in both approaches, the extended time required to actually carry out the study, and the need to keep research focused. As we noted in Chapter 2, however, it can sometimes be appropriate to collect both types of data, and often this can enhance a piece of research in a number of ways:

- As we have already mentioned, triangulation from using different data collection techniques can strengthen the validity of the research.
- The two types of data may complement each other, for example quantitative data may describe a phenomenon well, and qualitative data may be appropriate to gain an understanding of the phenomenon.
- Quantitative data may throw up questions that are more suited to qualitative analysis, and vice versa.

You need to be careful in identifying your purpose in mixing data. For example will you be looking at the same phenomenon using different data collection methods, or will you use one approach to investigate findings that have emerged from an earlier stage of the study? In the second case it could be argued that you are not mixing approaches, but simply looking at two separate research questions!

ETHICAL CONSIDERATIONS IN RESEARCH DESIGN

Whatever research design, sampling techniques and choice of methods you choose to adopt, you will also need to consider the ethical issues associated with the research, that is the question of whether your research design is socially and morally acceptable. Certain research designs (for example experimental designs) often raise important ethical questions that need to be addressed, and you should do this before commencing any data collection from your sample. This is an area where it is better to be safe than sorry, especially if the research involves sensitive groups, such as children. You should always, therefore, allow your research proposal to be scrutinised by an ethics committee, and accept their decision if the research proposal is considered unethical in any way.

Voluntary participation, involuntary participation and informed consent

The obvious way to overcome ethical issues in terms of who participates may be that of asking for volunteers to take part. Unfortunately, a voluntary sample is unlikely to be representative, and your sample is likely to be more highly educated, more socially oriented, more interested or more knowledgeable of the subject matter than the population as a whole. If this is the case, then it is difficult if not impossible for you to generalise your findings to the population. The motives of those volunteering may also be questioned, for example a relatively common

practice in sports-related research in the USA is to require students to participate in research projects for course credit. The results from these findings cannot be generalised to the wider population without some degree of caution, as they are likely to possess certain characteristics that differ from the overall population.

Occasionally an involuntary sample may be adopted, where the subjects are unaware of their participation. This is generally acceptable if the researcher is making what is referred to as unobtrusive measures, for example taking a frequency count of the number of people using a particular sports facility. Obtrusive research, that is influencing their behaviour in some way, such as setting up a contrived situation and monitoring subjects' reactions to that situation, however, needs much more ethical consideration before proceeding.

The best approach to take is that of *informed consent*. The sample should be chosen using an appropriate sampling technique as described earlier in the chapter. Each participant in the research should then be informed as to the nature of the study, and the use of the data supplied before data is collected from them. Consent should be obtained from the participants, and from parents and schools in the case of research into children. Subjects must be given the right to withdraw from the study at any time. If it is highly likely that informing the participants as to the exact nature of the study would bias or invalidate the results in some manner, then the participants should be informed of the purpose of the study after data collection. Coercion should not be used under any circumstance to ensure participation in any way. Informed consent can suggest non-random samples to some extent, in that there is some suggestion that the subjects have volunteered. Provided, however, the overall response rate is reasonable, and the researcher analyses the reasons for dropout to assess any patterns of non-participation, then this is not a significant issue for most research projects.

Deception

The issue of deception is a complex one. The primary argument for deception is that if the subject is aware of the nature of the investigation, then this may affect the results. The argument against is that deception is basically unethical in society. Some deception may be acceptable, if there are no questionable outcomes to the subjects, or if the subjects are not harmed or affected in any way. Other deception is more questionable. For example in a well-known study in a non-sport context, Rosenthal and Jacobsen (1968) informed teachers which children were likely to show better academic performances and which were not. Despite the fact that the two groups were actually chosen at random, those expected to do better actually did so, compared to those who were expected to fare worse. Such an experiment, it could be argued, may have had an extremely harmful effect on the subjects, both in the short and long term. In this instance, we can suggest no justification for the research, and would take the overall view that such deception is very rarely justified. We again stress that, at the very least, if you feel that deception is warranted, you should ensure that your research proposal is assessed by an ethics committee at your university or organisation.

Confidentiality

All participants should be informed as to who will have access to research data. Ideally this should be as few people as possible, and only those that actually need access to such data (in many cases this may be only the researcher) and you must ensure that once data is collected, then no one will have access unless authorised to do so. A further recommendation is to ensure that individuals cannot be identified by using pseudonyms, or assigning numbers to individuals in the data set.

ASSESSING THE ETHICS OF YOUR RESEARCH

Carrying out research into social phenomena such as sport is difficult to do without coming across some ethical issues. Make sure you read the codes of conduct laid down by your specific discipline. For example if you are interested in the psychology of sport, then you should familiarise yourself with the guidelines of the American Psychological Association (APA) or the British Psychological Society (BPS). Such codes generally include the following key requirements:

- Risks to participants are outweighed by the benefits of the research programme.
- Participation should be voluntary.
- Risks to participants are eliminated or minimised as far as possible, including psychological and social, as well as physical risks.
- All information should be treated as strictly confidential.
- The participants have the right to be informed of the purpose of the study.
- Participants may withdraw at any time.
- Participants should be debriefed after the research programme.

You should ensure that you gain ethical approval from the relevant committee at your institution before any research programme involving ethical issues commences.

SUMMARY

1   You should have a carefully considered approach to the collection of your data, in terms of who you will collect data from, when such data will be collected, and how such data will be collected. This is your research design.
2   We have identified six research designs: experimental, cross-sectional, time series, longitudinal, case study, grounded theory and ethnography.
3   Whatever research design you adopt, it is unlikely that you will be able to collect data from the entire population. Thus you will have to collect data from a smaller group within that population – your sample.
4   You will also have to choose the methods by which you are going to collect data from that sample.
5   It may be possible to increase the validity of your research by undertaking some form of triangulation. Triangulation means collecting data from more than one perspective; for example it may involve collecting qualitative, as well as quantitative data.
6   You will also need to consider the ethical issues involved in your research. If in doubt, you should gain approval from the committee responsible for ethical issues at your institution.

ACTIVITIES

Look again at some of the pieces of research that you have already read. Can you answer the following questions about each article?

1   What research design has been adopted for the research? Do you feel this is appropriate for the research in question? Can you identify any alternative research designs that may have been considered?
2   What methods have been adopted in the study? Why?
3   Can you identify any ethical issues that may have arisen? If so, have the authors addressed these issues?

- Can you clearly identify and justify the research design you are using? Have you considered any alternative designs?
- Have you considered using triangulation as a technique to enhance the validity of your research?
- What are the ethical issues involved with your research project? How will you ensure that your research project will not breach any guidelines? Have you ensured that your research has been assessed by the appropriate ethics committee?

CHAPTER EIGHT

COLLECTING DATA I:
THE QUESTIONNAIRE SURVEY

In this chapter we will:

- Discuss the use of questionnaires as a method of data collection.
- Introduce some of the advantages and disadvantages of using questionnaire surveys in your research project.
- Outline some of the issues of questionnaire design and administration.

INTRODUCTION

So far, we have largely dealt with the 'background' to your research project in terms of reading and assessing the literature, clarifying the role of theory, completing the conceptual framework and deciding upon a research design. The next stage in most cases is to collect primary data to test your hypothesis, or answer your research question. The next few chapters deal with issues of data collection, beginning with an examination of the use of questionnaires in sports research in this chapter.

Questionnaires are perhaps the most commonly used method in sport-related research. Defined simply, a questionnaire is a standardised set of questions to gain information from a subject. They are often associated with quantitative research designs, when relatively simple measurements are required from a large sample group (although you can collect qualitative data using questionnaires, it is not desirable in most cases and other methods are generally more appropriate). Questionnaires generally fall into one of three categories:

1   *Postal questionnaire*. The questionnaire is given or posted to the participant, who completes it in his or her own time. The participant then posts the completed questionnaire back to the researcher.
2   *Telephone questionnaire*. The researcher questions the participant over the telephone and the researcher fills in the responses.
3   *Face to face questionnaire*. The researcher and participant are in the same location, and the researcher asks the questions 'face to face'.

Questionnaires can be designed for completion either by the researcher (interviewer completion) or by the subject (respondent or self-completion). Interviewer completion surveys are effectively the same as *structured interviews*, and the issues associated with this particular technique will be dealt with in the next chapter. This chapter will provide an overview of respondent completion surveys, the type of questionnaire that you are most likely to use.

WHEN IS THE USE OF A QUESTIONNAIRE APPROPRIATE?

The first consideration that you must make is whether a questionnaire is actually an appropriate method to collect the data you need. Once you have developed and focused your research question, considered the relevant concepts (see Chapter 6), and determined your choice of research design, you should be able to list your information needs, that is the information you require to answer your research question. Three questions can now be asked:

1   Can I get the information I need using data from a questionnaire?
2   Is a questionnaire the best or most appropriate method, or are other methods more appropriate to collect the data?
3   Are other methods excluded, for example interviews, because of time and cost restrictions?

Questionnaires are appropriate in a variety of contexts, where relatively simple, generally quantitative information is required from a large sample group. This data can then be summarised through the use of tables or charts, or analysed statistically to answer a research question. Research projects such as the FA Carling Premiership surveys (SNCCFR 1996–2000) are a good example of the use of postal questionnaires. The main aim of this research was to discover a wide range of relatively simple information about English soccer fans, for example measuring variables such as age, gender and spending upon football-related merchandise. Given the number of clubs in the Premiership (twenty in total) and combined attendances of many thousands, interviewing a sufficient number of fans was obviously impractical both in terms of time and cost. Simple observation would not have allowed the appropriate data to be collected. Questionnaires were, however, ideal to collect such a large volume of simple data. If more complex information had been required, however, questionnaires would have been unlikely to be able to yield such information, and other methods would have been more appropriate in such a case.

ADVANTAGES OF THE QUESTIONNAIRE SURVEY

As you will learn over the next few chapters, each of the methods you may adopt as part of a research project has its own advantages and disadvantages. In most cases you will have to assess these when considering your choice of method. What you will ultimately need to do, however, is to be able to justify your eventual choice. The advantages of using a questionnaire include the following:

- *Accessibility*. The postal questionnaire allows you to collect data from a geographically dispersed sample group at a much lower cost than interviewing a similar sample. In addition, as you are not needed to be present to ask questions yourself, using questionnaires allows a larger sample to be investigated.
- *Potential reduction in bias*. With a well-designed questionnaire there is little opportunity to introduce bias into the results as may be the case with interviews, for example through the way you respond to an answer, or your body language (see Chapter 9), or simply your presence in observational studies. You should be aware, however, that badly designed questionnaires can lead to bias in your data, hence using a questionnaire does not automatically mean a reduction in bias.
- *Anonymity*. The presence of the researcher interested in certain sensitive issues, for example player violence, or the use of drugs, or cheating in sport, may inhibit the respondent. A postal questionnaire allows anonymity, and may, therefore, improve the validity of your responses in certain cases.
- *Structured data*. Questionnaires tend to provide highly structured quantitative data that is easily comparable, either between subject groups, or between the same group studied over an extended time period. Such data is generally straightforward to convert into tables and charts, and to analyse statistically.
- *Increased time for respondents*. Respondent-completed questionnaires allow the respondent to fill in the questionnaire at a convenient time if necessary, or to be able to go back to the questionnaire at a later time if they recall anything further.

DISADVANTAGES OF THE POSTAL QUESTIONNAIRE

- *Potential problems over complex questions.* The questions have to be clear enough for all participants to understand, as there will often be no opportunity for the respondent to seek clarification, especially in a postal questionnaire. If complex questions are required, then you may need to be present to explain them. Thus, to a large extent, you are restricted to relatively simple questions.
- *No control over who completes the questionnaire.* Unless you specify exactly who is to fill out the questionnaire, it may be completed by an inappropriate party. Even if you do specify that it has to be completed by a particular individual, it may be that the respondent delegates the task to somebody else without your knowledge.
- *No opportunity to probe.* Once the respondent has answered the question there is no opportunity to get him or her to expand upon or explain any of the points that may have been made.
- *Potentially low response rates.* Response rates from questionnaires are notoriously poor, and can range from as little as 5 per cent or so upwards. Low response rates may have a serious effect on the reliability of the study. Potential means of improving your response rates are highlighted later in the chapter.

DESIGNING YOUR QUESTIONNAIRE

Once you have decided that it is an appropriate data collection technique, the second stage of questionnaire-based research is that of the initial design of the questionnaire. A good questionnaire is difficult to design, and takes considerably more time than is often anticipated. Whilst it is relatively easy to put together a questionnaire that may seem to have some relevance towards the research objectives, designing questions that actually fulfil all of the researcher's needs is more time consuming. As Oppenheim (1992, p.7) notes:

> Too often, surveys are carried out on the basis of insufficient design and planning or on the basis of no design at all. 'Fact-gathering' can be an exciting and tempting activity to which a questionnaire opens a quick and seemingly easy avenue; the weaknesses in the design are frequently not recognised until the results have to be interpreted – if then!

Three questions need to be asked at the beginning of the design stage. These are:

1   What information do I need to answer my research question?
2   What questions can I ask that will provide me with data that will, when analysed, give me such information?
3   How am I going to analyse the data that I get from such questions to give me the answer to my research question?

Thus, before designing the questionnaire, it is important that your information needs have been clearly identified. As a rule of thumb, you should try to keep the questionnaire as short as possible, yet ensure that it will provide all of the necessary data. Do not be tempted to include questions that are not required, even if you consider them to be interesting! You should be able to justify the inclusion of each question, and identify how that question will help answer your research question. You also need to think ahead in terms of how you intend to analyse your data, which will influence you in the type of data that you decide to collect (for example ordinal or ratio data).

WHAT TYPES OF QUESTION CAN I ASK?

There are a number of different question formats that you can adopt when designing your questionnaire. The most common formats are described below.

Simple open and closed questions

Closed/pre-coded questions

The respondent is asked to choose one or more responses from a series of choices predetermined by the researcher, for example:

Q.1 How many competitive matches have you played so far this season? (please tick one box)

Less than 10

Between 10 and 20

21 or more

If the question involves relatively simple information, and you know all of the available responses beforehand, such as a question on the sex of the respondent, then use a closed question. This will provide you with the information in its simplest format, which will be easy to analyse, and provide easily structured data. Such questions are also easier for respondents, and take less time than other question formats to complete.

Open questions

Sometimes it is not possible to anticipate all of the answers you are going to receive, or you may anticipate a wide variety of different answers. Here you will need the respondent to write their answer with no prompting, for example:

Q.2 What, in your opinion, are the attributes of a good coach? . . . .
. . . .
. . . .

You can use open questions within a questionnaire to obtain limited amounts of qualitative data, although you need to be careful, as participants are unlikely to be willing to write down lengthy answers to your questions! Open questions can be harder to analyse, as a wider range of answers can be given by the respondent. The answers to any open questions will need to be coded, or converted into numbers if you are going to quantitatively analyse your data (see Chapters 12 and 13 for an overview of data analysis).

THE USE OF OPEN AND CLOSED QUESTIONS

Often, you will have the choice between using open and closed questions. Rather than make an arbitrary choice, you should think about the purpose of your questionnaire. The following guidelines may be of use.

Use closed questions if:

- You require quantitative data.
- You have a clear idea of the likely responses.
- Responses are likely to be simple.
- It is important for respondents to answer using a predetermined set of responses.

Use open questions if:

- You require qualitative data.
- You are unsure of the likely responses.
- Responses are likely to be complex.
- The respondent's own words are important.

An alternative approach is combine open and closed questions, so that a number of responses are provided but the respondent has the opportunity to respond in an alternative manner if none of the responses are appropriate, or to elaborate on a particular response, for example:

Q.3 Who was the most important influence on you in your decision to take up your chosen sport?

Father ▫

Mother ▫

Brother ▫

Sister ▫

Teacher ▫

Other (please state) . . . .

Scales

Occasionally you may need to measure a concept using a *scale*. A scale is a series of questions designed to gain a single measure of a concept, such as an attitude towards or opinion on something. A number of different scaling techniques exist.

Likert scales

These are generally used to assess attitudes. A Likert scale allows the respondent to indicate the extent to which they agree with a certain statement. At its simplest level, such a scale may provide a statement and the respondent may be asked whether they agree or disagree, for example:

Q.4 Do you agree that sponsorship of major sporting events is an effective marketing strategy for major corporations?

Agree ☒

Disagree ☒

Often, however, a respondent will be unhappy about being forced into such an extreme choice. Likert scales can be used to measure the *extent* to which participants agree or disagree with a particular statement, and are useful for questions where there may be no clear responses, such as 'yes' or 'no'. An example of this is the Sport Spectator Identification Scale (Wann and Branscombe 1993). This scale is a seven-item scale using an eight-point response designed to measure how strongly an individual identifies with a certain sports team. Two of the seven items are as follows:

	Not at all						Very much so

Q.5 It is important to me that
X team wins ☒ ☒ ☒ ☒ ☒ ☒ ☒ ☒

Q.6 It is important to me that
other people see me
as a fan of X ☒ ☒ ☒ ☒ ☒ ☒ ☒ ☒

Respondents tick the appropriate point on the scale that matches most closely their feelings. A score is assigned to each possible response, from one when the box on the far left is ticked, through to eight for a tick on the far right box. This allows an overall score to be calculated. For the Sport Spectator Identification Scale, the maximum score for each item is eight. Being a seven-item scale, this allows a minimum score of seven (scoring one on each of the seven items) and a maximum score of fifty-six (scoring eight on each item). The average score per question is then taken, which means potential scores of identification with a team ranging between one (little, or no identification with the sports team) and eight (very highly identified with the sports team). These scores can then be correlated with other characteristics such as perceptions of influence on game outcome, or reactions to opposition fans, for example. Occasionally you can reverse your items. For example, Q.5 could be reworded 'It is not important to me that X team wins'. For reversed items, the scales are scored from right to left, rather than left to right. This can be a useful measure to stop people simply ticking the same box for each question.

Semantic differential

This format measures the respondent's reaction to a specified concept using a scale with contrasting adjectives at each end, for example:

Q.7 Just before I start a football game I feel

Relaxed   ▢   ▢   ▢   ▢   ▢   Anxious

The responses are scored in the same way as for a Likert scale. Semantic differential scales are also useful to assess respondents' attitudes towards a particular phenomenon without forcing them into an extreme choice.

Other question formats

Ranking

Ranking questions ask the respondent to place responses in order of importance. These are appropriate when you want respondents to consider the relative merits of particular items.

Q.8 Please rank the following sports in order of preference 1 to 3, with 1 signifying the sport you like most, and 3 signifying the sport you like least:

Field hockey   ▢
Basketball   ▢
Tennis   ▢

List questions

These questions allow the respondent to indicate several responses to one question, for example:

Q.9 Which of the following companies have sponsored sports events to your knowledge in the last twelve months? (please tick as appropriate)

General Motors   ▢
Ford   ▢
Gillette   ▢
Coca-Cola   ▢

Filter questions

It is important that you don't alienate potential respondents through asking them to read through and respond to large numbers of irrelevant questions. Filter questions can be used where appropriate to prevent this. Often some of your questions will be inapplicable to certain respondents. Rather than forcing respondents to read each question and decide whether or not it is relevant, questions which are not applicable can be filtered out using the following format:

Q.10   Have you paid to attend a live sports event in the past seven days?

> No   ▪ – please go to question 11
> Yes   ▪
>
> If 'Yes' what event(s) did you pay to watch? . . . .
> . . . .

Using filter questions can minimise the time taken to complete the questionnaire, and reduce the potential frustration that respondents may feel when reading through a number of questions that don't apply to them. This can be a useful way of helping to increase your response rates.

SHOULD I USE EXISTING QUESTIONS OR SCALES OR DEVELOP MY OWN?

Inexperienced researchers often feel that to add to the originality of their research, they should always develop their own questions or scales, and that the use of somebody else's questionnaire lays them open to the charge of plagiarism. In reality, you are, in many cases, better off using existing questions and scales, especially if they have been designed to measure the same concepts that you are interested in (provided, of course, that you fully acknowledge the source of the original questionnaire!). These will already have been assessed in terms of their reliability and validity, and using existing questions allows you to compare your findings with those of others much more easily. Valid and reliable scales are difficult and time consuming to develop, and even apparently straightforward concepts may be difficult to measure using a scale. Sport is a complex social phenomenon, and the concepts within it are rarely unidimensional, that is they cannot be measured using a single question. Scales therefore have to measure the multidimensionality of concepts, and developing such scales can often be a task that is time consuming to even experienced researchers. Thus, when searching the literature, you should be prepared to look for information not only about the relevant concepts and ideas, but also about how such concepts and ideas have been measured in the past.

ORDERING THE QUESTIONNAIRE

Once you have designed the specific questions, it is then important to consider their sequence within the questionnaire. There is no set order, but you should consider the following points:

- Try to begin the questionnaire with a few straightforward, closed questions requiring factual answers if at all possible. It is important to get the respondent to actually start completing the questionnaire. Once the first few questions have been completed, it is much more likely that the respondent will persevere.
- You should therefore avoid putting complex questions, questions requiring detailed thought, or questions requiring lengthy responses at the beginning of the questionnaire.
- Group questions on a similar theme together, and avoid jumping from topic to topic.
- Ask personal, or potentially threatening questions at the end of the questionnaire (and include them only if they are actually necessary).

PROBLEMS IN QUESTIONNAIRE DESIGN

Unlike many other forms of data collection, questionnaire surveys generally allow the researcher a 'one-off' chance at research. If the questionnaire is badly designed, then it is unlikely that you will get another chance to collect the data due either to time restrictions, or the difficulties in finding further participants. Therefore, you should be aware of some of the potential errors in designing a questionnaire.

- *Ambiguous/complex wording.* Questions that may seem clear to the researcher may not be clear to the respondent, especially if the sample group is likely to be diverse. You should also avoid using technical, or 'academic' language. The questions should be understandable to the lowest level of education that the sample may encompass. For example if you are collecting data from a broad cross-section of the population, then your questionnaire must be understandable to children. Otherwise, you are likely to under-represent this group in your achieved sample, leading to non-response bias.

- *Incorrectly pre-coding closed questions.* An easy mistake to make is to incorrectly identify the predetermined responses that you provide for your respondents. An example of this would be the following question:

Q. 11 How many times a week do you train?

Never ▪   2–3 times ▪
1–2 times a week ▪   more than 3 times ▪

Those respondents who train twice a week could fill in more than one box, leading to problems of reliability and validity. Alternatively you may omit possible responses, so that none of the available responses are appropriate to the respondent.

- *Leading questions.* Questions such as 'do you agree that potentially dangerous performance enhancing drugs should be banned?' should be avoided as respondents may feel pressured to agree with such statements. Try not to influence respondents in any way by your question wording.

- *Double-barrelled questions.* Avoid asking for respondents' views on two separate issues in the same question. Questions such as 'do you agree that rugby is a dangerous sport and should be banned' ask two different questions, yet only allow for a single answer. Ensure that each question measures a single concept.

- *Threatening questions.* It is often difficult to obtain valid information if the respondent is likely to feel threatened at all. When undertaking research into violence in sport, or the use of performance enhancing drugs, for example, the respondent may well under-report, or even deny such activity. The researcher must first identify any threatening questions, and second, carefully word these questions to reduce bias. Try to word such questions in a neutral manner.

- *Incorrectly operationalising concepts.* If the concept has not been suitably operationalised, then it will be impossible to collect valid data. An example may be that you have operationalised commitment to playing for a particular amateur sports team in terms of how many times a respondent plays a season. It may be that an individual is extremely committed, yet can only play irregularly, perhaps due to work or family commitments. In such an instance, the data obtained would lack validity.

PILOTING THE QUESTIONNAIRE

No matter how well designed you think your questionnaire is, it is vital that it is piloted beforehand. A pilot survey refers to a small-scale administration of the survey prior to the main administration. The pilot survey performs a number of important functions, including:

- To check that the wording of the questionnaire is clear, unambiguous and understandable to the intended sample.
- To check that the sequence of the questionnaire is clear and logical to respondents.
- To assess the likely completion time of the questionnaire.
- To check the administration of the questionnaire, from its initial distribution to receiving the completed questionnaire.
- To allow you a 'dry run' at analysing the data collected from the questionnaire.

The last point is one that is often overlooked. It is worth inputting your preliminary data from the pilot questionnaires into whatever package you are going to use for analysis (see Chapter 12), and using this data to try and answer your question to ensure that the data you collect is suitable for your purposes.

Your pilot survey should be carried out in conditions as close to the main survey, and with as similar a sample group as possible. The results of the pilot should be closely monitored. Once changes have been made, then the survey must be re-piloted and the need for any further changes assessed. You should then continue to pilot your questionnaire until you are completely happy with its design.

CASE STUDY

MEASURING THE ECONOMIC IMPACT OF VISITORS TO SPORTS TOURNAMENTS AND SPECIAL EVENTS

UK Sport (1999) has provided a set of guidelines for those conducting research into the economic impact of major sporting events. These studies are generally done through visitor surveys, and the additional expenditure generated within a city as a consequence of hosting an event can partially be evaluated through self-completion questionnaires. Through examining the design of their questionnaire, we can develop an idea of how questionnaires should be designed to achieve their research objectives. It is important that a questionnaire of this type is kept as short as possible to maximise response rates. Thus, as with any good questionnaire, each question has a particular purpose related to the objectives of the research. The objectives of the research are as follows:

- *Objective 1*. To quantify the proportions of respondents who live in the host city and those who are from outside the host city.
- *Objective 2*. To determine the catchment area of the event by local, regional, national and international responses.

Economic impacts refer only to expenditure made by out-of-town visitors. Thus a question is required to differentiate between local and non-local respondents. This question also allows researchers to identify the proportion of out-of-town visitors to the event, as well as enabling the catchment area of an event to be identified.

Q.1 Where do you live? (Please specify town or city) . . . .

Note that an open question is used, as it is not possible to list all potential responses. It is important to specify the level of detail, by ensuring respondents specify the town or city, otherwise unhelpful answers such as 'England' may be returned. At this point, those who live within the host city can be identified, and the data collection terminated.

- *Objective 3*. To group respondent types by their role in the event, for example, media, spectators, competitors, officials, etc.

Different groups will show different characteristics, therefore it is important to have knowledge of which group the respondent belongs to.

Q.2 Which of the following are you?

Athlete	▪	Coach	▪
Official	▪	Media	▪
Spectator	▪	Other	▪

In this instance, all the appropriate responses are known, thus a closed question is appropriate. This allows easy analysis of responses, as well as being easier and quicker for the respondent.

■ *Objective 4*. To identify the basic characteristics of respondents.

Certain characteristics – such as gender – are easily observed. Other characteristics, such as the size of the group of which the respondent was a part, are included on the questionnaire. Note the use of a filter question to minimise the need to answer irrelevant questions:

Q.3 Are you attending the athletics alone?   Yes ▨   No ▨

If YES please go to question 4a

If NO: How many other adults (over 16)
are there in your party today?   ▨

If NO: How many other children (under 16)
are there in your party today?   ▨

■ *Objective 5*. To quantify the number of people from outside the host city staying overnight in the host city and from this subsample to quantify how many are staying in commercially provided accommodation.

Accommodation is by far the largest expenditure item, and those staying overnight are likely to spend more elsewhere. Thus, it is important to quantify such individuals. By using two questions, the location where respondents are staying, the type of accommodation utilised, and the proportion of day to overnight visitors could be ascertained:

Q.4a In which town/city are you staying tonight? . . . .
Q.4b Is this

    At home   ▨
    With friends/relatives   ▨
    A guest house   ▨
    A hotel   ▨
    A camp site   ▨
    Other   ▨

If Other; Please specify . . . .

Note the importance of allowing respondents an alternative option if none of the given options is appropriate.

■ *Objective 6.* To quantify how many nights those staying in commercial accommodation will spend in the city and how much per night such accommodation is costing.

The revenue from visitors staying in commercial accommodation is, as we noted, the largest source of economic revenue. To calculate this revenue, two questions are again needed:

Q.5a How many nights are you staying in town/city X? ■

   If you are not staying overnight in town/city X go to question 6

Q.5b If you are staying overnight in town/city X: How much are you spending on accommodation per night? ■

Simple analysis thus allows the number of commercial bed-nights (number of visitors x number of nights stayed) and revenue (commercial bed-nights x average cost per bed-night) to be calculated.

■ *Objective 7.* To quantify the amount spent per day on six standard categories of expenditure.

For such a study, it is also important to quantify the amount spent on other products and services by all respondents (not just overnight visitors). It is important that only expenditure made in the host town or city is included, and thus the question is designed to reflect this:

Q.6 How much will you spend in town/city X TODAY on the following?

Food and drink	■	Programmes/merchandise	■
Entertainment	■	Shopping/souvenirs	■
Travel	■	Other (parking, petrol, etc.)	■

- *Objective 8*. To quantify how much in total people have budgeted to spend in a host city and on how many other people this expenditure will be made.

People may combine an event with another activity, such as a mini-break or business, for example. To identify additional expenditure that would not otherwise be picked up, a question is included to quantify the total amount individuals have budgeted to spend in the host city. The final part of this question asks how many other people this expenditure is being made for. Response to this question enables any amount of expenditure already identified to be put on a per capita basis.

Q.7 How much have you budgeted to spend in TOTAL during your stay in town/city X?

Total expenditure
Does this include expenditure on others   Yes   No

If YES: how many others is this expenditure for? . . . .

- *Objective 9*. To establish the proportion of people whose main reason for being in the host city is the event under investigation.

It may be that, in certain instances, those attending the event are not in the host town or city specifically for that event. Thus, any economic impacts from such visitors can not be attributed to the sporting event itself. A question is needed to identify such individuals:

Q.8 Is event Y the main reason for your being in town/city X today?

Yes   No

- *Objective 10*. To determine if any respondents are combining their visit to the host city with a holiday.

For some, an event may lead to a decision to take a break, or a holiday. For example the World Cup may lead to supporters spending an extended period of time in the host nation. For such individuals, their economic impact is clearly greater than on the day or days of the event. Thus, it is important to have some data about these people:

Q.9 Are you combining your visit to event 'Y' with a holiday?

Yes ▓   No ▓

If YES: Where are you going . . . .
For how long . . . .

Can you provide us with a rough estimate of your total budget for this part of your trip? £ . . . .

The results of this question allow the wider economic impacts of an event to be assessed. For some events (such as the World Cup, Olympic and Commonwealth Games, etc.) such extended impacts are significant, and an important consequence of hosting them.

INCREASING YOUR RESPONSE RATE

As well as the design of the questionnaire itself, you need to be thinking about its administration, that is how it will be given to potential respondents, how it will be returned, and how you will ensure that as many are returned as possible. It is important to maximise the response rate for both academic and pragmatic reasons. Academically, a low response rate leads to the question of whether there are any particular groups that have not responded and why, what are the effects of the non-response on the findings, and whether there is bias in the data as a consequence. If children, for example, have not completed the questionnaire because it was too complex, then how can an accurate overview of the entire population be made? Taking a more pragmatic view, especially from the point of view of those undertaking student dissertations, low response rates can be expensive if you have to send out a considerably higher number of questionnaires than you originally anticipated (especially if you remember that each question-naire will involve not only the postage costs involved in sending it to the recipient, but also the cost of the pre-paid reply envelope). Frankfort-Nachimas and Nachimas (1996) have ranked the techniques that may be adopted to increase response rates (see Table 8.1). You should not focus on one or two of these techniques, however – all of them should be considered.

Table 8.1 Increasing response rates

Rank	Method	Optimal conditions
1	Follow-up	More than one follow-up.
2	Inducement	Questionnaires containing a monetary reward produce better results than ones without.
3	Sponsorship	People the respondent knows produce the best result.
4	Introductory letter	An altruistic appeal seems to produce the best results.
undetermined	Method of return	A regular stamped addressed envelope produces better results than a business reply envelope
undetermined	Format	Aesthetically pleasing cover; a title that will arouse interest; an attractive page format.
undetermined	Selection of respondents	■ Non-readers and non-writers are excluded from participation. ■ Interest in or familiarity with the subject is a major factor in determining the rate of return. ■ The better educated are more likely to return the questionnaires. ■ Professionals are more likely to return the questionnaires.

Source: Adapted from Frankfort-Nachimas and Nachimas 1996.

THE COVERING LETTER

You should always include a covering letter with any questionnaire. The covering letter is extremely important as one method of maximising the response rate. Postal questionnaires with no covering letter are unlikely to elicit a response. Covering letters have several key objectives.

■ To introduce the researcher, stating their position and to which organisation they are affiliated.
■ To introduce the research programme, including a statement of why the research is being undertaken and why it is important.

- To inform the respondent how they have been chosen to receive the questionnaire, stating the criteria if necessary, and why their response is important.
- To inform the respondent of the date by which their response should be returned.
- To stress anonymity for respondents if appropriate.

If you are carrying out a telephone or face to face survey, you should also cover these points. This can be done using a 'script' that has been prepared in place of the covering letter. Covering letters should also be piloted, to ensure that you have not been ambiguous, or said anything that lacks clarity or relevance to your sample.

THE COVERING LETTER

Covering letters should be tailored to each individual piece of research; however below is a hypothetical example:

Dept of Sport
University of Newtown

Dear Mr Johnson,

I am a researcher at the University of Newtown, where I am carrying out an investigation into sports participation. With your co-operation, this study will determine a number of facts about today's sports participant, and his or her experiences of taking part in sport. From the investigation it will be possible to find out what *you* as a participant value, and whether your needs are being met. Questionnaires are being given to a selected number of individuals such as yourself, who will provide a representative sample.

The questionnaire may appear to be quite complex, however it is quite easy, and should only take about ten minutes to complete. There are no right or wrong answers. In most cases it is simply a matter of ticking a box. There are, however, a number of opportunities for you to say more about certain issues. Try and answer all the questions if possible, as accurately as you can.

▼

For those that complete and return the questionnaire, there is also the chance to win some prizes. If you would like to enter the draw, please fill in the section at the end of the questionnaire. Please note that all information will be used for *research purposes* only.

THE COMPLETED QUESTIONNAIRE WILL BE TREATED WITH ABSOLUTE CONFIDENTIALITY. INFORMATION IDENTIFYING THE RESPONDENT WILL NOT BE DISCLOSED UNDER ANY CIRCUMSTANCES.

Therefore you should not worry about how you answer the questionnaire. Other parties will not *at any time* have access to the completed questionnaires. I would be grateful if you could return the questionnaire in the pre-paid envelope provided by November 19th.

Thank you in advance for your co-operation. I look forward to hearing from you.

JMSmith

J.M. Smith
Researcher
University of Newtown

ADMINISTERING THE QUESTIONNAIRE

Although having an appropriately designed questionnaire is important, it is not simply a case of distributing questionnaires wherever and whenever possible. If you have access to details about your population, then it is generally straightforward to provide them with the questionnaire. In many cases, however, you will need to distribute your questionnaire during a sporting event. The following process is suggested by the Sport Industry Research Centre (SIRC).

Preplanning

Each potential respondent group must be considered, so that a strategy can be implemented for optimum data capture. Thus the following issues need to be assessed:

- How many of each respondent group will there be?
- When will they be arriving?
- Where will they be staying?
- How will it be possible to get convenient access to them?
- Are there any unique circumstances relevant to any group which may have an effect on the research?

You will also need to consider how the questionnaires will be given to potential respondents, and how many assistants you will need to undertake this task.

Data collection

You then need to consider whether questionnaires will be left with the sample, to be returned at a later date through the post, or whether they will be completed face to face. Postal questionnaires (distributed either at the event or through lists of attendees where available) are considered cost effective, and allow participants to complete the questions in their own times. However, response rates may be low, and two or more follow-up letters may be required to achieve a desired response rate. An alternative is to hand participants the questionnaire, and wait with them while they complete it. This can be problematic as during the event spectators are unlikely to have the time or inclination to complete a questionnaire, and this method is also much more resource intensive. Unless you have a team of helpers, it is unlikely you will be able to collect sufficient data unless you are prepared to spend a considerable time within the field. One possible answer to this is to use the approach of Pol and Pak (1994) highlighted in the case study, and obtain names and addresses during the event, which can then be used after the event has finished.

CASE STUDY

USING A TWO-STAGE SURVEY DESIGN

Pol and Pak (1994) have noted that collecting data from people who are watching sport presents a number of major problems. First, those watching sport are generally unwilling to be distracted during the game, and thus unlikely to be willing to complete a questionnaire or be interviewed.

▼

Secondly, interviewing after the game is often difficult as spectators want to leave the event as quickly as possible, and they are often distracted by family and other fans. There are alternative methods, for example fans can be identified by mailing lists, but this is likely only to include season ticket holders, thus introducing sampling bias. To solve the problem, Pol and Pak describe the use of a two-stage survey. They selected seats at the stadium at random, and those in those seats were approached to be asked if they would consider taking part in a telephone survey within seven to ten days, and to provide contact details. 260 fans out of 270 (96 per cent) agreed to be surveyed. Of the 260 fans who agreed, 226 were finally surveyed (87 per cent). This method allowed Pol and Pak both a higher response rate, and more quality data to be obtained. The only shortcoming, as the authors note, is that respondents may forget details related to the event. However this could be minimised by reducing the time between initial contact and the telephone survey. This is an example whereby careful research design can help to identify and overcome potential problems with data collection.

FOLLOWING UP NON-RESPONDENTS

After the final date for questionnaire returns has passed, you will need to contact those who have not returned their questionnaires. This is usually done by sending a follow-up letter, and a copy of the original questionnaire, as well as a pre-paid envelope in which to return the questionnaire. Do not send the original covering letter, as this was obviously unsuccessful in eliciting a response first time round! Instead, one approach is to suggest that the failure to return a completed questionnaire was an oversight on the participant's part, rather than a straight refusal. Stress the importance of the study, and how valuable the contribution that would be made by completing the questionnaire. Include a further cut off date as appropriate.

SUMMARY

1   Questionnaires are generally an appropriate method to collect large amounts of relatively simple data.

2   The advantages of using questionnaires include the accessibility of your sample, reduced bias, anonymity, structured data and allowing time for respondents.

3   The disadvantages include the need for relatively simple questions, no control over the completion of the questionnaire, no opportunity to probe responses, and relatively low response rates.

4   The design of the questionnaire is crucial. Careful design and piloting are required.

5   There are a number of means whereby you can improve your response rate. Of these means, following up non-respondents, inducements, sponsorship by an outside body and an appropriate covering letter seem to be the most effective.

ACTIVITIES

■   You should use your research question developed in the suggested activity at the end of Chapter 4. Design a preliminary questionnaire suitable to obtain data to answer this research question, using a range of question formats.

■   Pilot this questionnaire to a sample of approximately five others. Get your sample to critically comment on the design of the questionnaire.

■   Redesign your questionnaire in light of the pilot study.

■   Produce a covering letter for the questionnaire. Again, pilot this to a small group, asking them to critically comment upon it, and redesign as necessary.

If you are thinking of using a questionnaire, consider the following points:

- Can I justify using a questionnaire as the most appropriate method by which to collect my data? How?
- What steps can I take to ensure the validity and reliability of the data that I collect using this method?
- What will be the effect of a low response rate on the reliability and validity of the data that I collect? How can I maximise my response rate?

FURTHER READING

Oppenheim, A. (1992) *Questionnaire Design, Interviewing and Attitude Measurement*, London: Pinter.

COLLECTING DATA II: RESEARCH INTERVIEWS

INTRODUCTION

It has been said that the simplest way to find out information from someone is simply to ask them! This is the underlying principle of the research interview. The one to one interview is undoubtedly the most common method by which qualitative data is collected in sport research. The interview method can be contrasted with the structured nature of the questionnaire survey (Chapter 8) in both the type of data that is collected, and how it is collected. Whereas the questionnaire collects highly structured data, and is often completed without the presence of the researcher, the researcher is a key element of the interview process, and his or her skills, attributes and interviewing technique are all an integral part of the success of this method in obtaining 'rich', qualitative data.

WHEN IS INTERVIEWING APPROPRIATE?

Interviewing is often associated with the collection of qualitative data, that is the 'why' and 'how' of a phenomenon. Interviews can collect data concerned with concepts that are difficult or inappropriate to measure, and tend to explore

questions of 'why' and 'how' rather than the 'how many' and 'when'. Interviews tend to provide much richer data than, for example, a questionnaire survey, where respondents are generally limited to short and relatively simple responses. Whereas questionnaires are appropriate for collecting limited data from a large sample group, interviews are better at gaining richer data from smaller sample groups. Veal (1997) notes three situations where interviews tend to be used:

1   Where there is only a low population, making the quantitative approach of the questionnaire inappropriate.
2   Where the information is expected to vary considerably amongst respondents, and such information is likely to be complex and thus difficult to measure using other methods.
3   Where the research is exploratory, and interviews may be used to identify information that could be used to refine and develop further investigation.

As always, the key questions are those of 'what information is needed?' and 'will this method provide such information?' If rich qualitative data is required, or you are looking for explanation, rather than description, then interviews are likely to be an appropriate method. If relatively simple data is required, then it is likely that questionnaire surveys will be a much more efficient method.

THE DIFFERENT TYPES OF INTERVIEW

Interviews can generally be classified under four categories: the structured interview, the semi-structured interview, the unstructured interview and the focus group, or group interview.

- *The structured interview.* This is essentially a questionnaire where the questions are read out by the researcher, who also notes the responses. This has the advantage over a respondent completion questionnaire that the respondent can seek clarification over questions that may be unclear or ambiguous.
- *The semi-structured interview.* This approach uses a standard set of questions, or schedule. However, the researcher adopts a flexible approach to data collection, and can alter the sequence of questions or probe for more information with subsidiary questions.
- *Unstructured interviews.* Here the researcher has only a very general idea of the topics to be covered, and the respondent tends to lead the direction of the interview. Further questions are developed by the researcher as the interview progresses. This allows the respondent to provide information from

his or her own perspective, and to develop areas that are important to them, rather than being led by the interview schedule. There is the danger with this type of interview that much of the data will lack focus.

■ *The focus group.* Essentially this is an interview involving a group, rather than one on one interaction, and interaction between members of the group is an important element in obtaining data. Focus groups tend towards being semi-structured in nature.

ADVANTAGES OF THE INTERVIEW METHOD

There are a number of methods that can be utilised within qualitative research, however the interview method has a number of advantages that make it appropriate in certain situations:

■ Interviews enable participants to talk about their own experiences in their own words, and allow them to elaborate on any areas of particular interest or importance.

■ The interview can be more insightful than other methods. As Yin (1994, p.80) notes, the interview 'provides perceived causal inferences' from the actor's, rather than the researcher's point of view. This allows the respondent to become more of an 'informant', providing data from their own perspective, which is often desirable, especially within inductive research.

■ Interviews allow unexpected data to emerge. Unstructured, or semi-structured interviews allow the emergence of important themes that may not emerge from a more structured format. This enables the subjects to reveal insights into their attitudes and behaviour that may not readily be apparent. Questionnaires are restricted to a series of questions developed by the researcher, and respondents are limited to these questions, with the occasional final question along the lines of 'if you have any further comments, please write these below', which can be less than ideal in persuading participants to introduce new areas of information.

■ A face to face interview allows you to assess the participant's body language, facial expressions, tone of voice, etc. which may be useful in some cases.

■ By using interviews, the researcher can introduce him or herself to the subject and establish trust and rapport, especially if any information is considered confidential, or sensitive.

■ Interviews allow you to investigate target groups that may be less able to complete surveys (such as the less well educated, or older or younger respondents for example).

- Interviews may allow the researcher to develop a sense of time and history, rather than providing a series of 'static' responses, which may be the outcome of a survey. They allow the responses to be put into context, rather than providing a 'snapshot' picture.

DISADVANTAGES OF THE INTERVIEW METHOD

As well as the undoubted strengths of interviewing as a data collection method, it does have a number of potential weaknesses that need to be considered before you carry out any interviews:

- Interviews require more resources than questionnaires. They may be expensive both in terms of time and travelling, and as a consequence the resulting sample may be small and unrepresentative of the wider population, especially if your budget is limited.
- It is possible that you may add bias as a result of your – often unconscious – verbal and non-verbal reactions, for example through nodding at certain responses, which may encourage the informant to answer in the manner that he or she thinks you want. It may be the case that the participant thinks that they have to provide the 'right' answers, rather than their own views, which may be exacerbated by you nodding or shaking your head after each response!
- One potential danger is that of the interviewee becoming dominant and leading the interview in unwanted directions. The researcher must be prepared to guide the interviewee back to the interview schedule.
- Analysis of the data may be difficult. The analysis of questionnaire data is often relatively straightforward, and requires little or no interpretation on the part of the researcher. Reliable and valid analysis of qualitative interview data may be more difficult, especially where there may be ambiguity. As Fontana and Frey (1998, p.47) suggest: 'Asking questions and getting answers is a much harder task than it may seem at first. The spoken word always has a residue of ambiguity, no matter how carefully we word the questions and report or code the answers.'
- As with all self-report measures, the quality of the data is dependent upon the responses of the interviewee. Interviewees are subject to problems of recall, misperception and incorrect knowledge.

Thus, as with all methods, the strengths of the interview need to be consolidated, and the weaknesses eradicated as far as possible. The use of appropriate probes, neutral body language and validation of your interpretation of the data by others (more on these points later) can be used to minimise such bias.

DESIGNING THE INTERVIEW SCHEDULE

Designing the interview largely follows the same process as designing a questionnaire, that is you need to identify what information is required, and how you will get that information using an interview. The key difference is that once you have determined the structure of your questionnaire, you are generally unable to alter it, whereas you may be able to continually develop and refine your interview schedule to some extent. A few points to note when constructing your initial interview schedule are as follows:

- Introduce the purpose and structure of the interview beforehand. In much the same way that a covering letter for a questionnaire provides the respondent with important information, your introduction should also 'set the scene', and you may find it useful to apply the guidelines given on covering letters in Chapter 8 to your introduction.
- Group questions about the same concept together, and try to avoid jumping back and forwards between topics.
- Begin with one or more 'easy' questions that will put the respondent at ease, and encourage them to begin talking comfortably. This question need not be directly relevant to the research – it is more important at this stage to gain the co-operation and trust of the interviewee.
- Ensure that the questions are clearly worded, unambiguous and understandable to the interviewee. Make sure too that the relevance of each question is clear to the interviewee. If the relevance is not apparent, or if the interviewee seems unclear, then take time to explain the purpose of the question.
- Ask personal, or potentially threatening questions (if necessary to the research) towards the end of the interview, once you have had a chance to develop trust between interviewer and interviewee.

Once a preliminary interview schedule has been developed, then it is important to pilot it, in much the same way as you would do with a questionnaire. As well as testing the questions, piloting an interview provides a further important function. It will provide a useful run through for the interviewer, and may increase confidence when it comes to the actual interviews, especially for the inexperienced researcher.

CARRYING OUT THE INTERVIEW

It is important for you to project professionalism, enthusiasm and confidence to the interviewee. Both appearance and demeanour are important in projecting these. As well as being smartly dressed, you should ensure that you appear knowledgeable about the subject under discussion, and can discuss this confidently. Thus, it is not a good idea to rush into interviews before you have become proficient in your field of study.

The location of the interview is important. It needs to take place where the interviewee is comfortable answering questions, such as their own home or office. The location should be relatively private so that there will be no bias from the presence of others (ensure that the interview cannot be overheard, as this can be extremely off-putting to the participant). Finally, the interview should take place in a location free from high levels of background noise, especially if it is being recorded.

The skills required by an interviewer are more than those of simply being able to talk to others. Always remember that the overall objective of the interview is to gather valid and reliable data to answer your research question. To achieve this, Hannabus (1996) suggests the following techniques:

- Establish rapport – this should start from when you first contact your interviewee.
- Keep the discussion going. Short periods of silence may actually be beneficial, in that the interviewee may be persuaded to provide further data, but try to avoid periods of lengthy silence. Know when not to interrupt and let silences work for you, but be prepared to step in with a comment on further question if appropriate.
- Avoid asking questions which can be answered with simply a 'yes' or a 'no'.
- Avoid jargon and abstractions with which the interviewee is unlikely to be familiar.
- Avoid double negatives and loaded expressions.
- Be non-judgemental in your reactions to the interviewee's responses, and avoid reacting in any way that may influence further data collection.
- Remember to keep focusing on your research objectives, and try not to stray from them.

In addition, Fontana and Frey (1998) provide some useful guidelines that may seem obvious, but are often overlooked by researchers. These include:

- Never deviate from the introduction, sequence of questions (if it is a structured interview) or question wording unless you feel that you will be able to obtain better data from the interviewee.
- Never let another person interrupt, or offer their own views on the question.
- Never suggest an answer, or show agreement or disagreement with a response. Your own views should not be apparent to the interviewee.

These skills do need to be practised. Although they may be relatively easy to achieve in an informal or social setting, the artificial nature of an interview makes them harder to attain, and it is likely that you will feel after your first few interviews that perhaps things didn't go quite as well as they could. Don't worry – your technique will improve as you persevere. If you have videoed your initial interviews, then it can often be a good idea to observe your own interviewing technique. Otherwise, you may be able to gain feedback from interviewees, and develop your technique accordingly.

MOTIVATING THE INFORMANT

The overall objective of the interview is to ensure that the respondent feels willing to provide the desired information, otherwise it is likely that the data will lack validity, especially if the interviewee feels pressurised into taking part, or just wants to get the interview finished as quickly as possible. Frankfort-Nachimas and Nachimas (1996) identify three factors that will help motivate the interviewee to co-operate with the researcher:

1   *The respondent must feel that the interview will be enjoyable and satisfying.* Three factors are important here. First the personal demeanour of the researcher must be such as to create a good impression. Secondly, the informant must be briefed as to the nature of the interview and how it is to be carried out, and given an indication of the likely length. Thirdly, the location and timing of the interview are important, and it is advisable to let the respondent choose these as far as is practical.
2   *The respondent needs to see the study as worthwhile.* The respondent should feel that they are making a contribution to a worthwhile study. This can be done when individuals are initially approached to take part in the interview, as well as in the briefing beforehand.
3   *Perceived barriers in the respondent's mind need to be overcome.* Trust needs to be developed. This can be done by explaining who you are and why you are doing the study, as well as how the respondent came to be chosen, and

by ensuring the confidential nature of the research. Here, you also need to project your competence to be undertaking such research.

PROBING

One key advantage of the interview as a research method is that of your opportunity to *probe*. A probe is where the researcher can gain additional information from the respondent through using particular techniques. Two types of probe can be used:

- *Clarification probes*. These allow you to clarify any point that was not clear, or open to misunderstanding by the interviewee, or to clarify your understanding of a point made by the interviewee.
- *Elaboration probes*. These are used to elicit a more in-depth response about a particular point related to the interview. For example using phrases such as 'why is that?', 'could you expand on that?' or 'could you tell me more about that?' will often enhance the richness and quality of your data.

ASKING SENSITIVE QUESTIONS

You may, at some stage in the interview, need to ask questions that the interviewee may perceive as sensitive, or even potentially threatening in some way. It is often tempting simply to play safe and not ask these questions, however it may be that such sensitive information is important to your research. If you do have to ask sensitive questions, you should ensure that you follow a number of guidelines:

- Be careful in your use of language when you first approach the interviewee for help. Avoid phrases such as 'I want to investigate . . .', which may imply that you are looking to uncover something underhand, and use neutral language, such as 'I am hoping to explore . . .' instead.
- Don't ask sensitive questions at the beginning of the interview. Wait until you have established trust and rapport with the interviewee.
- Try not to ask such questions in any way that could be construed as 'loaded'. This is one area where piloting of the interview can be extremely useful.
- Ensure that it is clear to the respondent, if at all possible, why you are asking the question. If the respondent can see the face validity of the question, then they are more likely to give you a response.

■ If you are seriously worried about asking a particular question or series of questions, then acknowledge this to the interviewee.

HOW TO BECOME A GOOD INTERVIEWER

Baker (1994) notes five basic rules that you should follow for every interview. These are as follows:

1 *Understand the interview.* You need to know the purpose of the interview, and also clearly understand the concepts under investigation.
2 *Be committed to completing the interview.* There may be the temptation to complete the interview in the shortest possible time, or to end the interview early. You should be committed at every interview to spend sufficient time to gather enough data (although the participant must be able to withdraw at any time).
3 *Practise the interview.* In the same way that a questionnaire survey is piloted, or pre-tested, an interview must be rehearsed beforehand.
4 *Minimise the effects of your personal characteristics.* Factors such as your age, dress, demeanour and so on may all affect the responses given. Depending on the nature of the interview, you should minimise these through appropriate dress, language and so on.
5 *Use common sense.* Be prepared to use common sense if things seem to be going wrong, or problems arise. Take each situation as it comes, and be prepared to exit the interview if things do go wrong.

RECORDING THE INTERVIEW

Interviews must be recorded in some form – it is simply not possible to rely on recall alone. The choice is generally between that of written notes or tape or video recording. Sometimes the respondent will determine the choice of method, in that certain individuals may be uncomfortable being taped. Taking written notes has two main advantages: first, it precludes potential problems created by using recording equipment, such as ensuring responses are audible, battery failure and so on. Secondly, if the researcher records only data that is relevant to the research question, then time may be saved in identifying and discarding irrelevant data. Writing notes can, however, result in a loss of rapport between interviewer

148

and interviewee, and the interviewer's focus may be divided between the respondent and writing down notes. Recording the interview will allow more rapport to develop, which may result in more information being divulged from the respondent. This will, however, result in much more data to be analysed, and a great deal of irrelevant material to be identified and discarded. As you are likely to have only one chance to undertake each interview, we would suggest that the best option is to record it on tape (with the interviewee's permission), as well as making limited notes.

USING INTERVIEWS TO EXAMINE WOMEN'S EXPERIENCES AS SPORTS COACHES

West *et al.* (2001) wanted to explore issues related to women's under-representation in sport coaching roles. Using Witz's (1990) model of occupational closure, they were interested in examining the social processes involved with regard to power and subordination. Interviews were an appropriate method in this regard as:

■ The information sought was rich, complex and subjective, and relied upon women being able to voice their own experiences. It is unlikely that a method such as a questionnaire would have been able to provide such information.
■ The data collected was extremely variable. The flexibility of the interview method enabled the researchers to cope with such variation.

The interview schedule was designed by carrying out a number of unstructured pilot interviews with six coaches. This allowed semi-structured interviews to be developed which were then undertaken with a further six coaches. After each interview, the schedule was revised until, as the authors note, 'a logical and fluent sequence of questions had been devised that was capable of eliciting the information required' (p.86).

A purposive sample was used, whereby twenty coaches were chosen, with five coaches coming from each of the levels of the coaching continuum (foundation, participation, performance and excellence). This allowed experiences from across all levels of coaching to be ascertained.

149

Transcripts of each interview were made, and the data was organised into topic areas reflecting the theoretical model used. Common themes were drawn out from the transcripts. The researchers were thus able to find out that women were limited in their coaching roles through both exclusionary and demarcationary strategies, such as gendering the role of coach as a masculine one, and reducing the access of female coaches to coach networks. The researchers were also able to discover that such strategies were challenged by women using a variety of approaches, such as emphasising coaching qualifications, focusing on their own experiences as successful athletes, and emphasising the success of athletes that they coached.

RELIABILITY AND VALIDITY OF THE INTERVIEW

As with survey research, the issues of reliability and validity in interview research need to be addressed. Reliability can be enhanced through a standardised interview schedule, maintaining a consistent interviewing environment, and recording with the interviewees' permission, which should then be transcribed within as short a time as possible by the researcher.

Validity is harder to ensure, given that transcriptions are a tool for interpreting the interview, rather than an analysis in themselves. The methods of obtaining the transcripts need to be stated clearly so that the validity of the transcripts can be evaluated. A number of problems need to be considered at the outset. These are:

- Will the informant interpret the question correctly? This will be more of an issue with younger or less educated participants.
- Are informants able to verbalise their thoughts, to say what they actually feel? That is, are they able to accurately convey their feelings through their own command of language? Responses need to be critically questioned by the researcher. The researcher's own experience through participant observation will be important in this respect in being able to tacitly assess responses.
- Is the informant giving a response that is applicable only to that moment in time, or are his or her views more long term? Although their behaviours may be relatively stable, responses may be affected by events or occurrences at the time of the interview.

- Will the informant's own values affect the response? That is, will people provide information based upon what they think is the correct response, rather than their own attitudes?

Dean and Whyte (1978) have noted that the interviewer needs to take into account four major factors prior to the interview. These are:

1   Does the informant have any motives that may influence his or her responses? This may be the case if the informant stands to benefit in any way from a particular response. Thus the researcher should stress the confidential, or 'blind' nature of the interview.
2   Are there any 'bars to spontaneity', that is are there any instances where the informant hesitates to mention things that will show him or her in a negative light? Again the confidentiality of the interview may ensure reliability.
3   Will the informant attempt to please the interviewer?
4   Are there any idiosyncratic features that may affect a response? An example of this potential effect may be a particular news story related to a sporting event on a particular day that will have a short term effect on the respondents' attitudes.

All of these considerations need to be accounted for before each interview. Two suggestions are made by Dean and Whyte (1978) to maximise the validity of the data obtained. First it is important to ensure that the subject is aware of the confidentiality of the interview. Secondly, it is generally a good idea to structure the interview so that a range of questions may be asked on any areas that may cause concern in terms of validity, thus using a form of 'within-interview triangulation'. The interviewer cannot always assume a relationship between responses and actual behaviour. This framework will allow a more reasoned evaluation as to what is reality, and what is distortion.

INTERVIEWING CHILDREN

Interviewing can be a fruitful data collection technique when you are researching children. However, there are a few things that you should bear in mind. Holmes (1998) makes a number of relevant points:

- The most important factor when researching children is the desire to be with them and to be interested in what they say.

- To establish rapport it is important to play a 'friend' role, rather than a role of authority.
- Alternative strategies – such as role play – should be considered as alternatives to interviewing.
- Informal or unstructured interviewing works best.
- Never take children out of a classroom to interview them, as they associate this with getting into trouble.
- Ethical issues are of paramount concern to the researcher.

Gender and race can be important issues when collecting data through this method. Watson and Scraton (2001) discuss both of these issues, demonstrating that the researcher must be aware that their own personal characteristics may have implications in terms of the data obtained. Will a white female collect the same data as a black male in a certain context for example? They stress the need for reflexivity throughout the research process, and it is an issue that you should consider. As well as the personal characteristics, the ability of the researcher should also be critically questioned. Before undertaking interviews, the question of whether the interviewer has the appropriate skills and experience to undertake the interview needs to be evaluated. This is rarely done, and, as Biddle *et al.* (2001) note, it is rare for this issue to be addressed, even in research published within international journals.

THE TELEPHONE INTERVIEW

Not all interviewing is carried out face to face, and telephone interviewing can be an appropriate method in some cases. Cost is greatly reduced, especially if the participants are geographically dispersed, and in certain cases telephone interviewing may be the only feasible option. Secondly, some individuals may prefer to be contacted by telephone, rather than by the interviewer in person. Finally, telephone interviews may be appropriate if face to face interviewing would involve access to restricted or potentially dangerous locations. There are disadvantages with telephone interviews however. It may be more difficult to develop a rapport, and trust from the participant. Secondly, it is not possible to observe non-verbal reactions to questions. Finally, it can be difficult to record interviews without specialist equipment.

INTERVIEWS AND SAMPLE SIZE

The issue of sample size in the collection of qualitative data is a common area of confusion. Unlike quantitative analysis, where there is often a requirement for the largest possible sample size, qualitative research has different requirements. Quantitative methods such as questionnaire surveys tend to obtain relatively shallow information from a large sample. The purpose of qualitative research is to generate 'rich' data, from a small sample group. It has been argued that a large sample group in qualitative research may actually be detrimental. Kvale (1996, p.103) suggests, with reference to qualitative research, that many research projects:

> would have profited from having fewer interviews in the study, and from taking more time to prepare the interviews and analyse them. Perhaps, as a defensive overreaction, some qualitative interview studies appear to be designed on a quantitative presupposition of 'the more interviews, the more scientific'.

As a qualitative researcher, the issue of sample size is not one that you should determine at the beginning of a study. Instead, you should aim to achieve what is referred to as 'saturation'. This refers to the stage in the fieldwork where any further data collection will not provide any different information from that you already have, that is you are not learning anything new. This point can be difficult to determine, however. If you undertake, for example, three or four interviews consecutively where no additional data is obtained, then this would be a good indication that saturation has occurred. Occasionally you may find that saturation does not occur, and in certain instances other considerations such as time or cost may be more important factors. If you do not reach saturation in your data collection, then the advice is to complete as much data collection as possible within your constraints.

CASE STUDY

QUALITATIVE SAMPLING

Andrew Sparkes (2000) was interested to find out the 'complex ways in which a strong athletic identity can act as an achilles heel in terms of both shaping an individual's reactions to a disruptive life event, and the consequences of these reactions for personal long-term development'

153

(p.15), that is how an elite sports person would react to the ending of their athletic career. The objective was not to generalise the findings to a wider population – rather to gain an understanding of the processes by which the athlete coped with the termination of their athletic identity. In this instance a *purposive*, rather than a *random* sample was chosen – consisting of a single subject – Rachel. Through examining Rachel's reactions to the end of her sporting career, Sparkes was able to explain some of the issues, which could then be generalised to other athletes. By having a small ($n = 1$), non-random sample, Sparkes was able to discover a great deal of information, and demonstrated that, in qualitative research, it is the amount of *data* that is important, rather than the amount of subjects.

THE KEY INFORMANT INTERVIEW

You may be able to identify one or more key informants, who will be able to supply you with specialist knowledge, based upon their position or relevant experience. Often, the key informant interview can complement data collected from other sources, for example you may be researching the impact of a change in policy upon sport participation, and you may be able to collect data from the individual responsible for such a change. This, whilst not answering the question itself, will be able to provide you with useful background information, as well as developing your own knowledge of the subject matter. Be careful to assess their perspective on the issue, so that any particular views can be taken into account. An employee of a sports organisation, for example, is unlikely to provide an opinion that may go against the organisation's policies, or show that organisation in a bad light. We must provide a word of warning about key informant interviews. Do not assume that simply by contacting potential key informants they will automatically make themselves available to you – they will generally be extremely busy, and if you are researching a popular area, yours will not be the first request that they have had!

FOCUS GROUPS

Focus groups are similar in many ways to interviews, with the key difference being that a small group of people, rather than a single respondent, is used. Members of the group are able to interact with each other, with the interaction leading to a greater depth of discussion, in that ideas can be generated and discussed between group members, allowing for 'richer' information to be gathered than if participants were asked individually. The interviewer will take on the role of facilitator, and will stimulate discussion whilst keeping it relevant to the topic being investigated. Focus groups are often used when the information collected would be richer than that from an interview. An example of this would be research into youth groups, where young people may be unwilling to talk to a researcher on their own, but would be happy to discuss things as part of a group of other young people.

A focus group will normally consist of between six and twelve people (although you should really aim for no more than eight, so that everyone has a chance to make some sort of significant contribution), who have not met beforehand if possible. It is important to ensure that everyone within the group contributes, and the discussion is not dominated by one or two individuals. Your role is to channel the discussion in much the same way that you would with a semi-structured interview, to ensure that the discussion is relevant, and all participants have the opportunity to contribute. This can be a difficult task, and as a consequence it is unlikely that you will be able to make any notes during the discussion. Thus you should ensure that you record the focus group, and also use a colleague to make notes of the most salient points. It is preferable to video record focus groups rather than record sound only, as this will allow you to identify which data came from which participant much more easily.

Although focus groups are a valuable means of collecting information, they can require much more in the way of organisation and resources than other methods. Successfully running a focus group is difficult to do, and you will often need to carry out a number of them before you feel totally confident, especially if the group needs a lot of guidance. Therefore you should think carefully about the use of focus groups as a method. If you do decide to use focus groups, then much of the guidance given above on interviewing applies.

Focus groups and difficult to research populations

Focus groups can be particularly useful to collect data from groups that may otherwise be unwilling to provide it. Children, for example, may be uncomfortable discussing issues with an adult interviewer. However they may well be more willing to discuss those issues with other children as part of a focus group guided by the researcher. You should be careful as to the validity of the data you collect in some circumstances, as participants may be tempted to provide false data to make an impression upon others in the group, so do be aware of this.

SUMMARY

- Interviews can be an appropriate method to collect qualitative data. They are especially useful when the information to be collected is varied or complex, or the study is exploratory.
- Three general types of interview can be used – the structured, semi-structured and the unstructured.
- Data collected from interviews can be rich and varied, especially if the interviewer is skilled at using 'probes' to elicit such information.
- Undertaking an interview is a skilled task, and one that should not be approached lightly. The quality of the data can often be dependent upon the skill of the interviewer.

ACTIVITIES

You should gain interviewing experience by undertaking an interview with a colleague on a sports-related topic of your choice. Try to ensure that you use a range of questions, and practise your use of probes to maximise the information obtained.

You should also carry out a focus group, again on a topic that you decide. You should try to ensure that data is obtained from all members of the group, and that the group is not dominated by certain individuals.

In both cases, obtain feedback from those involved. Try to assess your strengths and weaknesses as an interviewer and focus group facilitator, and identify how your performance could be improved.

If you are using interviews as a data collection tool, then consider the following points:

- Think about the design of your interview schedule. How are you going to ensure reliability and validity of the data that you collect?
- Are there any personal characteristics that may affect the quality of data that you collect? If so, how will you deal with this issue?
- Can you justify your choice of the sampling method that you used to obtain your interviewees?

FURTHER READING

Kvale, S. (1996) *Interviews: An Introduction to Qualitative Research Interviewing,* London: Sage.

Seidman, I. (1991) *Interviewing as Qualitative Research,* New York: Teachers College Press.

CHAPTER TEN

COLLECTING DATA III:
UNOBTRUSIVE METHODS –
OBSERVATION AND CONTENT
ANALYSIS

In this chapter we will:

■ Introduce two forms of unobtrusive method – observation and content analysis.
■ Introduce some of the advantages and disadvantages of using unobtrusive methods in your research project.
■ Outline the procedure by which each of the methods described can be carried out.
■ Briefly outline the various sources of data that may be used for a content analysis.

INTRODUCTION

An analysis of sports-related journals published in the last decade reveals that two main methods – the questionnaire survey and interview – dominate the research literature. As Kellehear (1993, p.1) suggests, this may be due to the fact that these are the obvious methods by which to elicit information from others. As he says: 'There is today, in social science circles, a simple and persistent belief that knowledge about people is available simply by asking. We ask people about themselves, and they tell us.' There is, however, an ever increasing acceptance of other methods, especially those that we can refer to as *unobtrusive methods* (sometimes referred to as *non-reactive measures*). Unobtrusive methods are methods which do not have any effect upon the social environment under investigation, and require no interaction between subject and researcher that may otherwise influence the data collected. This chapter introduces two forms of unobtrusive method, observation and content analysis, and outlines their potential use in sports-related research.

ADVANTAGES OF UNOBTRUSIVE METHODS

- Unobtrusive measures do not disturb or affect the social environment in any way. Because the methods are unobtrusive, participants are unlikely to react to them, and alter their behaviours. As a consequence, they are often repeatable, and the researcher can revisit the research site to collect additional data.
- Unobtrusive measures may therefore be stronger in measuring *actual* behaviour, which is not always the same as *reported* behaviour. Interviews and questionnaire surveys are always prone to the possibility that respondents will provide false or incorrect data. Thus it could be argued that the validity and reliability of such approaches may be enhanced.
- Access to data may often be easier. For some unobtrusive measures, such as certain observational data collection, permission will not always be required.

DISADVANTAGES OF UNOBTRUSIVE METHODS

- As the researcher is not interacting with the participants in the same way, then it may be difficult to understand or explain the phenomenon under investigation. Whilst it may be relatively straightforward to describe what is happening, it may be more difficult to gain a clear understanding of why it is happening.
- In the same way that interview responses can be distorted to present a particular image or viewpoint, data collected by unobtrusive measures can also be subject to distortion, especially if the subjects are aware of the research.
- For unobtrusive methods such as observation, data collection may be difficult without the use of specialist photographic or video recording equipment.

OBSERVATION AND PARTICIPANT OBSERVATION

Observation is, arguably, the most neglected research technique in sport, yet it has a number of advantages. Questionnaires and interviews rely on self-reporting by participants in research. This may lead to bias from respondents who may wish to alter information about themselves, or from those who can cannot accurately recall or verbalise events. An alternative is to observe behaviour, rather than to question people about it. Observation is often classified as either *participant* or *non-participant* observation. Non-participant observation is the simplest form, and is where the researcher will observe the phenomenon 'from outside' with no engagement with either the activity or the subjects. An example of this would be observing how many people used a particular sports facility at a particular time. This could be done using various techniques, for example video, photography, or simply watching with the naked eye, and recording the data on an appropriate sheet.

The second form is that of participant observation, where the researcher actually takes part in the phenomenon being studied. An example could be where the researcher investigating issues of customer care may actually use a sports facility, and collect data about his or her own experience as a user, to try and gain an 'insider's' understanding. Data in this instance would be recorded by the researcher in the form of field notes, whereby the researcher's experiences would be recorded. This is not, technically, an unobtrusive method, as the researcher may have some effect upon the social environment, although it could be argued that this impact should be minimal, and that the researcher should not set out to alter the behaviour of others in any way.

WHEN IS OBSERVATION APPROPRIATE?

Non-participant observation is an appropriate method when the phenomenon under investigation can be directly observed. Thus, if you are interested in researching whether sports fans are more likely to wear clothing related to their team after they have won, as Cialdini et al. (1976) found out, then observation is a suitable method. If, however, you want to identify why they are more likely to wear such clothing, then observation would be inappropriate, as it would not be able to collect data to answer such a question. Observation is generally more suitable for descriptive research rather than for explanatory research. A second justification for the use of observation would be when other methods are inappropriate. A good example of this would be investigating patterns of play in children's sports. Children themselves would almost certainly be unable to accurately describe how they play sport, therefore interviewing or using a questionnaire would be unreliable. Observation would allow you to describe the children's play more accurately, especially – as an unobtrusive researcher – you would be less likely to influence their behaviour in any way. Observation can also be a useful method if researching contentious issues, such as violence in sport. Respondents may be unlikely to accurately report their own violent or aggressive behaviour, or may even over-report such behaviour in some cases. Unobtrusive observation would allow you to assess the validity of such claims made by participants. It is often used in combination with other methods, and such triangulation (see Chapter 7) will help strengthen the validity of your research. Observation can also be used in a non-triangulation manner with other methods. Take, for example, the case of the sports clothing described above. Observation would allow you to identify that individuals do wear their team's clothes more after they have won. Another method, such as in-depth interviews, may allow you to explain why they do so. Thus such methods can be complementary.

THE USE OF OBSERVATIONAL METHODS – 'TWO-FOOTEDNESS' AND SOCCER

Carey *et al.* (2001) hypothesised that elite soccer players should be more 'two-footed' (that is able to use either foot with equal proficiency) than the general population. The authors noted an earlier study which had asked players to complete a questionnaire regarding their differing use of feet, and suggested that it was possible that questionnaire respondents may have inadvertently provided results that were not accurate, with a tendency to overestimate their 'one-footedness'. It may also be the case that certain players may wish to present a picture of being able to perform with either foot equally well. Thus, carrying out such a study using either interviews or questionnaires raises immediate concerns regarding the validity of the information.

To carry out a more accurate study the researchers decided to use an unobtrusive approach, undertaking direct observation of soccer players whilst playing in competitive matches. To do this, they videotaped a number of games from the 1998 football World Cup. This allowed them to identify and measure successful and unsuccessful actions by each player, which could then be analysed with reference to whether the preferred or non-preferred foot was used. The researchers actually found that elite players were equally skilled with their non-preferred foot as they were with their preferred foot, although they used the non-preferred foot considerably less.

Provided the concepts (successful action and unsuccessful action) were operationalised correctly, the researchers were able to have a high degree of confidence in their findings.

Such a study is useful in demonstrating how observation may – in certain cases – be useful in obtaining more 'truthful' data than other methods, and in demonstrating the potential weakness of other methods in certain situations.

Participant observation is appropriate when you are interested in uncovering some of the more subtle features of group behaviour, and trying to uncover meanings that are not directly observable. The researcher experiences, rather than observes what is going on, and it is this experience that provides the data for the researcher.

CASE STUDY

PARTICIPATION OBSERVATION TO INVESTIGATE GROUP MEMBERSHIP IN SPORT

Glancy (1986) was interested in whether the behaviour of members of a sports team would be incongruent with positive social relations amongst the group, that is whether it could be the case that individuals joined the group for social reasons, yet their positive experiences were dependent upon the competitive success of the team. To do this, she joined a local softball team, and took part in games as well as social events, such as parties at other players' houses. She recorded data immediately after each event, and used two informants from the group to verify her findings at regular intervals. Through her subjective experiences, she was able to conclude that there was no conflict between the two factors, and that competitive success or failure was strongly entwined with feelings of friendship and group membership, which seemed to be dominant overall.

Participant observation was especially useful for Glancy's study as it allowed her to see and to experience the concepts in practice, rather than as described by someone else. Her interpretations could then be applied to further occasions, to check their appropriateness, strengthening the validity of her conclusions.

ADVANTAGES OF OBSERVATIONAL METHODS

Participant and non-participant observation both have a number of advantages that make them well suited for data collection in certain circumstances. The advantages can be listed as follows:

- *Directness*. It is possible to record a phenomenon as and when it happens, rather than having to rely on an individual's recall of a particular event.
- *Takes place in a 'natural setting'*. The researcher is able to observe the phenomenon in its natural setting, rather than in the rather 'artificial' surroundings of an interview or whilst completing a questionnaire. This allows the researcher to observe the context in which such behaviour takes place, and – in the case of participant observation – to experience that context for themselves.
- *The identification of behaviours not apparent to the subject*. The individual may simply be unaware of how they behave in a particular situation, or believe that they act in an entirely different way. Observation will allow the researcher to identify the 'true' behaviour.
- *The identification of behaviours that the subject may be unwilling to disclose.* This is an issue when researching potentially sensitive subjects. Respondents may be unwilling to incriminate themselves in an interview or questionnaire. It may be possible to observe such behaviours, however.

DISADVANTAGES OF OBSERVATIONAL METHODS

Although observational techniques do have their advantages, there are also a number of potential disadvantages of which you need to be aware:

- *Misunderstanding of the phenomenon*. A drawback to observational methods is the likelihood that the researcher may simply misunderstand what they are seeing, especially if they are researching a subject in which they have little or no experience. This may be overcome to some extent through using observation in conjunction with other methods, such as interviewing, to ensure that the phenomenon has been correctly understood.
- *Difficulties in data recording*. What to actually look for, and how to ensure that nothing of importance is missed are key issues in observational research. The use of technology, such as video recording, may prevent this to some extent, but this is often an unrealistic option for many researchers. An alternative is to have a number of researchers each recording the

phenomenon, in which case inter-observer reliability becomes an issue (see Chapter 6).

■ *The effect of the observer on the subjects*. It is always possible that the researcher will affect the subjects' behaviour to such an extent that it may invalidate the entire research. The option of covert observation exists, where the subjects are unaware that they are being watched, however this raises two issues: first the ethical question, that is whether it is ethical to undertake research on a group without them being aware of the research, or without the option of not taking part in the research, and second the issue of how the researcher records their data without making the subjects aware that they are doing so.

CARRYING OUT AN OBSERVATIONAL STUDY

As with any other means of data collection, it is important that you don't rush into the data gathering stage of the research without careful consideration of what data is required. It is often tempting to observe a sporting phenomenon and collect reams of data, only to find that such data is inadequate for the purposes of the research. Thus, you should carefully plan and pilot your data collection (especially if you are observing a one-off event). A number of planning stages can be identified:

1 *Defining the variable(s) under investigation.* The first stage is to identify the variable(s) to be observed. Are you interested in a particular behaviour for example? Ensure you are clear about what exactly you are recording. If you are observing usage at a particular sports facility, then are you interested in quantitative measures such as the number of users, the breakdown between male and female users, etc., or are you more interested in qualitative measures such as how they use the facility, their patterns of behaviour and so on? You should relate these issues back to your research objectives, that is determine what information is required to achieve these objectives, and what data is needed to provide such information, and identify the variables as appropriate.

2 *Decide on your sample.* Your sample should, ideally, be systematically chosen. Once you have decided upon your variables, you need to decide from which individual or group you will collect your data. As well as sampling particular individuals, behaviours and so on, you will also need to choose a sample of times. Sometimes you will be able to sample an entire event, such as a single sports match. Otherwise you will need to choose when you will make your observations.

3   *Decide how the variables are to be recorded.* Will you use video recording equipment or rely upon making notes with a pen and paper? Can you produce a predetermined data sheet that simply needs to be filled in, or will you collect all data longhand?
4   *Pilot your study.* In exactly the same way that you would pre-test a questionnaire or interview schedule using a pilot study, then you should pre-test your observation, and identify any potential factors that may affect your data collection beforehand.

RECORDING DATA

Provided you have clearly identified the variables under investigation, the recording of quantitative data should be relatively straightforward. Generally it will involve the recording of information using a simple checklist, for example the checklist shown in Figure 10.1, which is taken from a study into basketball tactics and strategies.

It is difficult to record more than one variable at a time, so you should avoid recording large numbers of variables, unless you are using techniques such as video recording. If you do need to record more variables without the use of such technology, then you should either alternate between variables, that is record one variable for a specified period, and then another, or use multiple observers.

For each play made by the sampled individual, tick the relevant action								
Player no. X								
• Dribbled then shot	✓	✓	✓					
• Dribbled then passed	✓	✓	✓	✓				
• Immediate shot	✓	✓	✓					
• Immediate pass	✓	✓	✓	✓				
• Lost possession	✓	✓						

Figure 10.1   Recording data using an observation checklist

Data can be recorded directly on a pre-produced recording sheet, or dictated into a recording device. The danger with the second option is that, in many sports contexts, the level of background noise will make the recording inaudible.

Qualitative observation records data using *field notes*. Field notes are a summary of the observations made by the researcher, and follow a less structured format. Field notes should be:

- *Descriptive*. They should include a description of the setting, the participants, and the relevant actions and behaviours, as well as any other features that may have relevance for the research.
- *Detailed*. The description should be as detailed as possible. It is not possible to be able to rely on memory to recall all of the important occurrences.
- *Reflective*. The field notes should also contain the researcher's account of the situation, and any information that may help later interpretation.

CASE STUDY

USING OBSERVATION WITH OTHER METHODS

Dennis and Carron (1999) were interested to find out whether the location of an ice hockey game had any influence on certain decisions of the coaches, in this case the extent to which they told their team to forecheck assertively (i.e. in a more attacking manner) or passively (more defensively).

A questionnaire was distributed to coaches from the National Hockey League ($n = 23$) and the Ontario Hockey League ($n = 17$). The data from the questionnaires suggested that more assertive forechecking was carried out whilst playing at home, and against teams of lower ability. The authors noted, however, that questionnaires may be limited in collecting such data in that what the coaches reported may not reflect the teams' actual play. Dennis and Carron therefore used observation to collect data, videoing a random sample of games. The forechecking style was recorded for each game, and a random sample was analysed by a second observer to ensure reliability. Through the use of such observational methods, the data collected by the questionnaire was shown to be an accurate measure of the team's forechecking style, thus confirming the findings from the questionnaire survey.

unobtrusive methods

MISTAKES MADE IN OBSERVATIONAL STUDIES

There are a number of mistakes that are regularly seen within observational studies. You should ensure that these are not an issue within your research!

- Attempting to observe and record too many variables.
- Not evaluating the effect of the researcher on the subjects.
- Not taking a sample of times and/or locations.
- Making inadequate field notes and over-relying on recall.

CONTENT ANALYSIS

Content analysis refers to the analysis of the content of *communications*. It involves the use of systematic procedures to describe the content of a *text*. This text can be written, audio or visual, for example a television programme, a newspaper, a sports autobiography or a radio broadcast. Content analysis generally involves the researcher determining the presence, meanings and relationships of certain words or concepts within the text. In many cases, the advantages and disadvantages of this approach reflect those of observational approaches, for example in terms of misunderstanding meanings associated with such texts and so on. Thus, you should be aware of those issues when considering undertaking a content analysis.

Stages in doing a content analysis

1. Identify the text to be used. The choice of text will, of course, be largely dependent upon your research objectives.
2. Identify the data set to be used. If you have chosen a newspaper as your source text, for example, then which newspaper(s) is to be used, which editions, how many and so on.
3. Identify your categories, or *codes* into which the data will be placed. Codes can be taken from existing theory, or you may develop your own. Ensure that your codes are appropriate to fulfil your research objectives (see the Jones *et al.* case study on page 169)
4. Place each relevant statement/article/other data unit into the appropriate code
5. Analyse the resultant data.

Fishwick and Leach (1998) carried out a content analysis of BBC television commentaries of the 1994 Wimbledon Tennis Championships. They wanted to find out whether there was any gender bias within the commentaries, for example whether the male tennis players were perceived as powerful and important, whereas female players were seen as subordinate. The coding grid that they used was as shown in Figure 10.2.

Men/Women	Match	Round
Comments	Male commentator	Female commentator
• Positive		
Fitness/athleticism		
Play		
Misc.		
• Negative		
Fitness/athleticism		
Play		
Misc.		
• Victories		
• Defeats		
• First name calling		
• Emotions		
• Character flaws		
• Beauty and fashion		
• Patronising		

Figure 10.2 Sample coding grid for content analysis

The authors also undertook qualitative analysis of the commentaries to investigate not only *what* was being said (as identified by the quantitative analysis), but also *how* it was being said, to try to identify the meaning of the commentary. By using a combination of quantitative and qualitative content analysis, they were able to demonstrate that men's tennis was considered superior to the women's game, and that the women's game was almost always judged in relation to the men's game. One finding, for example, was that male players were referred to by their first names a total of 12 times throughout the tournament. Female players, on the other hand, were referred to in this way 589 times, reflecting what the authors refer to as 'gendered hierarchy of naming', or the establishment of a dominant/subordinate relationship through the differential use of forenames and surnames.

THE PRINT MEDIA COVERAGE OF US WOMEN'S OLYMPIC GOLD MEDAL WINNING TEAMS

Jones, Murrell and Jackson (1999) examined how descriptions of female athletes reflected attitudes towards gender in wider society using a content analysis of newspaper articles related to gold medal performances by the US women's team. They tested three hypotheses:

1   Articles about females were likely to convey beliefs about gender.
2   Articles about females involved in traditionally 'male' sports were more likely to include irrelevant statements, male stereotypes and comparisons to males than those involved in feminine or neutral sports.
3   Descriptions of females playing feminine sports are more likely to include female stereotypes than those playing masculine or neutral sports.

To test these hypotheses, seven newspapers/magazines were sampled. The following procedure was then adopted:

1   Articles were identified that described female gold medal winning performances.
2   Performance-related statements in each article were identified and transcribed so that the source of the article and names of athletes could not be identified.
3   The data was coded under the following headings:

- *Sports coding.* The sport covered was coded as male appropriate (basketball, hockey and soccer), female appropriate (gymnastics), and neutral (softball).
- *Task relevance.* The passage was coded as either task relevant (if it described the performance in winning the gold medal), relevant to sport (if it described the athlete in a sports-related context other than the gold medal performance), or non-task relevant (no relevance to the sports performance at all).
- *Depiction of gender.* The passage was coded as to whether it described stereotypical female characteristics (beauty, passivity, etc.), stereotypical male characteristics (physicality, determination), or whether the performance was compared to male athletes.

Jones *et al.* found that all three hypotheses were supported by the content analysis, confirming their assumption that beliefs in society on the gender appropriateness of sport were likely to be reflected in the printed media.

As well as frequencies of occurrence, you can measure a number of other variables as part of a content analysis. You may wish to measure the *prominence* of a particular concept, for example where does the concept appear? Does it appear early or later within a text? How much *space* in the text is devoted to the concept? In what *context* does the concept appear? What you choose to measure should, of course, be chosen to achieve your research objectives.

Some sources available to you are as follows:

- *Public records.* These are generally produced by local or central government. Although records such as the census may seem to be objective sources of data, care still needs to be taken to assess such sources. The census, for example, may under-record certain groups in society. Other sources that may be of interest include summaries of information such as *Social Trends* or the *Annual Abstract of Statistics*.

- *The media*. The media can be a useful source of data, however you should be aware of the following issues:

  - The intended audience. You need to assess who the report was written for, and how the intended audience may influence the report.
  - Accuracy. It is generally difficult to check the accuracy of newspaper reports. If you use one particular newspaper, it is useful to cross-check reports with another as far as is practically possible.
  - Distortion. The reporting of news follows a complex path, along which it is highly possible for distortion to take place. Occurrences may be distorted by witnesses, who misreport incidents, journalists, who try to make a story 'newsworthy', editors, and so on. Again, cross-checking is important here.

- *Advertisements*. Advertisements can provide extremely useful data, not only in terms of the words used, but also the imagery presented. Lucas (2000), for example, examined three television commercials produced by Nike demonstrating how Nike portrayed itself as being actively involved in the decision of women to participate in sport, yet at the same time could be seen to be constraining such participation by directing them towards certain types of sporting activity. In this research it was not just the words or the imagery, but a combination of the two that was analysed to allow the author to conclude that such advertising disempowers sportswomen by telling them the 'right' way to play sport. Company brochures may also provide a wealth of useful data.
- *Private papers/diaries/letters*. These can be extremely difficult to obtain, and there may be ethical considerations in using such documents. In reality, private papers are generally only an option if you have clear and agreed access to such documents before the research commences – you should not commence a research project and hope to gain access to such papers. Diaries have the added advantage of recording information significant to the diarist at, or very close to, the time that events took place.
- *Autobiographies and biographies*. Accounts of the lives of many well-known sportsmen and women are freely available. Autobiographies (provided they are actually written by the individual concerned) can provide an insightful account of an individual's sporting experiences, and give an understanding into differing areas. Biographies tend to be less reliable, but they may still provide some useful information. As with analysing media reports, you need to take into account issues of audience, accuracy and distortion when assessing your sources.

- *Photographs, films and video.* It is not just words that can be analysed. Pictures can provide a wealth of descriptive data, and may be used in a similar manner to non-participant observation.

You should be aware of a number of issues before you decide to undertake documentary or archive research. If you require permission to access official documents, the timescale may also be inappropriate – gaining permission to use government documents may take a number of months, therefore if you are constrained by time, you should reconsider your approach. You may also have to gain permission even to photocopy material. Retrieving the documents also takes time – often you will have to spend considerable time identifying and locating the appropriate source. On many occasions, what you think is appropriate will turn out to lack relevance for your research, hence such research can be extremely time consuming. We are not trying to deter you from documentary research, but it is important that you consider the potential pitfalls beforehand!

MISTAKES MADE IN CONTENT ANALYSIS

Again, you should be aware of some of the more common errors seen within content analyses. The two main issues for you to be aware of are as follows:

1 Not collecting a representative sample of texts. Consider your sampling method clearly, and ensure that it fulfils the objectives of your research.
2 Not considering the validity of the data from the context of the text. Do not unquestioningly use data from sources such as newspapers without critically assessing the validity of such data.

SUMMARY

1 Unobtrusive methods are those where the researcher does not interact with the subjects or environment under investigation.
2 Such methods are advantageous in that they may be stronger in measuring actual, rather than reported, behaviour. They are also generally much easier to undertake.
3 The lack of interaction may, however, make it difficult for the researcher to be able to clearly interpret the phenomenon being investigated.

4   The two main forms of unobtrusive investigation are those of observation and content analysis.
5   Observation can be used to collect qualitative and quantitative data from subjects in their natural environment.
6   Content analysis is used to collect data from texts, such as newspapers, television, photographs, etc.

ACTIVITIES

Observation

Identify a research question for which observational data is appropriate. Undertake a brief observational study paying particular attention to the following points:

■   *Sampling.* What is the best location? Who or what will you observe?
■   *Data collection and analysis.* How will you record your data? How will you analyse the data you do collect? (You may want to read Chapters 12 and 13 before you do this.)
■   What other additional means could you use to strengthen the reliability and validity of your findings?

Content analysis

Choose a contemporary sporting issue. Identify two contrasting newspapers, and undertake a content analysis to determine differences in how the issue has been covered. You should pay particular attention to how you operationalise your variables, for example what exactly will you be trying to measure or identify within the text? How does this relate to your overall research objective?

If you are using unobtrusive methods for your research project, consider the following points:

1   Why is the method you have chosen the most appropriate one for your research project?
2   Consider the issues of validity and reliability. How will you ensure that your observational or content analysis study is both reliable and valid? What are the threats to reliability and validity?

FURTHER READING

Kellehear, A. (1993) *The Unobtrusive Researcher*, St Leonards: Allen and Unwin.

CHAPTER ELEVEN

COLLECTING DATA IV: ETHNOGRAPHIC RESEARCH IN SPORT

In this chapter we will:

- Outline what is meant by an ethnographic approach to sports research.
- Describe the characteristics of an ethnographic approach.
- Describe the stages of undertaking a sport-related ethnography.
- Discuss some of the issues of writing up an ethnographic research project.

INTRODUCTION

> *I once heard a distinguished anthropologist say something that I have shamelessly plagiarised ever since. 'There are', he declared, 'only two basic methods of social research. One is called "asking questions" and the other is called "hanging out".' (Dingwall 1997, pp.52–3)*

One of the consequences of the growing maturity of sports research has been the use of an increasing number of different methods and methodologies, often as a reaction to the historical dominance of positivist approaches. One such methodological approach that has become increasingly popular is that of the sport ethnography. Defining the term 'ethnography', as Atkinson and Hammersley (1994) note, is a difficult task, and different authors will provide differing definitions. Ethnographies are generally characterised by their focus on a particular group, or subculture, the collection and use of extremely 'rich' data, and depth of information, often using several data collection methods, most notably observation, participant observation and in-depth interviews with key informants. Atkinson and Hammersley (1994, p.1) themselves suggest that:

> We see the term as referring primarily to a particular method or set of methods. In its most characteristic form, it involves the ethnographer participating, overtly or covertly, in people's daily lives for an extended period of time, watching what happens, listening to what is said, asking questions – in fact, collecting whatever data are available to throw light on the issues that are the focus of the research .

Thus, an ethnography investigates a group through collecting data over a substantial period of time, generally – although not always – using a number of different methods. Holt and Sparkes (2001) approach their definition from a slightly different angle, and suggest that the defining feature of an ethnography is its purpose. This purpose is the study of a group of people and their culture, where understanding of the group is obtained through examining behaviour from the group's, rather than the researcher's perspective. To achieve this, the researcher has to take on the role of 'insider', and spend an extended period of time within the group, during which time data is collected.

AN ETHNOGRAPHIC INVESTIGATION INTO BOXING SUBCULTURES

The aim of the researcher undertaking an ethnographic approach is that of immersion within the group. As Sugden (1996, p.201) remarks:

> It is only through total immersion that he or she can become sufficiently conversant with the formal and informal rules governing the webbing of the human interaction under investigation so that its innermost secrets can be revealed.

Sugden's (1996) own research into various boxing subcultures required him to become part of each subculture himself, so that the values, norms and behaviours otherwise hidden from the researcher could be uncovered:

The essence of good sociology is making sense of the mysterious. Here was a social universe which was buried deep within a sub-cultural envelope about which I knew next to nothing and about which there was virtually nothing written. (pp.2–3)

To 'make sense of the mysterious', Sugden became immersed within the group over an extended period of time:

For the next two years I led a dual existence: in the semi-rural idyll of the University campus as John Sugden, the anonymous college postgraduate student; and in Hartford's ghetto and in the base-ment gym as 'Doctor John', the idiosyncratic English ethnographer and the boxing club's odd-job man. (p.3)

By becoming part of the subcultures – albeit not completely immersed as a boxer, but rather as observer – Sugden was able to uncover many of the otherwise hidden values held by the group. During one bout in Havana, for example, it was noted that:

Despite the fact that there is a lot at stake and that the fights themselves are conducted with furious intensity, the young boxers show incredible self-discipline and emotional restraint. There is little overt sign of anger, even in the most bruising encounter. After the fight the two boxers hug one another, thank the referee and the opposite corner men and skip out of the ring without further ado. (p.162)

Such a scene may prove difficult for the non-ethnographic researcher to understand, yet through immersion into the group, Sugden was able to explain that Ajo (their coach):

Tells me that while winning and losing have some significance, at this level he is more interested in combinations of technique and temperament, believing that if the balance between these can be established early in a fighter's career, then the victories will automatically follow later. (p.162)

Thus, by a combination of immersion within the group for an extended period of time, and the use of different data collection methods whilst immersed, Sugden was able to both describe, and more importantly, explain the behaviours of members of the particular boxing subculture by collecting data that would – in all likelihood – be unavailable to the non-ethnographer.

CHARACTERISTICS OF AN ETHNOGRAPHY

Ethnographies generally have a number of common characteristics:

- They investigate human behaviour, and how such behaviour is related to the values and attitudes of the particular group under investigation. These 'cultural patterns' can then be used to explain the behaviour of members of the group.
- The ethnographer studies the group on its own ground, observing natural behaviours in a natural setting.
- The ethnographer will often use a range of methods to collect data. Often these methods will be flexible, and data is collected from whatever sources are available or appropriate at the time.
- The ethnographer is generally more interested in taking an holistic perspective than in focusing on individual aspects. It is the complex networks of interdependencies rather than isolated areas that are of interest to the ethnographer. Thus, it may be that the normal, mundane behaviours are more important than the extraordinary or unexpected behaviours.
- Ethnographies focus on the *emic* perspective. The emic perspective is that of taking the point of view of the people being studied, rather than the *etic*, or researcher's perspective.
- To gain understanding of the complex relationships within a culture, immersion is often necessary for a considerable period of time. Time is needed to gain access, to develop trust with those being studied, and to develop an understanding of what is actually going on within the group.

AN ETHNOGRAPHIC STUDY OF A COLLEGE SOCCER TEAM

Holt and Sparkes (2001) were interested in the factors influencing the cohesiveness of a college soccer team. Cohesiveness is the process reflected in the tendency of members of the group to maintain commitment to the group, and to the group's aims and objectives (for example commitment to training). An ethnographic approach was considered suitable, as the researchers were interested in studying a complex aspect of a group or culture's behaviour. The key ethnographic points of the study were as follows:

- *The objective of the study.* Ethnographies are not just about studying a group; they do need to have an overall research objective. In this case, Holt and Sparkes' objectives were to find out the influences upon team cohesion.
- *Entry to the field.* One of the researchers was able to use his personal characteristics as a graduate, soccer-playing student to enter the group. After a period of time, the objectives of the research were announced to the group, who agreed to participate. Rapport with the group was obtained through spending considerable time immersed within it, leading to trust and therefore more quality, 'rich' data.
- *The use of multiple roles.* The researcher was able to take on different roles, those of player and coach, allowing access to differing settings (training sessions, social events, etc.).
- *The use of multiple methods of data collection.* A variety of methods were used over an extended period of time including observation/participant observation, interviews and the examination of documentary sources.

Through using the ethnographic approach, Holt and Sparkes were able to determine that cohesion was a dynamic process, changing over the course of a season. Such a finding was unlikely had a more 'static' method – such as a questionnaire survey – been adopted. The ethnographic method also allowed the researchers to identify the importance of communication within the team as a key influence on cohesion. Thus, the ethnographic approach was able to provide a significant contribution to the literature on team cohesion.

UNDERTAKING A SPORTS ETHNOGRAPHY

A sports-related ethnography is a very flexible methodology, in that data collection is often unstructured, unplanned and even unexpected! Thus, unlike an experimental study, for example, it is difficult to provide a precise framework with which to approach such an undertaking. The following provides a generalised series of stages for undertaking an ethnographic piece of sports research.

1 Identifying the problem

The researcher cannot enter the field without having some sort of idea what the research problem is. Although a characteristic of these types of study is their inductive nature, that is where the theory emerges from, or is grounded in the data (see Chapter 2), some concept of the overall objective of the study has to exist so that the researcher will know what to observe in the field. What the researcher should not do, however, is impose a theoretical framework upon the research prior to data collection. As Holt and Sparkes (2001, p.242) suggest:

> An important requirement of ethnography is that researchers suspend a wide range of common-sense and theoretical knowledge in order to minimise the danger of taking on misleading preconceptions about the setting and the people in it. . . . In researching settings that are more familiar, it can be much more difficult to suspend one's preconceptions, whether these derive from social science or from everyday knowledge. One reason for this is that one finds it so obvious. . . . Therefore, while the ethnographic insider has the problem of making the strange seem familiar, the ethnographic insider has the task of making the familiar seem strange in order to maintain analytical distance.

2 Deciding upon an ethnographic approach

The next stage is to determine whether an ethnography is actually a suitable research design. If a rich understanding of a group or subculture is your objective, then an ethnography may be appropriate. If you require more descriptive data, or wish to assess a large population using statistical techniques, then other methods are more appropriate.

3 Considering your personal characteristics

Your own characteristics will be an important consideration. Your age, gender and even sporting experience or ability may all have a potential impact on your choice of ethnography. Look again at the case study in this chapter of Holt and Sparkes (2001). Could this ethnography have been carried out if one of the authors had not been a footballer himself? Could a female researcher have carried out the ethnography and collected the same data? In both cases, it seems unlikely that this would be the case. You may wish to allow your personal characteristics to dictate your choice of sample. For example if – such as with the Holt and Sparkes study – you are already a member of a group such as a football team, then consider using this opportunity to undertake an ethnographic study of your team. It is not always the case that your research question should determine the sample. In certain cases, the sample may determine the choice of research question!

4 Selecting the setting

As stage 3 suggested, although the setting is often chosen after the research question has been determined, it may also be the case that the setting is chosen first, maybe because it is familiar, or accessible to the researcher. The important issue is that the choice of the setting and the research question are compatible. Some settings, such as a sports organisation, may have clearly defined boundaries. Others, for example that encountered when undertaking an ethnographic study into a particular sporting community, have much less clearly defined boundaries. It is relatively easy for the researcher undertaking an ethnography into a sports organisation to identify the setting in terms of both the physical location and the members of the group being studied. In other cases this can be more problematic, and this needs to be considered so that the boundaries of the ethnography do not become too broad and unmanageable.

5 Consider the time frame

Ethnographies are characterised by the researcher spending a considerable duration of time within the setting. Unlimited time and resources are not generally available, however, and the researcher needs to delimit the time spent on the study. The time frame needs to be evaluated against the objectives of the study – will there be sufficient time for you to collect the data you need to achieve your research objectives?

6 Gaining entry to the setting

Gaining entry to the group from which you want to collect data is a key stage in ethnography. The method of entry has implications for the subsequent reliability and validity of data obtained, and thus must be approached with care. One method, as used by Giulianotti (1995 – see the case study *an ethnography of sports fans* later in this chapter), is to find a 'gatekeeper', trusted by group members, who can then introduce you to other members. Other methods may be more fortuitous, such as Gallmeier (1988) who was able to use his father's position as sports editor of the local paper and associate of the owner of the local team to gain access to the otherwise inaccessible players of a professional ice hockey team. You need to consider how you enter the setting, and the information you provide to members when you do enter. As Grills (1998) suggests, your access to informants, and thus data, will be strongly influenced by how those in the group interpret your motives and interests as a researcher. Entry is a crucial stage in ethnography, and one you should consider at length. Ultimately, there is no one 'best practice' that we can recommend, it is dependent upon a number of variables related to the characteristics of the group, and you as a researcher.

7 Consider your sample

Sampling in this respect takes on a slightly different meaning from that we have already encountered. A group may have many members, many behaviours, values, artefacts and so on. The researcher – especially if constrained by a limited time frame – simply cannot record all the potential data, and thus choices need to be made about what data to measure. In terms of who you should collect data from, Hammersley and Atkinson (1995) suggest two categories. First there are those that you, in your initial fieldwork, identify as suitable informants. Secondly there are those who volunteer themselves, or are volunteered by other members of the group. It is one of your roles, as ethnographer, to assess the most appropriate sample. Unlike methods such as questionnaire surveys, or in-depth interviews, the choice also needs to be made about *what*, as well as *who* to collect data from. The types of things you should be observing will vary, depending upon the research objective, but can include:

- ▪ *The history and context of the setting*. What background information will be useful to explain the data you collect? What is the history of the group? Are there any idiosyncratic features that may influence your observations? Do similar groups exist elsewhere?

- *The physical environment.* You should note the location and its appearance. You can also note the other physical factors, such as the smell, the noise and so on. You should aim to gather as much data as possible to allow the reader of your ethnography the sense of what it is actually like to be within that setting.
- *Artefacts within the setting.* Artefacts such as pictures, posters, décor and so on can all provide useful data in an ethnography. Where are they located? What is their purpose? Asking questions such as these can be extremely useful to the ethnographer.
- *The people within the setting.* Be descriptive – how many people are there, what do they look like, what are their characteristics?
- *The relationships between people.* How are people interacting? What norms and values are governing their behaviour? Does their behaviour seem to follow any patterns or rules? Why are they behaving in the way that they do? As well as listening to what people say, perhaps through interviewing them, observe what they do, and how they are doing it.

8 'Learning the ropes'

This refers to being able to fit in with the group, without arousing suspicion, standing out or antagonising those within the group in any way. As Gallmeier (1988) notes, there are no explicit guidelines for this, however it is an 'absolute necessity' (p.220) to establish trust and rapport with those being investigated. This will enhance both the amount and the validity of the data that you collect. Without establishing such trust and rapport, you will find collecting useful data a difficult task indeed.

9 Collecting the data

A range of data collection methods is often employed, with observation and participant observation extensively used, as well as key informant interviews. Data is generally written in the form of field notes, although you may – with the participants' consent – wish to use tape recorders, cameras or even video recorders. If you rely on recording equipment, always back up against possible technological failures by making written notes as well. Detailed notes should be made using your field notes as soon as possible (preferably whilst you are in the field, unless circumstances dictate otherwise). At the beginning, don't restrict yourself in the data that you collect – quite often it is a case of collecting as much data as you can. As your analysis of the data proceeds, you can become more selective in what you record.

AN ETHNOGRAPHY OF SPORTS FANS

Richard Giulianotti (1995) carried out participant observation with two groups of rival football hooligans in Scotland. Some of the issues that he faced were as follows:

- *Gaining access.* Gaining entry to these groups was difficult in that they were cautious of 'unsympathetic reporting', that is the possibility of condemnation by the researcher. Giulianotti struck a 'research bargain' to gain entry, by providing limited information on the opposing group to develop trust with the groups. Further entry was gained by the technique of 'snowballing', whereby one individual will provide access to another, who will then provide access to another and so on. This method is useful as trust can be further enhanced if the researcher is introduced by an existing member of the group.
- *Risks whilst conducting research.* Giulianotti encountered some initial hostility. However, the use of snowballing as a means of gaining access was instrumental in reducing risk – it is likely that a researcher obtaining an entrée to the group by other means would have been much more at risk. Giulianotti also notes that the researcher needs to be aware of the difference between threat and banter.
- *Validity of data.* Giulianotti's research posed a number of questions with regard to its validity. As he notes, each group were keen to portray themselves as the 'hardest' fans in Scotland, thus providing motivations for each group to over- or misrepresent their activities to the researcher.

---

10 Data analysis

Although we have put this stage as the final stage, data analysis in reality is a continual process and takes place during, rather than at the end of, the ethnography. Interpretation emerges from the data, and then further data can be collected to support or refute the interpretations. Thus explanations can be continually developed, tested and refined.

ETHNOGRAPHIC METHODS

Although there are a number of methods traditionally associated with ethnography, it is not possible simply to say which methods should be used. The choice should, as always, be made in terms of which method, or methods will provide valid and reliable data to investigate the research problem. The following methods are the most commonly used within ethnographic research:

- *Observation*. Simply watching the group can provide a wealth of information, especially if you can observe different members of the group within their 'natural' environment. This is often an appropriate method during the early stages of an ethnography.
- *Participant observation*. In most cases, participant observation will be an essential element of ethnographic research, to try to gain an empathetic understanding of the group's behaviours that you may observe.
- *Structured and unstructured interviews*. You should consider the use of both forms. Structured interviews will allow you to collect predetermined data, yet you should not limit yourself – you should allow new and important data to emerge from your informants through unstructured interviews.
- *Life histories*. Essentially this is the informant narrating his or her experiences to the ethnographer, so that a detailed picture of the culture or group can be developed. Life histories are an excellent method of understanding the group, and changes within the group. You should, however, be aware of the possibilities of forgetfulness, biased recall, exaggeration and so on.
- *Unobtrusive methods*. We have examined the use of unobtrusive methods in Chapter 10, and such methods can help enhance understanding of a group or culture as part of an ethnographic approach, for example through undertaking a content analysis of any documents or texts produced by members of the group.

You should also be flexible in how you collect your data, and be prepared to collect data at any time. Sands (2002) has noted how, as an ethnographer, he interviewed a sprinter almost immediately after a race. Sands recalls that: 'in that brief five minutes, what he told me was more succinct and from the heart than what I could have received in a two-hour interview' (p.67).

As the quote from Sands suggests, you must, as an ethnographer, be prepared to be flexible, and grasp opportunities as they arise. Always carry a notebook with you when you are in the field, to take advantage of unexpected data collection opportunities.

REFLEXIVITY

As Brackenridge (1999, p.399) notes, 'reflexivity is becoming an increasingly important research skill'. Defined simply, reflexivity is a process whereby the effect of the researcher, and their own characteristics, background, values, attitudes and so on, upon the subject matter is taken account of. As Brackenridge notes, an assessment of the position of the researcher, and the power relations between the researcher and participants is important towards an evaluation of the 'truth' of any findings.

METHODOLOGICAL AND ETHICAL ISSUES IN SPORT ETHNOGRAPHY

The sports ethnographer may face a number of methodological and ethical issues. Palmer (2000) summarises a common ethnographic issue that she faced when researching La Société du Tour de France. The issue was that of gaining access – access was only available to accredited journalists, and not to researchers. Palmer was able to use her contacts with an Australian television network to obtain a press pass, and thus fraudulently gain access, raising key ethical issues regarding deception. As she notes, 'the researcher needs to be able to work with whatever is available' (p.371) and justified her approach on the grounds that the accounts she would have obtained otherwise would have been 'nothing short of fraudulent'. By posing as a journalist she gained access to situations where the influence of La Société was visible. Unfortunately, by posing as a journalist, she was unable to use many of the tools of ethnography, such as participant observation or detailed interviews, as to do so would have been inconsistent with her role as journalist. This is a good example of an ethnography where it is simply not possible to use the full range of ethnographic methods, and the researcher must weigh up the issues involved, and make the decision that would provide the best data. In this case, the justification was made on the basis of the validity of the data obtained.

EXPERIENTIAL ETHNOGRAPHY

A relatively new term that has emerged within sport research is that of 'experiential ethnography'. Sands (2002) views this approach in terms of the researcher becoming a complete participant within the study. To do this, the researcher will have to go through a number of stages: learning about the group (anticipatory socialisation); becoming a member (recruitment); learning about the norms, values and behaviours of the group (socialisation), and finally acceptance as one of the group. Each of these stages, in itself, may provide understanding about the group. Experiential ethnography may allow the researcher to collect otherwise 'hidden' or inaccessible data, for example as Sands (2002, p.131) suggests:

> In my research with sprinters and football players, I experienced sensations and feelings through participation that would have lain outside the non-experiential ethnographer's boundaries of observation. In effect, my body's lived experience of performance and competition not only allowed me access to sensations of pain, elation, adrenaline rushes, and wild swings of emotion generated through cognitive appraisal of performance but also brought me closer to the cultural experiences of my team mates and other like athletes.

Thus experiential ethnography would seem to have strengths in uncovering sports experiences. However, you must approach this methodology – as with any methodology – with some caution in terms of assessing its potential weaknesses as well as strengths. It can be easy to simply become autobiographical in your write-up, with no real theoretical or explanatory framework within which to place your own experiences. Secondly, the danger of 'going native', or taking on the beliefs and values of the group may be an issue. Giulianotti (1995), for example, noted that each of the groups of football hooligans he investigated was keen to be presented as the 'hardest' in Scottish football. In the unlikely event of Giulianotti going native, then the value of his findings could have been questioned in terms of his own subjectivity, in perhaps selecting evidence to show that 'his group' was 'harder' than other groups. Perhaps the key for the researcher is to be 'objectively subjective' in being able to assess conflicts between his or her roles as participant and researcher.

WRITING THE ETHNOGRAPHY

During your fieldwork, you may collect large amounts of data in the form of written field notes, taped interviews, photographs, videos, analyses of documents and so on. It is now that you need to make the move from viewing ethnography as a methodology to that of the written report. The process of producing a meaningful report – often restricted by time and word counts – can be, at the beginning, an extremely daunting task. Unfortunately, there is no set procedure that exists to guarantee success!

The first stage of reporting is that of making sense of the data. The best way to do this is through the process of coding. You should read Chapter 13, which deals with the issue of making sense of qualitative data. Through a systematic process of coding and analysis, you will soon begin to make some sort of sense of the data (you should, ideally, begin this process during the fieldwork). By being systematic in your coding, you can soon make the task seem less daunting than it initially appears.

Although there is no one correct way to present your findings in an ethnographic report, as a general guideline your write-up should include the following:

1 Statement and justification of the research problem.
2 Literature review, and its use in refining research questions and research design.
3 Detailed review of the study design, including a detailed description of the setting.
4 Presentation of the data.
5 Explanation of the findings.

Gall et al. (1996, p.607) provide a statement that should guide you in your writing up: 'If an ethnography has been done well, readers of the final report should be able to understand the culture even though they may not have directly experienced it.'

ISSUES OF VALIDITY AND RELIABILITY

One criticism often levelled at ethnographic research is that it is difficult to objectively assess validity and reliability. Although validity and reliability are important, there are also a number of other factors you can assess when evaluating your report:

- Is your ethnography contextually complete? Does it make full reference to the context within which the group exists?
- *Verisimilitude*. Does it provide the reader with a sense of almost being there, and give them some understanding of the culture?
- *Triangulation*. Have you used data from a range of methods to strengthen the validity of your claims?
- *Plausibility*. Does the report ring true? Does it provide a plausible account and explanation of the group or culture?
- *Member checking*. Does your account provide a plausible explanation to those actually being investigated? Allow members of the group to read your analysis, if appropriate, and obtain their assessment of your written report.

ETHNOGRAPHY AND STUDENT RESEARCH

Although it is unlikely that those undertaking research as part of an undergraduate degree will have the time and resources to undertake a 'classical' ethnography, do not immediately rule it out as an approach. Even in relatively limited studies, an ethnographic approach can be fruitful. It is entirely possible for the student researcher to become immersed into the group – although not to the same extent as the 'true' ethnographer – and to collect data using different methods to develop an understanding of the group in question, especially if they are already associated with the group in the first place, such as undertaking an ethnographic study of a sports team to which they belong. In such studies, it may be possible to collect a quantity of extremely rich and informative data. As always, consider your information needs, and identify the best approach to obtain data to supply such information.

SUMMARY

1 Ethnography involves the study of a group, whereby the researcher becomes 'immersed' within the group's natural environment for an extended period of time.
2 Data collection is generally flexible and varied, being undertaken at whatever times are appropriate, often using a variety of methods.
3 The researcher needs to be aware of certain issues such as entry to the group, and their particular role within the group, as these may have implications for the validity of the findings.

4   Ethnography may be an appropriate research design in certain cases, but where time and resources are limited – for example in the case of a student research project – it needs to be carefully considered.

ACTIVITIES

Locate a sport-related ethnography using Sport Discus. Critically evaluate the ethnography, and try to determine why the ethnographic method was chosen, and how such an approach allowed the researcher to gain understanding of the group. Try to answer the following questions:

■   Would the use of a different methodology have allowed the same understanding to be developed?
■   What was the chosen setting? How and why was it chosen?
■   How did the researcher gain access to the setting?
■   What methods were used to collect data?
■   What were the main conclusions of the study?

ABOUT YOUR RESEARCH PROJECT

If you are undertaking an ethnography, consider the following points:

■   Can you justify the use of an ethnographic approach? What will the ethnographic approach provide that other research designs will not?
■   What is the justification for your choice of setting? Can you justify the choice in academic terms?
■   How could your personal characteristics influence the data collection process? How will you take this into account when undertaking your research?

FURTHER READING

Brewer, J. (2000) *Ethnography*, Buckingham: Open University Press.
Sands, R. (2002) *Sport Ethnography*, Champaign, Ill.: Human Kinetics.

If you intend undertaking ethnographic research, it is also worth locating and reading as many ethnographic studies as you can, even if they do not relate directly to your own subject area.

CHAPTER TWELVE

ANALYSING DATA I:
QUANTITATIVE DATA ANALYSIS

In this chapter we will:

- Describe how to prepare your quantitative data for analysis.
- Introduce *SPSS for Windows* as a data analysis software package, and briefly run through its use.
- Introduce some of the different statistical tests that you may wish to use to analyse your data.

INTRODUCTION

Data itself will not provide you with the answer to your research question. The data needs to be interpreted, and to be interpreted, it needs to be organised and analysed. If you have collected quantitative data, you need to analyse it so that it may be meaningfully used to answer your research question. This is the process of quantitative data analysis. It is often at this stage that panic – especially among non-statisticians – may set in! From your reading of the related literature, you may already have encountered terms such as 'multiple regression analysis', 'repeated measures ANOVA', 'factor analysis', and so on, and found them difficult to comprehend, let alone to interpret. Ideally, as a researcher, you would have a detailed understanding of the entire range of statistical tools and techniques. In reality, however, it is unlikely that you will have the time, energy or resources to become a statistics expert, especially if you have not had the chance to undertake a specialist statistics course during your studies. It is, however, useful to have some idea of what the different tests you may encounter are measuring, so that you can interpret the research that you read, as well as undertake your own analysis. The field of statistics is a large and complicated one, and a book of this type can only provide you with a broad overview. We would strongly recommend that, if your research involves detailed statistical procedures, you should read one of the many available specialist texts such as Vincent (1995).

Statistical analysis can be broadly separated into two forms, descriptive and inferential. Descriptive statistics organise your data, for example in terms of producing frequency counts of participation in sport, or calculating the average points scored per game by a particular team. Inferential statistics allow you to infer relationships between two or more variables, such as calculating a correlation between the variables of experience and ability at a particular sporting task. In terms of your own use of statistics, you will have to ask the following questions:

■ What exactly do I need to find out from this data to answer my research question?
■ What statistical test will give me this information?
■ What do the results from this statistical test mean?

A final point to note, and one that we will repeat, is that statistics in themselves have no meaning. Thus, simply to report the results of a statistical test is only the first stage. The importance lies in how such statistics are interpreted, and how that interpretation is related to your research objectives.

THE USE OF COMPUTER SOFTWARE IN QUANTITATIVE ANALYSIS

A number of computer packages are available to assist you with quantitative data analysis. The most commonly used package is *Statistical Package for the Social Sciences for Windows (SPSS for Windows)*, and it is worth learning to use this. It is relatively simple to pick up the basics of the program, and a lot of the functions are intuitive if you have used other Windows software before. *SPSS for Windows* allows large data sets to be used, it has a wide range of statistical tests available, and it can produce professional looking graphs and tables. It is the standard package used globally, and a knowledge of SPSS is a valuable skill to have. There are other alternatives you could consider, for example spreadsheets such as *Microsoft Excel*, but you may find other packages less flexible or user friendly. Whatever your choice of software, you should remember, however, that it is not the case that certain software will produce 'better' results (the results produced should be the same whether you use *SPSS for Windows*, *Excel*, or calculate them by hand!). Your research project will not be assessed on what package you used to analyse your data, but rather on your interpretation of the statistical results.

Throughout this chapter, we will assume that you will be using *SPSS for Windows* to analyse your data, and will provide guidance on carrying out the tests using this package. The underlying statistical principles of what follows, however, will apply whatever method you choose.

DATA PREPARATION

The first stage in analysing your data is to prepare the data for input into SPSS (or other appropriate statistical package). There are four steps that you need to undertake before the process of analysis begins.

1 Coding data

Coding refers to translating the responses that you receive into common categories, each of which can be assigned a numerical value, allowing subsequent statistical analysis. Coding can be relatively straightforward; for example a question on age worded 'how old are you?' is already numerical in format (thus providing a ratio variable – see Chapter 6 for a reminder of the different types of data). Non-numerical responses should be assigned numerical values, for example responses to a question on gender could be coded so that answers of 'Male' are coded as 1, and 'Female' coded as 2 (thus providing a nominal variable). Open questions are slightly more problematic. Here, each response should be grouped together (coded) by the researcher. For example responses to the question 'What is your favourite sport?' could be as follows:

tennis
hockey
soccer
basketball
association football

Each group would then be assigned a numerical value. Tennis would be coded 1, hockey 2 and so on. Soccer and association football would have the same numerical value as, although different responses were given, conceptually they are the same response and they would thus be coded together. Thus, each response is converted into a number. Occasionally you may encounter difficulties in deciding whether to code differing responses together or separately. The answer to this is dependent upon whether they are conceptually similar in terms of your research question. If in doubt, code the responses differently, as you can always combine different codes together as one afterwards, which is a lot easier than separating one code into two!

Responses from the other types of questions we discussed should be relatively straightforward in terms of converting responses to numerical values. If you are using scales, then each potential response is allocated a number. Have a look at the following question, for example:

	Never	Seldom	Sometimes	Often	Almost always
I take a positive attitude towards myself as a sportsman or woman				✓	

Each response can be allocated a logical numerical value. Thus a response of 'never' is coded as 1, 'seldom' as 2, 'sometimes' as 3 and so on. Therefore, in the above example, the response would be coded as 4. Occasionally a question may be 'reversed', that is asked in the opposite way, for example the question above may be asked as 'I take a negative attitude towards myself as a sportsman or woman'. The scoring is also reversed, thus 'never' is scored 5, 'seldom' as 4 and so on. You may also need to add up the scores from all of the items in a scale, and include that score.

2 Data entry

The numbers produced from step one should then be input into whatever software package you choose. Depending on the package used, you may have to set up your data entry sheet beforehand. We will run through data entry in *SPSS for Windows* later in the chapter.

3 Data checking

Once data entry has been completed, then a careful check should be made for accuracy. It is easy to make inputting errors, for example inputting making a double keystroke by accident and entering '11' rather than '1'. The data set should be checked beforehand as far as possible to minimise the effect of such errors, and any unusual or unexpected results that occur after the analysis (such as having three different response sets for a question on gender!) should also be checked in case of mistakes in data entry.

4 Dealing with missing values

The general practice is that questions that have not been answered should be assigned a value (for example '99' or '999') in the data set. This will allow you to distinguish between actual missing values and those that have been inadvertently omitted. You can inform *SPSS for Windows* that you have used a particular response for missing values so that your analysis will not be affected.

USING SPSS FOR WINDOWS[1]

The following section will give you a brief guide to the use of *SPSS for Windows*, which we would recommend for your quantitative data analysis. It is, once you have picked up the basics, a user friendly package, and allows you to undertake any statistical test that you will realistically need. It will also provide you with high quality tables, charts and graphs which can be imported into your word processing package. You should ensure that you use the tutorial provided with SPSS as this will be extremely helpful. Another good way to learn about SPSS is to practise using hypothetical data sets. You may also want to have a look at Ntoumanis (2001) for an overview of the use of *SPSS for Windows*.

There are four basic steps to analysing data using SPSS. These are:

1 Inputting your prepared data into the data editor.
2 Selecting an appropriate test, graph, chart and so on from the menus.
3 Selecting the variable(s) for analysis.
4 Interpretation of the results from the output file.

Upon opening the program, you will encounter a window that asks you whether you wish to open an existing file, or create one of your own. For the first time, you should create a new file, and give it a name that summarises the contents (i.e. *sport participation study* as opposed to *data*). You will be faced with

---

1 Please note that this edition refers to *SPSS for Windows* version 10. There may be slight differences with later versions. If you are using a later version, use the *help* command to find out what is different.

a screen that resembles a spreadsheet. This is the data view. This is where the data is to be entered, and is essentially a grid that displays all of the responses for all of the participants. Each of the grey boxes running along the top of the screen (containing the letters *VAR*) refers to a different variable. Each of the boxes down the left hand side, numbered from 1 onwards, refers to a participant. Thus, you are able to include each variable response for each participant on this screen.

To help you keep track of variables, both during data entry and in later analysis, SPSS also allows you to provide more detailed information about each variable. If you go towards the bottom of the screen, you will see that you are in the *data view* window. By clicking on *variable view* (next to *data view*), you will bring up a different screen. On this screen, each row represents a different variable. The grey boxes along the top represent some of the characteristics of the variable. The most important ones are as follows:

- *Name*. This refers to the name you assign the variable. Try to make this as simple yet as meaningful as possible, so name your variables 'age', 'score', 'weight' and so on, rather than 'question 1', 'variable 1', etc.
- *Type of variable*. This allows you to specify whether your data is in numeric form, date form, currency and so on.
- *Label*. This allows you to give a more detailed label to your data, for example your variable may be titled 'score' and your label may be 'what was the participant's score on the basketball shooting task'. This label will then be attached to whatever output you produce, such as graphs or tables.
- *Values*. Here, you can enter detail about the codes that you have used for each variable. By clicking on the small grey box within the cell under *labels*, a small window will open. Under label you should enter the codes you have used, and what those codes refer to under value label, for example if you coded males as 1 and females as 2, you should enter '1' for value, and 'male' for value label, then click *add*. Repeat the action, except entering '2' for value, and 'female' for value code. Once you have done this, your output will automatically include the labels such as 'male' and 'female', rather than just '1' or '2'.
- *Missing*. This will allow you to identify which values are missing, for example you may wish to enter '99' for missing values. You can enter up to three codes for missing values, so you can distinguish between reasons for their omission. For example '99' could be entered for those questions that were not applicable, and '999' could be entered if the participant failed to respond.

You are now in a position to enter your data. Return to the data view window, and enter your data carefully, trying to avoid any errors, which may affect your analysis. Remember to enter missing values. Once you have entered all of your data, you are ready to undertake statistical analysis.

ANALYSING DATA USING SPSS FOR WINDOWS

There are several steps that you need to follow when analysing your data. These are:

- *Decide what you need to find out.* List your requirements beforehand. What do you need to know? What variables do you need to compare?
- *Choose the appropriate test.* Decide the appropriate statistical test to use to give you that data. Then, using the menus across the top of the screen, select *analyse*, and choose your test accordingly. There are a range of available options, including the production of tables as well as descriptive and inferential statistics.
- *Select the variables to be tested.* Once you have selected your test, you will be asked which variables are to be tested. Highlight the appropriate variables in the box in the left of the small window (the dialog box) that appears when you choose your test. Move them across to the appropriate sections, for example into the independent variable box. You may also need to select which groups to compare, for example the independent sample t-test asks you to enter your grouping variable. Simply enter the codes for the two groups you want to compare, e.g. '1' for males and '2' for females.
- *Interpreting the output.* SPSS will produce an output window where the results are presented. Depending upon the test used, various information will be presented. The information that will be of most interest to you will be the level of significance. *SPSS for Windows* will state the level of significance, and if this is below the threshold that you have set, then you can assume a significant relationship between your variables. You may find out that the level of significance produced is 0.03, and you have set 0.05 and below as the level at which you will reject your *null hypothesis* (more on this later). As your level of significance is lower than that of the predetermined threshold, the null hypothesis can be rejected.
- *Producing graphical output.* This follows the same procedure as analysing your data. Rather than select *analyse*, you should select *graphs*, and follow the instructions as above. Graphs can be copied and pasted directly into a word processed document, and you can link the chart with the data file, so

that if you update your data file, you can also update your chart in the document.

ANALYSING YOUR DATA

This section will present an overview of some of the commonly used methods of statistical analysis. As we have said, *descriptive* statistics are those which organise and summarise numerical data. *Inferential* statistics allow inferences to be made about the wider population from your sample by analysing the associations or differences between two or more variables.

DESCRIPTIVE STATISTICS

Measures of central tendency

A measure of central tendency is a value that describes a particular characteristic of a set of scores. The most commonly used measures are those of *mean*, *mode* and *median*.

The *mean* is the average score of all observations of a variable. You may, for example, be interested in the attendances of a particular sports team. Rather than select one attendance figure (which may be misleading), a better approach would be to average out the attendance figures over a period of time, for example a single season. The mean is calculated by the following:

Mean = sum of scores/number of observations

USING SPSS TO MEASURE THE MEAN

1 Select *analyse* from the menu.
2 Select *descriptive statistics*.
3 Select *descriptives*.
4 Select the variable for which you want to know the mean. Move that variable into the central box.
5 Click *OK*. SPSS will produce the results in a separate output window.

199

Thus, for the example above, the average attendance would be the entire sum of attendances over the period of time, divided by the number of matches. Thus, three matches, with attendances of 481, 375 and 425 would result in an average attendance of the three attendances (481 + 375 + 425) divided by the number of occurrences (three), providing an average attendance of 427.

Sometimes, you may come across grouped data, as shown below:

Points scored	Frequency
0–2	3
3–5	5
6–8	6
9–11	1

In this instance, the mean is calculated by multiplying the midpoint (halfway between the upper and lower score) by the frequency, and then dividing by the total number of observations.

Points scored	Midpoint	Frequency	Midpoint × frequency
0–2	1	3	3
3–5	4	5	20
6–8	7	6	42
9–11	10	1	10
	Total	15	75

Thus the average points score was 75/15 which is 5 points.

A second measure of central tendency is the *mode*. You may be interested to find out the most common age for individuals to drop out from competitive sports. In this type of research, a modal score can often be more useful than a mean score. The mode refers to the category with the largest number of observations. Thus, the mode for the above example of grouped data would be 6–8, as that was observed 6 times, more than any other category.

Finally, the *median* is the point that divides the observations, once ordered, into two equal parts. If the weekly hours spent training for a sport were measured as 2, 2, 4, 5, 6, 10, 10, 11, 15 then the median would be 6, as there are four values above this value and four below. A *median split* can be used to split one group into two subgroups for the purposes of comparison. It may be that the researcher is interested in the relationship between the time spent training and self-efficacy whilst competing. In this case, a median split could be used to divide the group into 'low' trainers (those scoring below the median) and 'high' trainers (those scoring above the median).

Measures of dispersion

Measures of dispersion indicate the spread of the data around the mean or other measure of central tendency. The most commonly reported measure is the *standard deviation*. The standard deviation (SD) measures the extent to which scores deviate from the mean. Thus, two samples may have identical means, but differing standard deviations. The researcher is then aware that the measures from the sample with the larger standard deviation are likely to be deviate from the mean score to a greater extent, that is they will be more spread out. A further, although less commonly used measure of dispersion is that of the range. The range is simply the difference between the lowest and highest score in the distribution.

Relational measures

Rate

Rates can be useful in comparing different populations. For example you may want to find out differences in sports participation between two countries with significantly different populations. Rather than simply provide figures as to overall participation (which would effectively be meaningless), a rate would provide a more useful comparison. A rate measures the frequency with which a value occurs compared to the maximum frequency with which it could occur. The calculation is simple:

Rate = number of actual occurrences/number of possible occurrences

The rate of regular participation in sport in the UK may be 0.15 (that is fifteen people from every hundred participants) whereas the rate in the USA may be 0.18 (or eighteen in every hundred).

Ratio

You may be interested as to the proportion of different groups undertaking a particular activity. A ratio describes the numerical relationship of parts of a group to each other; for example it could describe the numbers of males compared to females in a sports crowd. It is calculated using the following formula:

Ratio = number of members of subgroup one / number of members of subgroup two

If there were 32,000 males and 24,000 females watching a sporting event, then the ratio would be 32,000/24,000, which is 1.3 males for every female.

Percentage

A percentage (%) compares a subgroup to the total group, for example, using the above scenario, the percentage of male fans in the entire crowd. This is calculated by:

% of subgroup = (number of members of subgroup / number of members of entire group) × 100

So the percentage of male fans is (32,000/56,000) × 100, or 57.1 per cent. You may also wish to use percentages to ascertain levels of performance, for example one individual may score seventeen points out of twenty, compared to another who scored eleven points out of fifteen. Because both scores were from different totals, it is not possible to compare them directly. One way to compare them is to convert them into percentages. Player one scored seventeen out of twenty, which equals 85 per cent. Player two scored eleven out of fifteen, which equals 73 per cent. The percentages can then be compared rather than the raw scores.

PRESENTING DESCRIPTIVE STATISTICS

Descriptive statistics are generally presented in the form of tables and graphs. Tables should be included where the information is appropriate to the research question (you should not include every single result unless it is relevant to your research!).

Tables should include percentages as well as raw scores – this allows easier comparison between groups of different sizes (you should also include the raw

Table 12.1 Age of respondents

Age category	Per cent	n
0–10	18.1	17
11–20	26.6	25
21–30	29.8	28
31–40	14.9	14
41–50	6.4	6
Over 50	4.3	4
	100	94

Table 12.2 Gender comparison of sport preference

	Prefer contact sport (%)	Prefer non-contact sport (%)
Male	79	21
Female	22	78

scores, and an indication of the total number of responses). You must also label each table accordingly. The format of your table should be similar to that presented in Table 12.1.

Cross tabulation simply involves producing a table with the responses from the dependent variable across the top, and the responses from the independent variable down the side, as demonstrated in Table 12.2.

Using SPSS to create tables

1 Select *analyse* from the menu.
2 Select *custom tables*.
3 Select either *basic* or *general* tables.
4 Select the appropriate variable(s). Move those variables into the central box.
5 Click *OK*. SPSS will produce the table in a separate output window.

Bar charts may be useful to present data visually. They consist of a 'bar' for each response (either horizontal or vertical), the length of which represents the size of response. A scale is placed along the side or bottom of the chart to indicate the size of response.

USING SPSS TO CREATE BAR CHARTS

1   Select *graphs* from the menu.
2   Select *bar* from the options.
3   Decide the type of bar chart you want using the options provided.
4   Move the appropriate variable into the *category axis* box.
5   Decide what you want the bars to represent (number of cases, percentage of cases, etc.).
6   Click on *titles* if you want to add any titles to the bar chart.
7   Click on *OK*, and the chart will be produced. If you want to edit the chart at a later date, then double click on the chart.

Graphs are useful for showing changes over time, or across groups. As well as being useful in highlighting trends, line graphs enable you to include more than one variable at a time, allowing easy comparison.

USING SPSS TO CREATE LINE GRAPHS

1   Select *graphs* from the menu.
2   Select *line* from the options.
3   Decide the type of line graph you want using the options provided.
4   Move the appropriate variable(s) into the *category axis* box.
5   Decide what you want the lines to represent (number of cases, percentage of cases, etc.).
6   Click on *titles* if you want to add any titles to the graph.
7   Click on *OK*, and the graph will be produced. If you want to edit the graph at a later date, then double click on the graph.

Pie charts are used to show the relative size or importance of different responses. The size of each 'slice' of the pie is proportional to the number of responses, thus if one response accounted for 50 per cent of responses, then the 'slice' would be equivalent to half the pie.

USING SPSS TO CREATE PIE CHARTS

1 Select *graphs* from the menu.
2 Select *pie* from the options.
3 Decide the type of pie chart you want using the options provided.
4 Move the appropriate variable into the *category axis* box.
5 Decide what you want the slices to represent (number of cases, percentage of cases, etc.).
6 Click on *titles* if you want to add any titles to the pie chart.
7 Click on *OK*, and the chart will be produced. If you want to edit the chart at a later date, then double click on the chart.

Histogram is similar in appearance to a bar chart, but it shows the relative distribution of scores achieved on a particular variable. Whereas bar charts have discrete, or separate bars, the bars on a histogram are connected. A histogram is useful to assess whether the data follows a normal distribution, which is an important assumption of some of the statistical tests that are outlined below.

USING SPSS TO CREATE HISTOGRAMS

1 Select *graphs* from the menu.
2 Select *histogram* from the options.
3 Move the appropriate variable into the *category axis* box.
4 Click on *titles* if you want to add any titles to the histogram.
5 Click on *OK*, and the histogram will be produced. If you want to edit the chart at a later date, then double click on the chart.

Whatever method you choose to describe and present your data, you need to ensure that the results are clear to the reader. Do not over elaborate when producing tables or charts, and often you should consider if they are actually needed. In many research projects it is a case of less, rather than more, is better! If you do not actually refer to any of your tables or charts in the text, then it is almost certain that they are not needed. Do not be tempted into using an excess of charts to 'pad out' a piece of research! If you think that a chart is required, then it is often the case that the simpler the presentation the better. Ensure that each table or chart has a clear title, that any axes are clearly labelled, and that you provide a legend if appropriate, showing which line/slice, etc. belongs to which data set.

INFERENTIAL STATISTICS

The measures discussed above investigate single variables, such as team scores, hours spent training in a week and so on. Much explanatory research, however, is interested in the relationship between two or more variables. This is the realm of inferential statistics. Inferential statistics assess the association between independent and dependent variables (you should go back to Chapter 6 if you are not clear about these terms). These may be bivariate (measuring the effect of a single independent variable upon a single dependent variable) or multivariate (involving more than two variables). There are two categories of inferential test:

1   *Parametric tests*. These tests use interval or ratio data (see Chapter 6 for a reminder). Parametric tests assume that the data is drawn from a normally distributed population (i.e. the data is not skewed) and has the same variance (or spread).
2   *Non-parametric tests*. These are used with ordinal or nominal data.

Inferential statistics require you to test a hypothesis, or more accurately, a *null hypothesis*. A null hypothesis suggests that there is no relationship between your variables. Thus, you are assuming no association, and it is the role of the test to contradict this hypothesis. Assume the null hypothesis is true until the evidence suggests otherwise.

INTERPRETING THE RESULTS

Inferential statistics do not, as such, tell us whether there is a relationship between two or more variables. Instead, they calculate the likelihood of whether an apparent relationship or difference between two or more groups is down to chance or not. Inferential statistics provide a 'p-value'. The smaller the p-value, the less likely the result was due to chance, and that there is an actual relationship between the variables. A p-value of 0.10 indicates that in ninety cases out of a hundred, the result was due to an actual association, rather than chance findings. Thus there is a 10 per cent chance of rejecting the null hypothesis when it is true. The probability of this being the case is indicated by a 'p' value. For example $p < 0.1$ indicates a likelihood of incorrectly rejecting a true null hypothesis one time in ten, whereas $p < 0.01$ suggests that this would be the case less than once in a hundred times. A value of 0.05 is the generally accepted level of significance in sport studies, thus a p-value of 0.05 or less strongly suggests that you have a relationship that is not due to chance. If you have a larger p-value, then you could not really be confident enough that the results do show an actual difference or relationship.

KEY TERM

P-VALUE

You may be interested in the difference between male and female ability at a sporting task. You want to know whether that difference in ability is due to the independent variable (gender in this case). Measuring the mean scores from each sample (male and female) will not be enough on its own to conclude that the wider populations have different means. It is possible that the populations have the same ability and that the difference you measured is simply a coincidence or chance finding. You cannot be sure if the difference you measured is representative of the wider populations, or if it is just a one-off result. All you can do is calculate the probability that it is indeed representative. This probability is the *p-value*.

The p-value ranges from zero to one. If the p-value is small (for example 0.05 or below), you may conclude that the difference between sample means is unlikely to be a coincidence. Instead, you'll conclude that the populations have different means, and that there is an effect related to the independent variable. If the p-value is higher (above 0.1), then it is very possible that your findings were, indeed, coincidence, and that no true difference exists between the groups.

It is important that you decide the level of significance before you undertake the statistical test. Although common practice, it is not good research to await the outcome of the test before deciding upon a significance level! You should also report your p-value in your results. In the past, precise values were not presented (due to the method of working out statistical significance, researchers reported the probability levels as either less than one in ten ($p < 0.1$), less than one in twenty ($p < 0.05$), or less than one in a hundred ($p < 0.01$). Nowadays, packages such as *SPSS for Windows* allow you to report the exact p-value, and this is generally accepted as good practice.

When selecting a particular level of significance at which to reject the null hypothesis, be aware that there is a possibility of two types of error. These are:

- *Type I error*. This occurs when you reject the null hypothesis when it is, in reality, true. Thus, you would suggest a relationship where, in reality, none exists.
- *Type II error*. This occurs when you accept the null hypothesis when it is false. Thus, you would suggest no relationship, where a relationship does actually exist.

The likelihood of making a type I or II error depends on the level of significance that you choose. Thus, if you choose to operate at the 0.1 level of significance, then you are more likely to make a type I error. If you choose a level of significance of 0.01, then a type II error becomes more likely.

TESTS OF ASSOCIATION

Tests of association refer to those tests that measure whether two or more variables are related, that is as the independent variable changes, then the dependent variable alters accordingly. Thus, you may be interested to examine whether there is a relationship between participation in sport and income. You are seeking to assess whether the two variables of participation and income are associated. There are a number of tests that you may consider using.

Correlation

Correlations investigate the relationship between two variables consisting of interval or ratio data, for example the relationship between advertising spend and sales of a particular sports product. A correlation can indicate:

- Whether there is a relationship between the two variables.
- The direction of the relationship, i.e. whether it is positive or negative.
- The strength, or magnitude of the relationship.

A positive correlation exists where higher scores on one variable correspond with high scores on another, for example performance may increase with self-efficacy. A negative correlation is where higher scores on one variable correspond with lower scores on another, for example performance in a complex sporting task may decrease with increasing levels of anxiety. The strength of correlations range from −1.00 to +1.00. A score of −1.00 represents a correlation that is a perfect negative correlation, that is as the score on one variable decreases, then the score on the other variable increases. A score of 0.00 represents variables that are not correlated, or have no relationship with each other, and a correlation of +1.00 represents a perfect positive correlation, that is the variables increase or decrease together.

CORRELATIONS USING SPSS

1   Select *analyse* from the menu.
2   Select *correlate* from the options.
3   Decide the type of correlation you would like to undertake (normally, but not only, a bivariate correlation).
4   Move the variables you want to analyse into the appropriate box.
5   Decide what type of correlation you need to use, for example a Pearson's or Spearman's correlation.
6   Click on *OK*, and the correlations will be produced.

Whilst correlations are useful to identify relationships, they are unable to determine *causality*, that is the extent to which variable X causes variable Y. This is because it is often unclear whether it is actually X causing Y, for example does increasing anxiety lead to a reduction in performance, or does Y cause X? Could it be that decreasing performance leads to increasing anxiety? A further possibility is that they are interrelated. Finally, there may be an unidentified variable that is leading to an increase in both X and Y. Thus you should be extremely cautious in assuming causal relationships from correlations.

Regression analysis

Although a correlation may indicate a relationship between two variables, it does not provide any indicator of the magnitude of effect, for example what a likely outcome would be of an increase in the independent variable upon the dependent variable. Regression analysis between two variables effectively calculates a 'best fit line'. This line will subsequently predict the effect of one variable upon the other.

REGRESSION ANALYSIS USING SPSS

1   Select *analyse* from the menu.
2   Select *regression* from the options.
3   Decide the type of regression you want using the options provided.
4   Move the appropriate variables into the dependent and independent variable boxes.
5   Click on *OK*, and the regression will be produced.

Using a Pearson or Spearman correlation

The Pearson correlation coefficient is used to analyse two variables collected at the interval or ratio level of measurement where the data is parametric in nature. Thus, a correlation between the height of a golfer and average drive length would use a Pearson's correlation. The Spearman's rank order correlation is the non-parametric equivalent of the Pearson's correlation, and is used with ordinal, or ranked data. Thus you may be undertaking a project into golf performance, and be interested in the relationship between position in driving accuracy tables, and position in final money tables. As the data is ordinal and non-parametric, a Pearson's correlation is inappropriate, and a Spearman's test is required.

TESTING DIFFERENCES

Tests of difference generally assess whether differences between two samples are likely to have occurred by chance, or whether they are the result of the effect of a particular variable.

The independent samples t-test

The independent samples t-test examines whether the mean scores of two different groups can be considered as being significantly different. For example, you may be interested to compare the effects of mental rehearsal on golf putting performance. You randomly assign your participants to either the rehearsal or non-rehearsal group, and compare their scores to see if there is a significant difference. It can be used when:

- The data is interval or ratio in nature.
- The groups are randomly assigned.
- The variance, or spread, in the two groups is equal.

THE INDEPENDENT T-TEST USING SPSS

1. Select *analyse* from the menu.
2. Select *compare means*.
3. Select *independent samples t-test*.
4. Select the independent variable and move it into the central box.
5. Choose the variable representing the groups you wish to compare. Move it into the *grouping variable* box.
6. Click on *define groups*.
7. Type in the codes for the two groups to compare (e.g. '1' for males and '2' for females).
8. Click *continue*.
9. Click *OK*. SPSS will now produce the results of the t-test.

Paired samples t-test

Whereas an independent t-test measures differences between two groups, the paired t-test measures whether the mean of a single group is different when measured at different times, for example whether the performance of a group on the putting task after mental rehearsal was significantly different from that before the rehearsal.

Analysis of variance (ANOVA)

ANOVA is similar in nature to the independent t-test, however it allows you to
ascertain differences between more than two groups.

Mann-Whitney test

The Mann-Whitney test is an alternative to the independent t-test, and is used
when your data is ordinal and non-parametric.

Chi-squared test

The chi-squared test is a useful test for non-parametric nominal data. The chi-squared test compares the actual, or reported, frequencies of a given variable with the frequencies that would be expected if the data was to suggest no differences between groups. As an example, you may be interested in whether preferences towards sport vary between genders. The results may be as follows:

	Prefer contact sport (%)	Prefer non-contact sport (%)
Male	79	21
Female	22	78

It would seem apparent from the table that there is a significant difference between the type of sports favoured by males and females. This can be confirmed by undertaking a chi-squared test.

WHICH TEST SHOULD I USE?

We have only included some of the more commonly used tests. You should make sure you spend some time reading around the different types of test available to you, and when such tests are appropriate. You should also read up on what the tests actually say. It is no good obtaining a highly significant result from a test without knowing what that significant result actually means! It is important that you do choose the right test, otherwise your findings will lack any meaningfulness. The type of data that you collect will be important in your final choice of test:

■ *Nominal*. Consider a chi-squared test if you are interested in differences in frequency counts.
■ *Interval or ratio*. Are you looking to identify relationships between two variables? If so, consider the use of a correlation. If there are three or more variables, then consider multiple regression. If you are concerned with differences between scores, then t-tests or ANOVA may be appropriate. If you want to identify differences within one group, then a paired samples t-test should be used. If you are comparing two groups, then use an independent samples t-test. If you are looking to compare three or more groups, then use ANOVA.
■ *Ordinal*. If you are interested in the relationship between groups, then use Spearman's rho. If you are looking for differences between groups, then a Mann-Whitney test may be appropriate.

The above is a very simple guide to the different statistical tests that you may use. We have not included every test, and it may be that there are other tests that will be more appropriate. If your research involves statistical analysis, we strongly recommend that you read a specialist text, so that you gain a fuller understanding of the principles underlying each test.

MISTAKES SOMETIMES MADE IN QUANTITATIVE ANALYSIS

- Choosing an incorrect statistical test.
- Designing the questionnaire so that the data is in the incorrect format for the appropriate statistical test.
- Misinterpreting a p-value, or deciding upon an inappropriate level of significance, and making a type I or type II error.
- Using parametric tests for non-parametric data.

A FINAL WORD ON STATISTICS

As a final note, we should stress that undertaking statistical analysis and producing significant results is not, in itself, that important. The important part is in being able to interpret your findings, that is being able to understand what they actually mean. Thus, if you have carried out a paired samples t-test, then what does a significant result actually suggest? The interpretation is just as important as undertaking the correct test!

SUMMARY

1   There are a number of ways in which you can analyse quantitative data. Descriptive statistics allow you to organise and summarise your data. Inferential statistics allow you to draw inferences regarding the association or difference between two or more variables. A number of computer packages exist to help you carry out descriptive or inferential statistics. *SPSS for Windows* is the most powerful.

2   Inferential tests will provide you with a 'p-value'. The p-value indicates the likelihood that any association or difference (depending upon the test) was

down to chance or not. A p-value of 0.05 indicates that in ninety-five cases out of a hundred you could be confident that there was an actual difference or association, rather than a chance difference or association.

3   The importance of statistical analysis lies not in the analysis itself – although that has to be done correctly. Instead it is the correct interpretation of the results that you obtain!

ACTIVITIES

You should try to gain some experience using *SPSS for Windows*.

- Using some of the sample data files available with the package, try to undertake some descriptive and inferential analysis. Don't be too concerned with the subject matter of the data. Instead, it is more important that you begin to understand the principles of the package.
- Try to produce some graphical output. Again, don't worry too much about what the data is saying, but simply try to gain confidence in using the program.

ABOUT YOUR RESEARCH PROJECT

If you are undertaking quantitative analysis, can you identify the following:

- What is the purpose of your analysis, that is, what exactly do you want to find out?
- What statistical test will provide you with the result that you need?
- Have you got the right data for this test (for example in terms of ordinal or interval data for certain tests, parametric data where such data is required and so on)?
- Have you assessed the likelihood of making a type I or a type II error?

FURTHER READING

Ntoumanis, M. (2001) *A Step-by-Step Guide to SPSS for Sport and Exercise Studies*, London: Routledge.

Vincent, W. (1995) *Statistics in Kinesiology*, Champaign, Ill.: Human Kinetics.

CHAPTER THIRTEEN

ANALYSING DATA II: QUALITATIVE DATA ANALYSIS

In this chapter we will:

- Introduce the basic principles of qualitative data analysis.
- Describe the different types of coding that form the framework for qualitative analysis.
- Describe one way of graphically representing qualitative data.

INTRODUCTION

Analysing qualitative data can prove to be much less straightforward – at least initially – than the seemingly more 'logical' and 'objective' analysis of quantitative data. This is partially due to the lack of a commonly accepted method of qualitative analysis, and also because, as you may have noted from your own reading, many researchers reporting qualitative research do not make it clear how the analysis has taken place. Thus, there is often an air of mystery about qualitative analysis, especially when compared with the seemingly more straightforward and objective approaches to quantitative data analysis. Essentially, the aim of both is the same, that is to make sense of your data so that evidence can be obtained to answer your research question. Although quantitative and qualitative data are different in their nature, as Table 13.1 shows, the principles of analysis of each are, however, not entirely different.

217

Table 13.1 Similarities and differences between quantitative and qualitative analysis

Similarities	Differences
▪ Analysis for both involves *inference* – that is they both reach a conclusion based on evidence. ▪ Both involve a *systematic* process. ▪ Both involve comparison, either internally or with related evidence from elsewhere. ▪ Both strive to avoid errors, false conclusions and misleading inferences and seek valid description and explanations.	▪ Quantitative analysis is highly standardised and varies little between projects; qualitative analysis has many more possible approaches. ▪ Quantitative analysis takes place at the end of data collection; qualitative analysis takes place during data collection. ▪ Quantitative analysis tends to test hypotheses through the manipulation of numbers representing 'facts'. Qualitative analysis blends empirical evidence and abstract concepts in the form of words to explain or illustrate a theory or interpretation. ▪ Qualitative analysis is less abstract, and does not assume that real life can be measured by numbers.

Source: Adapted from Neuman 2000.

STAGES OF QUALITATIVE ANALYSIS

As we have noted, there is no single accepted method of analysing qualitative data in sports research. This section will provide a brief overview of some of the methods of analysis. However, if you are analysing qualitative data it is worth having a look at a text such as Miles and Huberman (1994) for more detail on the various methods of analysis available to you. The key, as always, is to ensure that your analysis is appropriate to achieve your research objectives.

Miles and Huberman (1994) suggest that qualitative data analysis consists of three procedures:

1   *Data reduction*. This refers to the process whereby the mass of qualitative data you may obtain – interview transcripts, field notes, etc. – is reduced and organised, for example coding, writing summaries, discarding irrelevant data and so on. This process should begin almost as soon as you begin the data collection, and is often an ongoing process throughout much of the research.

2 *Data display*. To draw conclusions from the mass of data, Miles and Huberman suggest that a good display of data, in the form of tables, charts, networks and other graphical formats is essential. Again, this is a continual process, rather than just one to be carried out at the end of the data collection.
3 *Conclusion drawing/verification*. Your analysis should allow you to begin to develop conclusions regarding your study. These initial conclusions can then be verified, that is their validity examined through reference to your existing field notes, further data collection, or even critical discussion with your colleagues.

CODING QUALITATIVE DATA

The key process in the data reduction stage is that of *coding* your data. Coding is the organisation of raw data into conceptual categories. Each code is effectively a category or 'bin' into which a piece of data is placed. Coding is the first stage to providing some form of logical structure to the data. As Miles and Huberman (1994, p.56) note: 'Codes are tags or labels for assigning units of meaning to the descriptive or inferential information compiled during a study. Codes are usually attached to "chunks" of varying size – words, phrases, sentences or whole paragraphs.'

Codes should be *valid*, that is they should accurately reflect what is being researched, they should be *mutually exclusive*, in that codes should be distinct, with no overlap, and they should be *exhaustive*, that is all relevant data should fit into a code.

CASE STUDY

CODING IN PRACTICE – SPORT, NATIONAL IDENTITY AND THE MEDIA

Maguire and Poulton (1999) analysed the relationships between sport, national identity and the media during the 1996 European Football Championship. They were particularly interested in the media representations of football, and the relationships of those representations to European politics of the time. The authors undertook a qualitative content analysis of eight British newspapers. A number of appropriate codes were identified, providing a framework for analysis of the data. The codes identified by Maguire and Poulton were:

- National symbols/stereotypes.
- National identity/habitus and the use of personal pronouns.
- The vocabulary of war.
- Narcissistic language.
- The reference of invented traditions/nostalgia.
- Issues related to European politics.

Through analysing each of these themes, the authors were able to conclude that the media coverage of *EURO '96* actually served more to divide competing nations than to unite them. By reflecting underlying political tensions, the media may have simply reinforced existing stereotypes. The codes allowed the authors to draw out important points, and make a structured and systematic analysis that otherwise would have been unattainable.

STAGES OF DATA CODING

The following is a suggested framework for undertaking your coding:

1   The data is carefully read, all statements relating to the research question are identified, and each is assigned a code, or category. These codes are then noted, and each relevant statement is organised under its appropriate code, either manually or on computer, along with any notes, or *memos* (see below) that the researcher wishes to add of their own. This is referred to as *open coding*.

2   Using the codes developed in stage 1, the researcher rereads the qualitative data, and searches for statements that may fit into any of the categories. Further codes may also be developed in this stage. This is also referred to as *axial coding*.

3   Once the first two stages of coding have been completed, the researcher should become more analytical, and look for patterns and explanation in the codes. Questions should be asked such as:

- Can I relate certain codes together under a more general code?
- Can I organise codes sequentially (for example does code A happen before code B)?
- Can I identify any causal relationships (does code A cause code B)?

4   The fourth stage is that of *selective coding*. This involves reading through the raw data for cases that illustrate the analysis, or explain the concepts. The researcher should also look for data that is contradictory, as well as confirmatory.

MAXIMISING THE VALIDITY AND RELIABILITY OF YOUR DATA

After you have collected some initial data, you should ask a fellow researcher to code the same data set, and compare the findings. This will allow you to identify possible problems in your coding, and ensure that you have a clear and valid set of codes. You can also check the reliability of your analysis through comparing your coding with that of others. Miles and Huberman (1994) suggest that you should use the following formula:

Reliability = number of agreements /(number of agreements + disagreements)

They suggest that you may begin with a fairly low reliability score (for example about 60 per cent) but with continual discussion of findings, and clarification of differences, you should achieve a score of up to 90 per cent if not higher.

Krane *et al.* (1997) suggest that an alternative approach may be for one or more research partners to critically question the coding and analysis after it has taken place, acting as 'devil's advocate' in questioning the analysis. The two approaches to assessing your coding are not mutually exclusive, and there is nothing to stop you checking your coding both before and after analysis to ensure validity of your qualitative coding and classification.

Whilst you are coding your data, you should also be prepared to write *memos*. These are the ideas that occur to you whilst you are coding your data, for example concerning explanation, theorising, or other ideas about the data. They can be extremely helpful to you in trying to make sense of the data at a later date. You can write them directly on the transcripts, or keep a record of them elsewhere. Try and make your memos as detailed as you can, as this will help you with later analysis.

WHAT SHOULD I LOOK FOR WHEN I HAVE CODED MY DATA?

Once you have coded your data, you should look for patterns or regularities that occur. Within each code, look for data units that illustrate or describe the situation you are interested in. Try to identify key words or phrases, such as 'because', 'despite', 'in order to', 'otherwise' and so on and try to make sense of the data through interpretation of the meaning and values that respondents assign to the phenomenon that you are interested in. Look for statements that not only support your theories, but also refute them, and try to build a comprehensive picture of the topic. Frankfort-Nachimas and Nachimas (1996) suggest that you ask yourself a number of questions to assist in your analysis:

1   What type of behaviour is being demonstrated?
2   What is its structure?
3   How frequent is it?
4   What are its causes?
5   What are its processes?
6   What are its consequences?
7   What are people's strategies with dealing with the behaviour?

Another method of qualitative analysis is outlined by Biddle *et al*. (2001) whereby the data units (statements, sentences, etc.) are clustered into common themes (essentially the same as codes), so that similar units are grouped together into *first order themes*, and separated away from units with different meaning. The same process is then repeated with the first order themes, which are grouped together into *second order themes*. This is repeated as far as possible (see Figure 13.1).

An example of how this may appear is provided by Roberts *et al*. (2001), who were interested in how comfortable golfers felt with their clubs. Their analysis is shown in Figure 13.2. This mapping of data units suggests a logical sequence for your analysis working from right to left. For example, you may want to introduce your general dimension ('club control') first. You can then discuss the higher order theme of 'controllable feel', illustrating the theme with reference to any appropriate data units. You can then discuss the concept of 'uncontrollable feel' in the same way. As you will notice, there is no indication of any numerical analysis, and at no stage are numbers assigned to any category. As Krane *et al*. (1997, p.214) suggest:

> Placing a frequency count after a category of experiences is tantamount to saying how important it is; thus value is derived by number. In many

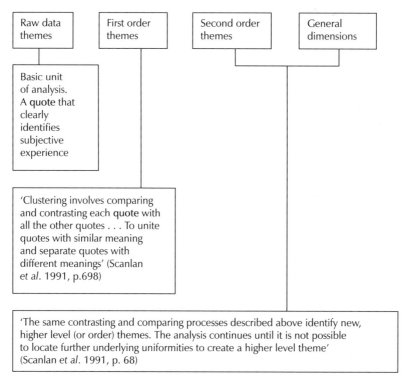

Figure 13.1 A framework for the thematic analysis of qualitative data

Source: Adapted from Biddle *et al.* 2001, p.797.

cases, rare experiences are no less meaningful, useful, or important than common ones. In some cases, the rare experience may be the most enlightening one.

USING RAW DATA TO SUPPORT YOUR ANALYSIS

Throughout your results and discussion, it can often be appropriate to include direct quotes from participants, or direct observations from your field notes. Using quotes in this way can enrich your report, and bring your findings to life, often making the report much more readable. You should resist the temptation to over-use quotes, however. As a rule of thumb, you should use direct quotes or observations:

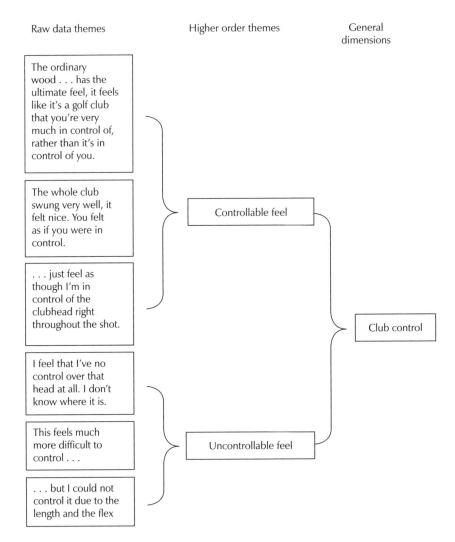

Raw data themes   Higher order themes   General dimensions

The ordinary wood . . . has the ultimate feel, it feels like it's a golf club that you're very much in control of, rather than it's in control of you.

The whole club swung very well, it felt nice. You felt as if you were in control.

. . . just feel as though I'm in control of the clubhead right throughout the shot.

I feel that I've no control over that head at all. I don't know where it is.

This feels much more difficult to control . . .

. . . but I could not control it due to the length and the flex

Controllable feel

Uncontrollable feel

Club control

Figure 13.2 A qualitative analysis of golfers' perceptions

- When they describe a phenomenon particularly well.
- To show cases or instances that are unusual.
- To show data that is unexpected.

You should also avoid including quotes without making clear reference to how such quotes refer to your analysis.

COMPUTER ANALYSIS AND QUALITATIVE DATA

A number of authors have suggested using computer software to analyse qualitative data, using packages such as NUD*IST or Atlas/ti. NUD*IST (or Non-numerical Unstructured Data Indexing, Searching and Theorising) allows you to import data files which can then be coded and patterns and relationships identified by the computer. NUD*IST can also be used to deal with the analysis of photographs and other visual material. There are a number of issues related to the use of computer software for qualitative data analysis. First, although computer analysis may allow much quicker, and seemingly more objective analysis, the process of manually 'tagging' specific quotations can often be considered desirable in that it gives you a 'feel' for the data, and allows increased familiarity with the transcriptions. Second, as Dey (1993, p.61) notes, 'the use of a computer can encourage a "mechanistic" approach to analysis. In this scenario, the roles of creativity, intuition and insight into analysis are eclipsed.' The research analysis may then become a routine and mechanical process (Lee and Fielding 1996). Third, much of the tagging that is carried out by such software requires words to be specified or coded beforehand by the researcher, which, given the wide range of possible answers, will be equally time consuming. Fourth, most of the available software only identifies the sentence within which a specific word or phrase occurs, and thus often fails to locate the context. Finally, the increased time incurred by manual tagging of transcripts is offset by the time required to develop competence in an appropriate computer software package. Some of the packages, although extremely powerful, do take some time to learn, even with specialised instruction. You need to weigh up the pros and cons of taking the time to learn such a package before deciding on a particular approach. If you are likely to be undertaking a considerable amount of qualitative research over a reasonable period of time, then it may be worthwhile learning one of the packages. If you are engaged in a one-off piece of research, then we would recommend manual analysis. If you do reject the use of computer software for analysis, you should not immediately assume that the quality of analysis is inferior to that done by computer. As Krane *et al.* (1997, p.215) note with regard to computer versus manual analysis:

> None of these procedures directly affects the value of the study; they are merely ways for the inquirers to work with their data . . . If individuals use NUD*IST or Hyperqual computer programs, or 3 x 5 cards and paste them to the wall, they are really doing the same thing conceptually.

Thus provided the analysis is carried out correctly, as outlined above, the method of analysis is not related to the quality of the information obtained, and, in effect, the researcher is doing the same process, whether using a computer program or manual methods. It is equally likely that computer analysis may be done as well, or as badly, as manual analysis.

MEMBER VALIDATION OF QUALITATIVE ANALYSIS

Whereas the analysis of quantitative data is, on the outside at least, relatively objective and transparent, qualitative data analysis is open to considerably more interpretation and debate, especially with regard to the validity of the interpretation. There are a number of techniques that can be used to validate the interpretations, and these are outlined by Bloor (1997). One particular method of note is to ask those being investigated to judge the analysis and interpretation themselves, by providing them with the analysis, and asking them to critically comment upon the adequacy of the findings. Whilst this is not a requirement of all qualitative analysis, it can be a useful exercise for the qualitative researcher to undertake. The issue arises, however, of what happens when subjects disagree with the analysis. In such instances, it is important to identify the source of disagreement, to assess whether such disagreement is indeed valid (it may be, for example, that participants have misunderstood some of the analysis, or they approach the analysis with a different agenda to the researcher). Thus, even agreement or disagreement with the analysis can be problematic. Despite this, however, member validation can be an important tool to the qualitative researcher.

SUMMARY

1   Although qualitative and quantitative data are different in nature, the analysis of both involves inference, systematic analysis and comparison. Both try to seek valid conclusions and avoid errors.
2   There are a number of ways of approaching qualitative analysis.
3   Analysing qualitative data should be an ongoing process throughout, as well as after the collection of data.
4   There are three key stages to qualitative data analysis: data reduction, data display and conclusion drawing/verification.
5   Data reduction takes place through the process of coding. Coding involves assigning units of meaning to data chunks, and can be open, axial or selective.

6   Your analysis can be done either manually or by computer. There are advantages and disadvantages to each, but the final analysis should be the same whichever method you adopt.

ACTIVITIES

■   Carry out and transcribe a short interview with someone you know who is keen on sport. Question them on their experiences of playing and/or watching sport. Now try to code the interview, first using open, and then axial coding.
■   Can you draw any conclusions from your coding?
■   Now undertake selective coding to explain, support or refute your conclusions.
■   Ask a colleague to undertake the same process in terms of open and axial coding. How reliable are the results?
■   Try to produce a graphical display of your findings.

ABOUT YOUR RESEARCH PROJECT

If your research project involves the analysis of qualitative data, you need to consider the following points:

■   How will you ensure the reliability and validity of your analysis? Will you use another researcher to help in your coding?
■   In your write-up of the research, have you made the processes by which your data was analysed clear to the reader?

FURTHER READING

Miles, M. and Huberman, A. (1994) *Qualitative Data Analysis,* Thousand Oaks: Sage.

CHAPTER FOURTEEN

WRITING THE RESEARCH REPORT

In this chapter we will:

- Introduce the process of writing up your research.
- Outline the structure of a typical research report.
- Identify some of the areas where you should be assessing the quality of your written report.
- Describe some of the issues related to oral presentations of your research.

INTRODUCTION

An important part of your research is being able to communicate your findings to others through the process of presenting the research, whether in the form of a report, dissertation, journal article, presentation or other such format. It does not matter how wide your reading has been, or how good your data collection, if the report is poorly written – you must ensure that you do not let yourself down in the final write-up. This chapter will guide you through the process of writing the report, and highlight some of the problems that you may face, so that you can present a final report that will do the many hours spent undertaking the research justice.

WRITING THE RESEARCH REPORT

Writing the research report allows you to communicate the research process undertaken to answer your specific research question to others. It is a difficult and time consuming task, and will generally take much more time than you think. The five main pieces of advice we can give are:

1 Begin writing up the report as soon as you can. Do not leave it until you have finished your data collection before you start writing up. Many sections, for example the literature review and the methodology, can be drafted during or even before data collection.
2 Write down ideas as soon as you get them, rather than leaving them to the writing up stage. Keep a research diary where you can safely note any ideas. Not all of your ideas will be useful, but it is certain that some of them will be! Don't imagine that you will be able to remember these ideas at a later date.
3 Be aware of the nature of the report and the intended audience. If it is for a student research project, then ensure you have read and understood the criteria laid down by your institution in terms of content, presentation, length and so on. If you are writing for a journal, ensure that your research fits within the scope of that journal's objectives as well as its editorial requirements. If you are producing a report or piece of consultancy, ensure that you are clear about the requirements of your audience.
4 You will not be able to write the final report out first time. You will need to rewrite it a number of times before it reaches completion. You should allow for this when planning your research timetable, and not become discouraged when the first draft is not perfect.
5 Make sure before you begin writing up that you have an adequate supply of disks, and that you make backups of your work at every available opportunity. Whatever you do, don't assume that whatever you save on a hard drive will be safe! You should keep your backup disks in a separate location. It is no good keeping them with your lap-top on whose hard drive your work is saved – if the lap-top does go missing, then you have lost all of your work, whether backed up or not! As a further safety measure, print out what you have written so far at regular intervals.

As we have already stressed, writing the report is a difficult task, and generally much more time consuming than most inexperienced researchers imagine. There are a number of stages that you will need to undertake:

- First clarify the nature of the planned report, and its intended audience. If any examples of past reports are available, read as many as you can – both good and bad!
- Identify any predetermined requirements, for example maximum word length, formatting, such as double spacing or required referencing style, and so on. Ideally you should familiarise yourself with past projects, etc. so that you have an idea of the final product before you start.
- Throughout the duration of the research you should be collecting together the information necessary to complete the report, such as your review of literature, analysis of the primary data, list of references and so on.
- Prepare an outline plan of the report. At the bare minimum, this should be a list of chapter headings. Ideally you should be able to have more detail – include likely subheadings as well. The more detailed your initial outline, the easier you will find the process of writing up the first draft of the report.
- Write a first draft of the report. You should not anticipate the first draft being your final submission!
- Evaluate the content of the first draft, either through reading it yourself or, preferably, getting somebody else to read it with a critical eye.
- Rewrite and re-evaluate the report as appropriate. You may need to do this more than once!
- Final editing and proof reading. Once you have got this far, the temptation is to skip over the final proof reading and simply submit the project. Do carefully read over to check spelling and grammar, and get someone else to do the same (once you have read your own work several times, it becomes very difficult to take in what you have read). Don't rely on the spellchecker that comes with your word processing package. It is a useful tool, but will not pick out every mistake, for example when you type 'there' instead of 'their'.
- Submission of the report. Now you can relax! Unless you are to be orally examined, then don't read a copy of the report for some time . . . you will only pick up errors that you didn't see, sections that you feel could have been written better and so on. Instead, you should enjoy the achievement of completing the research!

When writing the report, do not feel that you have to complete one chapter or section before starting another. It can be a good idea to be working on several sections at once, so that if you do – as is likely – get 'writer's block', then you can carry on writing. Often, it then becomes easier to go back to the problematic section. Neither should you attempt to write the report in the same order as it is to be presented. Early sections, such as the abstract and the introduction, for example, are better left until towards the end of the writing up process. There is no set way to write a report, and it is often a case of personal preference.

STRUCTURING THE RESEARCH REPORT

It is possible to structure a report in different ways depending upon the nature of the research. You may find that your approach lends itself to a different layout from the one we suggest, for example if you have undertaken an ethnographic piece of research, in which case you may wish to combine your results and discussion into a more integrated section. If you consider that a different approach is necessary, then discuss this with your tutor or research supervisor. We shall use as an example a commonly used structure for an undergraduate dissertation, which is as follows:

1 Abstract
2 Acknowledgements
3 Table of contents
4 List of tables and figures
5 Introduction
6 Literature review
7 Research methodology
8 Results
9 Discussion
10 Conclusions and recommendations
11 References and/or bibliography
12 Appendices

1 Abstract

This is, essentially, a summary of the research. It describes the topic under examination and outlines the research question or hypothesis, objectives, and methods of the study. It should also give a brief résumé of the main conclusions and recommendations. The abstract is a brief section, and should be within the word limits set down by your institution, journal, etc., often between 100 and 200 words (slightly longer for a postgraduate thesis). It is often the basis upon which others will assess the usefulness of the research, so you should ensure that you include all relevant details.

2 Acknowledgements

Your report should thank various people who have helped in the research. You might include specific individuals who have given information, offered insightful clues, or have been especially supportive. If funding has been provided, then acknowledgement should be made here. Gratitude may also be expressed to groups of people, such as those who formed the sample group. It is best to avoid tendencies towards the extremes of either flippancy or sycophancy. Sometimes, for example in a journal article, acknowledgements may be placed after the main body of the report as an endnote.

3 Table of contents

The contents page gives the reader the first view of how the report is structured and how you have attempted to develop the topic. It should list sequentially the chapters and the major subdivisions of chapters, each identified by a heading and located by a page number. Contents are not always required, for example for journal articles or similar reports.

4 List of tables and figures

Throughout the written report you may want to present material in tabulated (tables) or diagrammatic (figures) form. For example if you have undertaken any quantitative analysis you will need to report the analysis in the form of tables. The location of this material needs to be listed, with separate lists for figures and tables.

5 Introduction

The introduction should describe the subject under investigation, the purpose of the research and why you are doing the research. In the introduction you should provide some academic justification for the choice of topic if possible, as well as any particular personal justification. You should include a summary of how you are going to treat the chosen topic and, importantly, set out and explain (especially if your terminology requires clarification) your research question or hypothesis and your subsidiary questions or objectives, including defining any key terms or concepts. Finally, it may be useful to show your intentions by briefly running through your intended chapters or sections. What you must not neglect, or hide away, is what Creswell (1994) refers to as your *purpose statement*. The purpose statement is the statement that establishes the direction of the research, and highlights the objectives that are hopefully to be met. You can often start this with the phrase 'the purpose of this study is to . . .'. For a quantitative purpose statement, Creswell suggests including the following:

■ The theory or model that is to be used in the study.
■ The specific research design (cross-sectional, experimental, etc.).
■ The variables to be tested, and their relationship with each other (begin with the independent variable, followed by the dependent variable).
■ The unit of analysis, or the sample that you are investigating.

For a qualitative study, Creswell suggests the following:

■ Use words such as develop, understand and so on, that convey the emergent sense of the research, rather than words such as test, or measure.
■ Clearly state and define the central concept or idea being researched.
■ Describe the research design and method of data collection to be used, for example an ethnographic design, involving participant observation, etc.
■ Identify the unit of analysis, such as the setting, organisation, group and so on.

6 Literature review

After an introductory chapter, most reports will include one or more chapters where you draw upon and consider theories, arguments and findings from the literature and which obviously relate in some way to your question or hypothesis (see Chapter 5). As we suggested earlier, the literature review should not just be a list of all of the literature you have discovered, rather it should be a critical appraisal of existing work, and you should be explicit as to how your study is related to, or has emerged from this literature. As Veal (1997, p.85) maintains, 'a review of the literature should draw *conclusions* and *implications* for the proposed research programme'. It is, therefore, a good idea in your report – perhaps at the end of your literature review – to come to some conclusion over what other researchers have found and how this has impacted upon your research. A number of research objectives should emerge from your literature review. It is essential to state these clearly, and to show how they have developed. A common weakness in literature reviews is to list or summarise existing literature, then conclude with a number of research objectives that are unrelated to the literature.

233

You should ensure that there is a strong link between your written literature review and your research objectives.

7 Research methodology

The literature review should 'set the scene' in terms of your research objectives. The methodology should outline how these objectives are to be achieved. Although the methodology may be one of the shorter sections, it is crucial to the entire project. You must address the area of research methods including a justification of the methodology chosen and an explanation of how the data was gathered. Generally the methodology section or chapter will consist of a number of sections:

- *Outline of methodological assumptions*. You may wish to justify your epistemological stance, for example, or your use of qualitative rather than quantitative data. You don't, however, need to provide lots of basic description about the nature of positivist approaches, or the characteristics of qualitative data in general.
- *Your research design*. Explain your choice of research design, making it clear what data is to be collected, and at what times.
- *Methods*. You should describe your choice of method, such as a postal questionnaire, and outline some of the design issues. What questions were included and why? If you have adopted an existing questionnaire or interview schedule, then explain why you have done this. You may also – depending upon the nature of the report – include details about the piloting or pre-testing procedure.
- *Sample*. You should include details of your sample, how you achieved the sample, and any limitations of your sampling method.
- *Procedures*. Describe how the research was carried out, for example whether questionnaires were posted or handed to participants, what instructions were given and so on.
- *Methods of analysis*. You should briefly outline your methods of analysis, for example a description of the statistical tests to be used and a justification of their appropriateness.
- You may also consider including an *evaluation of the methodology*, highlighting the strengths and weaknesses, and making any limitations clear to the reader. The methodology section or chapter needs to include a lot of detail in a relatively short space (often about 1,500–2,000 words in a 10,000-word undergraduate project). One rule of thumb that you can use to check whether

you have included enough detail is whether another researcher, through reading only your methodology and armed with copies of your data collection instruments, could undertake the same research and gain similar results.

8 Results

Do not simply report every finding here – report those results that are relevant to your study. In terms of the presentation of results, think about how to put your findings over as clearly as possible. You may want to look at past research reports to see how they have presented their results. The purpose of the data analysis is to develop a series of logical and convincing answers to the research question(s) that have emerged from the literature review. You should not therefore present data that does not relate to your research, even if you think it would be 'interesting'. Be careful in your graphical treatment of data – it is very tempting to include as many charts and graphs as possible, and to try to make them extremely impressive in terms of colour, layout and so on. In practice, it is often the case that the chart with minimal detail is often the clearest to understand. You should only consider the use of colour if it clarifies a particular chart, a situation which is actually rare (and in many instances, such as when you submit to an academic journal, you will be restricted to black and white line drawings anyway!).

9 Discussion

The purpose of this chapter or section is to discuss the implications of your results in light of your research objectives. A common error at this stage is simply to discuss your own findings, what they mean and so on without any reference to existing knowledge. Do remember, however, that you are building on such existing knowledge, so refer back to that knowledge, which you will have reviewed in your literature review chapter(s). Do your results find support in the literature? Were they predicted by the literature? If they did and were, then how does your research add to the literature? If your findings differed from your expectations, then are there any possible reasons why? Does the particular theory or model you've used still hold true in light of your research? If not, to what extent is this a limitation of the theory or model, or a possible limitation of your research? If the theory or model seems flawed, then how can it be refined to explain your findings? When discussing such issues, it is important to ensure that the discussion is grounded on your own observations, analysis and reading of the literature. By doing this, your arguments are more likely to be well constructed and convincing.

10 Conclusions and recommendations

Your discussion of findings/literature should lead to a chapter or section on conclusions. Your conclusions are very important and often receive inadequate attention. Importantly, conclusions should stem from the findings/discussion, be feasible and lead to consistent, sensible recommendations if applicable. All the matters you wish to discuss and develop in the concluding section should be related to and follow logically from what's gone before. The conclusion should include a summary of your main arguments, drawing together the various themes and issues so that they can be brought to bear on the defined objectives or subsidiary questions of the study. The original research question or hypothesis should be revisited at this stage, and the dialogue would explain the extent to which this has been addressed within the context of the study. Limitations of your project and what, in hindsight, you might have done differently should be included. If you do include content on the limitations of your study, then you may also wish to include something about the strengths of your research as well.

When you have completed the first draft of your introductory chapter and your conclusions, then try to read them together. Ideally, reading the introduction followed by the conclusions should make sense without reading anything in between – remember, the introduction should set the scene to the research question, and the conclusion will provide the answers!

Depending upon the nature of your project, recommendations often follow a conclusion, but not in all cases. Recommendations are more likely to be included where your project is of a practical nature, e.g. in terms of the potential application of your findings to industry or education. In such cases, the recommendations should place your conclusions within a concrete, practical framework. In making recommendations you are constrained, however, by what is feasible and practical to do. Additionally, it can be useful to consider your recommendations in the context of possible human, financial, political, managerial implications and so on.

11 References and/or bibliography

Some confusion exists over the difference between 'references' and 'bibliography' and whether it is a requirement to include both lists. In reality, the terms are often used interchangeably – the minimum requirement is normally for a list of references, which contains all items cited in the text in alphabetical order of author. If you want to use both a list of references (references cited in your own text) and a bibliography (items not necessarily cited, but deemed relevant to the research), then this may be in order. Including the latter can be advantageous as a bibliography can demonstrate the width of literature that you have accessed, which may not always be clear from doing a reference list alone. You should check the requirements of your own institution if there is any doubt. Whatever you do, it is critical that you reference any work that you are citing accurately giving a detailed description of the source from which you obtained the information. You must acknowledge sources and clearly differentiate between ideas or words that are your own and those that originate from others.

Various conventions can be used for referencing with the one highly recommended for usage being the *Harvard system*. We have discussed this in more detail in Chapter 5, with specific reference to the literature review. The principles of referencing will, however, apply throughout your written report, not just in the literature review.

STANDARD REFERENCE FORMATS – HARVARD SYSTEM

You will, in all likelihood, have to reference a variety of sources in your list of references. Within the text, the format of the references should remain constant (such as (Johnson 1999) where you are using another's ideas, but not taking them word for word, or (Johnson 1999, p.213) when you are using direct quotes from the source). Each different source of information will require a slightly different format within your bibliography or list of references. The most common formats are outlined below:

Book

Author surname, author initial, year of publication, title of book, place of publication, publisher.

Coakley, J. (1998) *Sport in Society: Issues and Controversies*, Boston: McGraw-Hill.

Journal article

Author surname, author initial, year of publication, title of article, title of journal, journal volume number, part number, pages in journal.

Jones, R., Murrell, A. and Jackson, J. (1999) 'Pretty versus Powerful in the Sports Pages', *Journal of Sport and Social Issues* 23 (2), 183–192.

Chapter in edited book

Author surname, author initial, year of publication, title of chapter, editor of volume, title of volume, place of publication, publisher, pages of chapter.

Sloan, L. (1979) 'The function and impact of sports for fans', in J. Goldstein (ed.) *Sports Games and Play: Social and Psychological Viewpoints*, New York, Academic Press, pp. 219–62.

Internet journal article

Author surname and initial, year of publication, title of article, title of journal, journal volume number, part number, web address, date accessed.

Jones, I. (1997) 'Mixing Qualitative and Quantitative Methods in Sports Fan Research', The Qualitative Report [On-line serial] 3 (4). Available at: http://www.nova.edu/ssss/QR/QR3-4/jones.html (accessed 10/10/2001).

Other Internet resource

Title of author (if known) or title of article, web address, date accessed.

'Trends in Drug Testing', Australian Sports Drug Agency web page, http://www.ausport.gov.au/asda/trends.html (accessed 11/10/2001).

12 Appendices

You should locate in the appendices all that information which gives any additional support to the arguments you are constructing. It is important, however, that you put all the crucial information you wish to be read in the main text, rather than hiding it away in an appendix. All appendices that you do include should be referred to in the text. You may also want to include copies of correspondence, details of organisations, people you have contacted, details of interviewees, etc. Your research instruments such as copies of questionnaires or interview schedules should also be included in an appendix.

LANGUAGE AND WRITING STYLE

The issue of language and style can often be overlooked in a research report. What you should be aiming for is to present a well-written, readable report that will actually interest your readers. There are four, very general styles that can be identified:

1   *The 'dry' and objective style.* This is characterised by reporting everything in a totally objective manner, with no sense of humour or enthusiasm for the research. This style is difficult to read, especially in an extended report, and makes it quite difficult for the reader to actually complete the report! Try to avoid this style if at all possible.

2   *The informal style.* Here, the researcher feels that they have to chat to the reader. The language used is informal, as if the writer was explaining the research to his or her friends over lunch. Again try to avoid this style!

3   *The 'long-winded' style.* Some writers try to imitate some of the more complex pieces of literature that they have come across in their reading, or, alternatively, to impress the reader with their use of complex academic language. This type of report uses technical jargon when perfectly acceptable words in plain English exist, and will use fifty words where ten will do in an effort to impress. Such reports can be difficult to read, and it may be harder for the reader to accurately assess what the researcher is actually saying! Holt (1989, p.357) identifies an example of this style: 'Massification as the negation of publics designates that moral inter-subjectivity as a process of need expression and sublimation is replaced by corporatized, desublimating modes.' Remember – write to express, rather than to impress!

4   *The 'elegant' style.* This is the style towards which you should strive. It lies somewhere between the dry and informal, and it allows the information to be presented in a manner which is readable and interesting. Technical terms can be used where appropriate, but sparingly. This style often conveys the researcher's own sense of enthusiasm, and makes for an interesting, yet 'academic' read.

ASSESSING YOUR OWN RESEARCH REPORT

Before your report is read or assessed by others, such as your examiners, it is important that you critically evaluate its content beforehand. This can sometimes be a time consuming task, and you should allow yourself as much time as you can for this stage, especially if it is likely that you will find significant errors, or if you think that a significant rewrite is required. You should be aiming to fulfil four criteria, those of:

1   Validity
2   Reliability
3   Representativeness
4   Generalisability

Critically question these when reading your report. Have you considered them? Have you demonstrated to the reader that your research has all four characteristics? Have you omitted anything that may strengthen your claims? In addition to those four characteristics, there are a number of other, more specific questions that you should ask yourself with regard to the content of your report. These are as follows.

SETTING THE SCENE

✓   Does your abstract give a clear idea of what is in the report? Has it clearly described your objectives, the methodology adopted, and the main conclusions that have emerged?
✓   Is your table of contents well structured and does it give a picture of what's included? Have you included a list of tables and a list of figures if appropriate?
✓   In your introduction have you introduced your research adequately? Are you happy that you have 'set the scene' for the reader? What is the rationale behind your research report? Have you clearly identified this? Have you defined your key concepts?

FOCUS AND JUSTIFICATION

✓   Have you a clear focus? Is your research report tightly defined and contained or does it sometimes lack direct relevance, or stray off the point?
✓   Have you got a clearly constructed and suitable research question or hypothesis which leads to a set of clear and related subsidiary questions or objectives?

240

✓ If someone asked you what was the main point of your research report in terms of findings, and what were the main outcomes, could you easily direct them to these in your report?

✓ Why should the reader read your piece of work? Is it saying something worthwhile?

YOUR USE OF THE LITERATURE

✓ Is your issue or focus underpinned by theory? Is it clear which theory or model you have adopted?

✓ How up to date are your references? Have you included the most up to date work in your area?

✓ Have you managed to identify and get hold of the work of key writers in your particular area? Have you ensured that you have paid due attention to 'classic' sources?

✓ Have you used a variety of sources or are you over-reliant upon certain authors? Have you included or acknowledged competing theories or viewpoints, or simply selected literature that supports your hypothesis?

✓ Is it clear to the reader how your research relates to what has been done before, or builds upon existing knowledge?

✓ In your literature review do you merely identify and describe, with no real critical edge? Have you been analytical enough?

✓ How well have you researched the literature on your topic and on your specific focus? Have you explored all possible sources?

YOUR METHODOLOGY

✓ Do you clearly identify and explain your choice of research design?

✓ Are your research methods the most appropriate given your chosen hypothesis or research question, and your subsidiary questions or objectives?

✓ If you didn't use primary data collection methods, how substantial is your analysis of secondary data? Is it more than just a review of existing literature? Have you assessed the limitations of using secondary data?

241

- ✓ Have you made it clear who the subjects are? And to what population these subjects belong? Is it clear how they were selected?
- ✓ Have you explained the rationale behind your chosen means of collecting information? If it is an existing instrument, whose is it? Why did you choose it? Is it clear to the reader why your methods were the most appropriate ones for your research question?
- ✓ Did you undertake any piloting of your data collection instruments? What was the outcome of any piloting? If so, have you reported these in your write-up?
- ✓ Are you making assumptions? You know what you did in terms of research methods, but would the reader? Have you expressed yourself clearly and given adequate details? Would someone else be able to replicate your study on the basis of the information you've given?
- ✓ Have you clearly identified the strengths of your methodology? Are there any limitations to your methodology? Is there anything you might have done differently?

FINDINGS AND DISCUSSION

- ✓ Are your findings clearly presented? Have you included tables for your descriptive and inferential analysis of quantitative data?
- ✓ If you have included graphs, charts and so on, are these appropriate? Is the content of each chart clear? Is it clear how each chart relates to your research objectives?
- ✓ How have you analysed your findings? If you have undertaken quantitative analysis, which statistical tests have you used? Are you sure these are the correct tests? Have you interpreted the results correctly? For qualitative analysis, have you demonstrated that you have analysed your data in a systematic manner?
- ✓ In your discussion, do you adequately revisit the literature and relate your findings to the literature, or do you simply discuss what you found?
- ✓ Are your arguments coherent, logical and sound? Are they consistent with the evidence that you have collected?

CONCLUSIONS AND RECOMMENDATIONS

✓ Have your conclusions clearly emerged from the evidence collected and discussed? Have you acknowledged unexpected evidence, or evidence that contradicts your chosen theory or model?

✓ Do you return to your research question or hypothesis?

✓ Do you evaluate the research? Have you identified the strengths and the limitations of the project?

✓ Are any recommendations you make based upon your findings? Are they feasible and practical?

GENERAL PRESENTATION OF THE REPORT

✓ Is your content well planned and logically structured?

✓ Is the work well presented? Have you used an appropriate font, and followed the guidelines of your institution in terms of margins, double spacing and so on?

✓ Have you made appropriate use of supportive materials to enhance presentation, i.e. graphs, tables, illustrations?

✓ Have you conducted a thorough read through, to eliminate careless spelling and typographical errors, poor grammar and poor sentence construction?

✓ Are you writing in the most appropriate tense? Is your writing too informal?

✓ Are you writing in the first person ('I') rather than using the more appropriate third person?

✓ How well do you communicate your ideas? Does what you write make sense?

✓ Do you link your various chapters and make use of signposting to help the reader? Do you set out your intentions clearly in your introduction?

✓ Have you set out your references and/or bibliography with the required detail and in the recommended format?

✓ Have you acknowledged all sources used, and made it clear when it's your views that are being expressed, or the views of others?

✓ Have you made appropriate use of appendices? Are there any unnecessary appendices?

> ✓ Have you ensured that your report is as stimulating and as interesting as possible? Have you conveyed your enthusiasm to the reader throughout the project?

THE ORAL PRESENTATION OF YOUR RESEARCH

It may be the case that you are called upon to defend your research orally, generally through what is referred to as a *viva voce* (or just *viva*). This is still rare at undergraduate level, although it is a requirement of higher degrees such as a doctorate. Alternatively, you may be asked to give a short presentation about your research (this is often a useful way to answer questions where there are doubts about the authenticity of some aspect of the research).

The viva voce

The difficulty with preparing for an examination of this nature is that it is simply not possible to predict with total accuracy the questions that will be asked! The best advice is that you simply have to know your research inside out. You should be able to anticipate some of the questions, for example on the main findings of the research and so on, and prepare for them. If you are asked a question that you can't answer straight away, then stop and carefully consider your answer rather than rush into a response. Write down the question if necessary, and ask the examiner for clarification of what he or she means if you are not sure. If you really cannot answer the question, then don't panic! The examiners are not expecting a perfect response to every question anyway. You should put such questions to the back of your mind and concentrate upon the rest of the viva – remember, one question that you cannot answer will not lead to a failed exam!

COMMON VIVA QUESTIONS

The following are some of the questions that do appear regularly at viva examinations. It is by no means an exhaustive list, and you should always expect the unexpected, or unusual questions as well!

▼

244

- How did you come to research this topic?
- How has the research contributed to knowledge in this area?
- What were the important research decisions that you made? On what basis did you make these decisions?
- What are the next steps in this research?
- What are the most interesting findings from the research?
- And the most unexpected?
- Aren't the results all obvious anyway?
- What have you learnt personally from doing the research?

Presenting your research

An alternative to the viva is to present your research in front of a small audience. Not everyone in the audience may have read your work, and you may well be addressing differing levels of expertise. Presentations of this nature are often short, and need to be well rehearsed. There are a number of common errors in presentations that you should be aware of when preparing:

- *Putting too much detail on your overheads or slides*. Stick to the key points. Often people will put a lot of detail on each slide, and simply read the slides out loud. Sticking to the essentials will help prevent this, and help you maintain eye contact with your audience.
- *Using material that is difficult to read*. Ensure that you have a sufficiently large and easily readable font (fonts such as Arial are better for presentations than fonts such as Times New Roman. If in doubt about the font size, then err on the side of caution and use a minimum font size of twenty-four), and avoid complex models or diagrams. Use handouts for such material if they are to be included.
- *Having too many slides*. If you are presenting for ten minutes, then you simply will not get through ten or fifteen slides! Ensure you have a run through beforehand to check your timing, especially if you are presenting at an institution that will simply cut you off without warning at the end of your allocated time slot!

You may wish to adopt the following structure if you are called upon to present your research:

- Slide 1 – Introduction, main aims and objectives of the research.
- Slide 2 – A brief outline of your theoretical approach.
- Slide 3 – The key features about your methodology.
- Slide 4 – Your important/significant results.
- Slide 5 – Two or three bullet points for discussion.

You will find that using five slides, with only one or two points on each slide will be more than adequate, provided you are able to talk about your own research freely.

SUMMARY

1   Writing the report is the culmination of a lot of time and energy spent doing the research . . . make sure that you do yourself justice!

2   Writing the report will almost certainly take longer than you think. You will generally have to go through the process of writing and rewriting a number of times until you are happy with the result.

3   There is normally no single acceptable structure for your research report. A typical undergraduate dissertation may follow the order of abstract, acknowl-edgements, table of contents, list of tables and figures, introduction, literature review, methodology, results, discussion, conclusion and recommendations, references and/or bibliography and appendices.

4   Take care with your writing style. Avoid the extremes of informality, dryness or jargon.

5   Whilst you are writing the report, you have to be self-critical, and read your work with an eye to continually improving its content.

You should obtain, if appropriate, a copy of the marking criteria used by your institution. Carefully, and critically, assess your own performance against the criteria. Identify the areas where you are happy that you fulfil the criteria, and also those areas that you are not sure about. Identify what you see to be the strengths and the weaknesses of the research. Now is the time to look at the weaknesses – are they remediable? If the weaknesses are things such as a lack of literature, poor structure and so on, you should address these and redo the activity. Get a colleague to read your research report. What do they think? Often they will be able to spot things that you will be unable to – once you have read a section more than a few times, it becomes extremely difficult to take in everything you are reading.

CHAPTER FIFTEEN

SPORTS RESEARCH AND THE INTERNET

In this chapter we will:

■ Outline the use of the Internet to locate and access sources of relevance for sports-related research.
■ Discuss some of the means by which you can access the sites that you locate.
■ Provide links to some of the important sport-related sites available on the Internet.

INTRODUCTION

The Internet has seen rapid growth in recent years, and the implications of this growth for sports research are enormous. This chapter will outline the potential uses, and dangers, of the Internet as a research resource. The World Wide Web contains a vast amount of information, some useful, most irrelevant. Theobald and Dunsmore (2000) have estimated that in January 2000 there were over 40 million web sites, with further information being added at an astounding rate. One consequence is that much of the information relevant to the sports researcher is hidden away, and difficult to locate. The researcher may waste a great deal of time trying to locate relevant sites, with no guarantee of success. Secondly, the accessibility of the Internet means that anyone with the appropriate technical skills and equipment can publish on it, and therefore there is no guarantee of quality. This chapter will give a brief overview of using the Internet to provide some guidance for the researcher in finding relevant information.

WHAT IS THE INTERNET?

Whilst it is not necessary for you to have a detailed technical knowledge of the Internet, it is useful to have an awareness of what the Internet actually is. Put very simply, the Internet is a network of computer networks. Each network provides (or 'serves') information that can then be accessed by other networks. Thus, the Internet itself does not contain information. Rather, it is a tool to allow the sharing of information held on computer. Everything available on the Internet has its own unique uniform resource locator (URL). When you type in the URL or click onto a link to a URL, you send a request to retrieve that document, or web page, from its source.

SEARCHING THE INTERNET

The Internet essentially consists of a number of 'web pages', accessible through any computer with the appropriate software. You can 'browse' these pages using browsers such as *Netscape Navigator,* or *Internet Explorer.* Each page is accessed using its own unique page 'address', the uniform resource locator (URL). The key to searching the Internet is to be able to locate relevant URLs. This can be done in a number of ways.

Using uniform resource locators

The uniform resource locator is simply an address of a page. If you know the URL for a particular page, then this can be typed straight into the address bar, and the relevant page will be located, for example if you were to type in http://www.christiansinsport.org, then you would access the homepage for that particular organisation. Each web page will have its own unique URL, and this is the easiest way of locating a web page, provided that the URL is known. Often, however, the URL is unknown, or you are simply carrying out a general search for information.

Using search engines

A number of search engines exist. These include:

- Lycos – http://www.lycos.com
- Yahoo – http://www.yahoo.com
- Infoseek – http://www.infoseek.com
- Altavista – http://www.altavista.com

Within the United Kingdom, try:

- Yahoo – http://www.yahoo.co.uk
- Altavista – http://www.altavista.co.uk
- Google – http://www.google.co.uk
- The BBC web site also has a good search facility – http://www.bbc.co.uk

Each search engine will also provide a number of links on its own page, for example http://www.yahoo.com, or http://www.yahoo.uk will provide links to a number of relevant categories, such as sports and recreation, or social sciences. Further subcategories are given when clicking the appropriate links, ranging from the Olympic games to sport trivia. Most often, however, you will have to 'search' for web sites yourself.

Search engines use 'keywords' to locate web pages of interest. This is often more difficult to do than anticipated; for example if you are interested in the economics of sport, then the two logical keywords to use would be 'sport' and 'economics'. This would give over 68,000 matches on www.yahoo.co.uk alone, ranging from the highly relevant to those of no use whatsoever. You will obviously not have the time or resources to locate the relevant sites from this result.

You can also use what is referred to as Boolean searching to focus your search. This allows you to combine terms using the words AND, OR and NOT. By using sport AND economics as the search term, the search will be made for pages containing both words. Sport OR economics will search for pages containing either word, and sport NOT economics will search for pages containing sport, but excluding those also containing economics. You may also be able to use quotation marks to search for specific phrases, for example searching for 'the economics of sport'. This will search for pages containing that specific phrase, and it can be the most effective type of search, although there is a risk of missing out pages. It is advisable to search using a number of similar phrases, for example 'the economics of sport', and 'sport and economics' and so on to maximise the search. You should also use alternative spellings whenever they exist, for example searching only for information on 'socialisation into sport' will miss out on a number of potentially useful pages that contain the alternative spelling of 'socialization'. It goes without saying that you should ensure that your spelling is correct whatever search method you use!

There are a number of problems with search engines. As well as providing large numbers of irrelevant web pages, they can often be out of date, and may not identify recent additions to the web. A final point to note is that some web sites are incorrectly classified, and may not be picked up by search engines.

Hyperlinks

Many web pages will contain links to other pages, generally highlighted in a different colour from the rest of the text. These hyperlinks are an effective way of locating a large number of additional web sites without the need to search the web. For example, if you were to access the homepage of the International Olympic Committee (http://olympic.org) you would find a number of links to related web sites, such as a link to the homepage of the World Anti Doping Agency (http://wada-ama.org). Using this method, you can often identify a large number of relevant web pages in a relatively short period of time.

ASSESSING WEB SITES

Once you have located a web site, then it needs to be assessed in terms of its quality and usefulness. Any individual with the correct equipment can put a web page on the Internet, and being available on the Internet is no guarantee of accuracy or quality. Therefore it is your responsibility to assess each site. There is no foolproof way of doing this; however, there are a number of questions that should be asked:

■ Who produced the page? Was it:

– An academic institution or publisher?
– An official company or organisational web page?
– A personal web page?

■ What are their qualifications for producing such material?
■ What was their purpose in producing the page?

- Who was their intended audience?
- Has the content undergone any form of refereeing process?
- When was the page last updated?

As with more traditional sources, there are certain types of source that can be considered more reliable than others. Fully refereed online academic journals are often of equal quality to printed journals, and may often be more up to date (articles in printed journals may take up to two years to be published from their initial submission!).

INTERNET RESOURCES

There are a number of useful resources available for the sports researcher. The Internet is constantly being updated, so this is not an exhaustive list, and some of the sites may not always be operational. Some sites will require a personal *Athens* account to be set up – if you are in a higher education institution, your librarian should be able to do this for you. Remember, these are just examples of some of the resources available to you – you will need to undertake a much more detailed search of the Internet when it comes to undertaking your own research project.

Sport resources

- *Sport Discus* (http://biomed.niss.ac.uk/ovidweb/ovidweb.cgi). Sport Discus is an excellent research resource. As well as normally being available on CD-ROM via your library, Sport Discus is also available online, and will be one of your most important resources in locating appropriate literature.
- *Scholarly Sport Sites* (http://ucalgary.ca/library/ssportsite). This is a gateway containing links to a wide range of sport-related sites, including national bodies, research archives and various sport archives.
- *The Scholarly Journal Archive* (http://uk.jstor.org). This site provides access to a range of sport-related articles from peer-reviewed sources. An *Athens* account is required for access.
- *The Amateur Athletic Foundation of Los Angeles* (http://www.aafla.org/index.html). This is a very comprehensive site, focusing largely on the Olympics, but containing a wealth of information.
- *British Society for Sports History* (http://www.umist.ac.uk/sport/index2.html). This should be a starting point for anyone interested in researching sport

history. This site includes links to data archives, conferences, sport history societies and publishers.

- *Sportszine* (http://www.sportszine.co.uk). This site provides up to date information on a number of contemporary issues in sport. The site is not 'academic' in nature, and caution should be adopted.
- *The Centre for Research into Sport and Society* (http://www.le.ac.uk/crss). Based at the University of Leicester, this site provides a number of useful resources, including various publications from the centre, and links to other sites of interest.
- *The Virtual Library of Sport* (http://sportsvl.com). This page provides a wide range of links to various sport-related sites. The sites are variable in terms of their quality, but there are a number of useful resources here.
- *Yahoo! Sport categories* (http://uk.dir.yahoo.com/Recreation/Sport). The content of this site is similar in tone to that of the Virtual Library of Sport. Again, the quality is variable, but a number of useful links are provided.

Selected academic journals

- Cyber Journal of Sport Marketing – http://pandora.nla.gov.au/nla/pandora/cjsm.html (although no longer published, back issues of the journal are available at this site)
- International Review for the Sociology of Sport – http://www.nesli.ac.uk/
- Journal of Sport and Social Issues – http://www.nesli.ac.uk/
- Journal of Sport Management – http://www.humankinetics.com/products/journals/
- Sociology of Sport Journal – http://www.humankinetics.com/
- Sociology of Sport Online – http://www.brunel.ac.uk/depts/sps/sosol/sosol.htm
- The International Journal of the History of Sport – http://www.frankcass.com/jnls

Selected sport organisations

- Australian Institute of Sport – http://www.ais.org.au
- Australian Sports Commission – http://www.ausport.gov.au
- British Olympic Association – http://www.olympics.org.uk
- Department of Culture, Media and Sport – http://www.culture.gov.uk/sport/default.htm
- FIFA – http://fifa.com

253

- Football Association – http://www.the-fa.org
- Institute of Sport and Recreation Management – http://www.isrm.co.uk
- International Olympic Committee – http://www.olympic.org
- International Paralympic Committee – http://www.paralympic.org
- International Sport Sciences Organisation – http://issaonline.com
- Sport Canada – http://www.pch.gc.ca/sportcanada
- Sport England – http://www.sportengland.gov
- UEFA – http://www.uefa.com/uefa
- UK Athletics – http://www.ukathletics.net
- UK Sport – http://www.uksport.gov.uk
- United States Olympic Committee – http://www.olympic-usa.org/

A FINAL WORD ON THE INTERNET

The Internet is a useful resource for the sports researcher. It is, however, still in its infancy. Most of the literature on sport is not available on the web, and that which is may be difficult to locate. The Internet alone will not provide you with enough material to carry out a successful piece of research, and you will still need to undertake a literature search using the more 'traditional' sources, such as CD-ROMs and library catalogues, that were outlined in Chapter 5. The Internet is to be used to complement, rather than replace such sources. Some of the best sources of information are not yet on the Internet, and if you rely on the Internet for sources of information, you are almost certainly going to have an incomplete piece of research. We are not, however, suggesting that you avoid the Internet. There is a wealth of information available, and you may find vast quantities of relevant information. The key is to be open minded in your searches – what may be appropriate for one research project may not for another.

SUMMARY

1   The Internet is a large, rapidly expanding tool for the sports researcher. Because of its size and organisation (or lack of!) it can be both a good and bad research resource.

2   Because of its nature, finding pages can be difficult. If you are aware of the URL, then this simplifies finding the site. Otherwise, you are generally required to use keywords and a 'search engine' to locate sites. This can be a haphazard process, and there is no guarantee that you will locate the appropriate site.

3   Sites on the Internet are not – with few exceptions – subject to any form of reviewing process. Thus there is no guarantee of quality, and it will be your role to assess each site.

4   There are a number of sport-related resources on the Internet, and you should be prepared to use these resources when appropriate.

ACTIVITIES

Undertake a search for sport-related sources in areas of interest to you. Locate several sources, and assess the quality of each using the criteria we outlined earlier in the chapter. Using your assessment, decide whether any of the sites provides material that would be useful in an academic research project.

ABOUT YOUR RESEARCH PROJECT

Are you using any Internet sources within your research project? If so, you need to assess the quality of each of the resources using the criteria we outlined earlier in the chapter. Are you happy that they are of appropriate quality? Have you made full use of the Internet, or do you feel that you have over-used the Internet at the expense of other sources?

FURTHER READING

Theobald, W. and Dunsmore, H. (2000) *Internet Resources for Leisure and Tourism,* Oxford: Butterworth-Heinemann. This text provides a thorough introduction to the use of the Internet, and provides detailed guidance on areas such as searching the Internet, electronic discussion groups, and university and college resources online.

CHAPTER SIXTEEN

STUDENT ISSUES

In this chapter we will:

- Outline the different types of research that you may undertake as a student.
- Describe some of the initial considerations that you should make about your research project.
- Outline some of the issues that you may need to consider when trying to gain collaboration for your research.
- Discuss the role of your tutor or supervisor in your research project.

INTRODUCTION

This chapter is designed for those undertaking research as part of a taught degree, for example a final year dissertation at undergraduate level. If this is the case, then this is probably the first significant piece of research that you will have to do. This chapter will highlight some of the specific issues that you may want to consider before starting your research.

THE TYPES OF STUDENT RESEARCH

Student research takes on a number of forms, each with its own requirements, depending both upon the nature of the course and the institution within which the research is being conducted. This section can only give a broad overview of the issues, and you should ensure that you read your own institution's regulations carefully before you start the research.

Student research can be broadly separated into two forms. First, the research may be the culmination of a period of taught study, generally at undergraduate or masters level. The research produced for the purpose of these degrees is referred to as a *dissertation*. The dissertation gives students the

> opportunity to conduct an in-depth study of a particular topic, synthesising various course elements, yet pursuing one area of interest in depth. The dissertation allows students scope for expression of skills, knowledge and abilities, and offers the chance to develop – in an original and creative way – areas of particular interest. The dissertation also performs the important integrative function of bringing together different elements from the course, testing the ability and discipline of the student in producing a detailed study. (Jones 2002)

Other types of award are based entirely upon the production of a research report – in this instance a *thesis* – and an accompanying defence of the research with two or more examiners who are expert within the field (the *viva voce*). These awards are normally at masters level (MPhil) or doctoral level (PhD or DPhil). The objectives of these programmes are naturally considerably more advanced, with the criteria generally requiring the student to have

> satisfactorily completed a research training programme and to have investigated and evaluated or critically studied an appropriate topic over not less than thirty-three months of full-time study resulting in a significant contribution to knowledge, and has presented a satisfactory thesis. (Jones 2002)

The research project – at whatever level – is an important part of any programme of study as it allows you to both develop and demonstrate a number of key transferable skills. The skills that you could expect to develop and demonstrate as part of a research project are as follows:

- To demonstrate familiarity with the core knowledge base of a particular field of sport-related study.
- To be able to seek, describe and interpret information within a particular field of sport studies.
- To be able to complete an information search using a range of appropriate primary and secondary sources.
- To analyse data, using appropriate techniques.
- To use appropriate IT resources independently.
- To be able to communicate effectively in context.

- To be able to apply given tools/methods accurately and carefully to a well-defined problem and draw appropriate conclusions.
- To produce a complex piece of work which demonstrates a grasp of vocabulary of the subject and deploys a range of skills of written expression appropriate to the subject.
- To be able to decide on action plans and implement them effectively.
- To manage time effectively in order to achieve intended goals.
- To deliver a paper or presentation which succeeds in communicating a series of points effectively.
- To produce creative and realistic solutions to complex problems.

Thus, by undertaking a piece of research, you are likely to show a potential employer that you possess a wide range of desirable skills that you may not develop to the same extent elsewhere during your academic career. Potential employers are likely to look at any research project you have undertaken – especially a dissertation or thesis – much more closely than taught modules, and you should bear this in mind when you commence your research programme.

INITIAL CONSIDERATIONS

Whatever programme of study you are on, you will almost certainly have to present a proposal for your research project at an early stage, either in the form of a written or verbal presentation. It is at this stage that you should highlight any potential problems. You should remember that your research will be restricted in terms of time and resources, and poor planning can lead to difficulties later. At this stage, you may want to consider the criteria in Table 16.1, and assess your intended project against such criteria.

WHAT CHARACTERISES A GOOD PIECE OF STUDENT RESEARCH?

Identifying what makes a piece of research 'good' or 'bad' is an important skill to develop. First, it is important for you to be able to assess the work of others. Second, you will also have to assess your own research. Finally, it is important to know how others will be assessing your work. It is important to know upon what criteria you are to be assessed before you start your research. Although there are some general areas upon which your research will be judged, which we will outline later, there may also be specific requirements of your institution,

258

Table 16.1 Criteria for consideration at the planning stages

Research topic

■ Too broad
■ Unrealistic – will you get the co-operation you need?
■ Not related to your programme of study

Background

■ No theoretical background
■ What particular theories or models are you going to use?
■ Have you defined your concepts?
■ How will you measure these concepts?
■ You need to mention one or two key authors

Research design

■ What design will you use?
■ What type of data will you collect?
■ What methods do you anticipate using?
■ You need to justify your methodology

Sampling

■ Who will be your sample?
■ What is your desired sample size?
■ How will you choose them?
■ Have you got confirmed access to your sample?

General

■ Have you got the collaboration/access you need?
■ Do you have the appropriate skills to carry out such research?

organisation, etc., and you should familiarise yourself with these at the earliest possible stage. Generally speaking, there will be three areas upon which you will be assessed:

1   Your understanding of existing knowledge, the use of existing ideas, and the development of your own research question from relevant literature, based upon logical argument and rational thought.
2   The use of an appropriate methodology to collect valid and reliable data with which to answer that question.
3   The development of sound conclusions based upon your data.

ORIGINALITY AND GENERALISABILITY

There may also be the requirement with certain research projects (for example at masters or doctoral level) to make a 'contribution to human knowledge', through the development of new theories, methods, etc. At undergraduate level, there is not the need to make such a contribution, and the extent of 'originality' required is minimal (although you should aim to make your project 'original' in some way, for example in one of the ways suggested in Chapter 4). It is also a good idea in most cases to ensure that your project has some relevance beyond the setting within which it was carried out. This is generally straightforward provided you ensure that your research is theoretically grounded. Since a theory explains and predicts a particular phenomenon, behaviour, happening and so on, your theory should be able to be applied to other situations. Thus you should not be overly concerned in your research about how your findings would apply to other specific situations. For example, if you were interested in umpiring stress, you should not spend too much time thinking about how your findings would or would not apply to umpiring in other sports. Instead, you are better advised to think about how your findings illustrate, develop or modify a theory. It would then be the task of others (or yourself at a later date) to apply that theory to other situations.

THE RESEARCH TIME SCALE

You also need to consider the time scale for your research. From our experience, students often underestimate the time required to undertake a piece of research, and it is important to be realistic. Take for example the following activities:

- *Locating relevant literature using an online database*. This can be an ongoing, and seemingly endless task. You may need to spend an entire day locating literature on one specific area of the project. You may then have to order this (for example from the British Library) which could mean up to a fortnight before you even get a look at the key literature.
- *Reading a single journal article*. To read such an article could take you anything from an hour upwards, especially at the beginning of the research, when you are still developing your own understanding of the subject, where you may find yourself struggling with an article for three hours or more.
- *Designing an initial questionnaire/interview schedule*. A good questionnaire or interview will take a substantial period of time to develop, even once you have developed an understanding of the concepts that you are researching.

- *Piloting an initial questionnaire.* This may take several weeks – remember that it is up to your respondents to get the questionnaire back to you, which they may need to be reminded of several times!
- *Undertaking a postal survey.* Even using a pre-designed questionnaire, you will need to post the questionnaires to your sample (several days). They will then need to complete the questionnaires (up to two weeks for those who remember) and return them to you (several more days). You will then have to repeat the process for those who didn't return the questionnaires in the first round (another two to three weeks).
- *Writing up an interview.* Even if you are a good typist, you should allow yourself about five hours to transcribe a one-hour interview, often more, especially if the recording is not clear, or if there is background noise.
- *Entering the results from one hundred questionnaires onto a statistical analysis package.* Obviously this is dependent upon the length and complexity of the questionnaire, but you may need to allow yourself several days to do this.

These are just some of the activities you may find yourself undertaking as part of a research project. You need to timetable as many of the activities that you think you will be undertaking as possible, and ensure that your objectives are feasible within the time available to you.

GAINING COLLABORATION AND ACCESS

Developing a focused, feasible research proposal is, unfortunately, only part of the story. As part of your research, it is very likely that you will have to negotiate access to a sports-related body, whether it be a sports team, a school, sports organisation, local authority and so on. Securing good relations at an early stage can be extremely beneficial to you, and can make the whole research process seem a lot easier, so it is worth considering three questions:

1   What organisation/school/team, etc. do I need to gain access to?
2   How likely are they to provide access?
3   What is the best way to gain access?

The issue of access is important, and one that you should think about sooner, rather than later (it is no good completing your literature review, designing your questionnaire and so on, only to find out that you have no way of accessing your intended sample!). The two pieces of advice we can give are:

1 *Be realistic.* You may think that professional sports teams would be only too willing to distribute your questionnaires amongst their players and/or supporters. In reality, professional teams, governing bodies, etc. are often inundated with requests from students (often with requests such as 'please could you suggest an area for my dissertation'!) and your chances of a positive response are minimal in most cases. If you do require assistance, then consider regional or local – rather than national – bodies. They are much more likely to be interested in your research, and may be more willing to provide assistance.

2 *Try to gain the co-operation of whichever body you choose at the earliest appropriate stage.* This does not mean that you should approach them as soon as you have a rough idea of your research question. They are much more likely to be impressed if you can provide the following information:

   ■ What is the rationale behind the research? Why is it important?
   ■ What is the expertise of the researcher to undertake such a research project?
   ■ What are the benefits for the particular body if they provide you access?
   ■ What is the anticipated methodology? What data would you need to collect, and from whom?
   ■ What is the time scale of the research?
   ■ Will the organisation have the opportunity to view the research report before it is submitted?
   ■ Will a copy be available to them after the research is completed?
   ■ How will confidentiality be ensured if the research involves sensitive information?

The first step is generally to telephone the organisation to identify the appropriate person to contact. If you are using a personal acquaintance (for example you may know someone who works for a particular organisation), then you should also find out whether they are the best person to deal with, or if there is someone else in the organisation that you should be in contact with. (There is no harm at this stage in approaching several different organisations to maximise your chances of access. Do ensure that if you receive an offer of help that you have to decline, then you should respond in writing explaining your reasons and thanking them for the offer.)

Your next stage, even if verbal agreement has been given, is to write to the appropriate individual within the organisation. Include the information about the project mentioned above. Put as much detail as you can into this letter.

Following this, you should wait until you receive a response in writing before assuming that co-operation is assured! Finally, you should confirm your acceptance in writing, and make arrangements for the next stage, which will often be a face to face meeting with the organisation.

THE ROLE OF YOUR TUTOR

So far, it may seem the case that you are on your own, that coming up with a suitable proposal is your task, and that you are left to sink or swim. Thankfully this is not normally the case! Normally you will be allocated a tutor (also referred to as a supervisor) who will provide guidance throughout the research. The student–tutor relationship can be crucial to the success of the project in many cases. It is important to strike the right balance – a final year dissertation, for example, is designed to test the student's ability to carry out a piece of in-depth research independently, yet you are not expected to undertake the task without any help or assistance at all. Different institutions have differing guidelines. The following is a list of frequently asked questions regarding the student–tutor relationship taken from the dissertation guidelines of the university of one of the authors (Jones 2002).

Frequently asked questions on dissertation tutors and their role

Q. What will my tutor do?

A. Your tutor will help you complete the research by providing guidance on key areas of the research. Your tutor will tell you if you are on the right track, or if anything is wrong. It is not the tutor's role, however, to give you a topic to research, to suggest the detailed methodology, to interpret the results for you, or to keep in contact with you.

Q. How often should I see my tutor?

A. It is up to you and your tutor. Past experience has shown that no or minimal contact correlates with failed work. You should be aiming to see your tutor at least once every two weeks, sometimes more regularly, especially during key stages of the research. If there is a problem then you must make alternative arrangements with your tutor. You should always have an agenda for your meeting – do not turn up without a clear idea of what you want to discuss.

Q. What sort of things will I discuss with my tutor?

A. The function of meetings will differ depending upon the stage that you are at. Once you have decided upon your research question, it is often a good idea to produce written work on a regular basis, which can form the focus of the meeting. Do not expect the meeting to consist of your tutor giving you advice, or telling you what to do. It is up to you to discuss and debate your project with them, and to lead the meetings. You must have an objective for each meeting with your tutor. You should discuss progress and attempt to resolve any issues that might detract from your ability to work towards maximum performance. Examples of these issues are:

- Recommendation of suitable references.
- Amendment of project objectives.
- Advice on carrying out research.
- Advice on suitability of research instruments, e.g. questionnaire/interview schedule.
- Advice on planning/scheduling your work, setting deadlines.
- Debate about theoretical issues.
- Making personal contacts.

Q. Can I bring in work for my tutor to check on the day of my appointment, or should I hand it in prior to the meeting?

A. Usually you will have a relatively short time allocated to you, thus you should not expect your tutor to give you feedback on the spot. Often it is a good idea to give work to your tutor in plenty of time. To do this, you will need to be well prepared!

Q. Is the tutor responsible for getting me to complete the research?

A. No. Whilst the tutor acts as adviser and facilitator, the onus is clearly on you: to be responsible for your own progress; to keep in contact with your tutor; and to come to an agreement on frequency of attendance. Ideally, you should see your tutor at regular intervals. Whilst it is difficult to come up with an optimum amount of contact, as suggested before, past experience has shown that no or minimal contact correlates with failed project work. Equally, the tutor does not expect you to be camped on her or his doorstep, nor to do the work for you!

Q. *The skills being tested as part of the project include communication skills. Will my tutor check my spelling and grammar in my draft?*

A. No. They will not have time to check for grammatical errors. It is up to you to have this done, through the use of spelling/grammar checkers in your word processing package, and through using someone who is skilled in the use of English. You should not rely on spellcheckers, as they will not always pick out incorrect usage of words, e.g. there/their.

Q. *Will my tutor mark individual chapters for me before I hand in the final submission?*

A. No. Whilst tutors are prepared to look at drafts, or rough sections of your work, do not expect any pre-marking. You should also be aware that even if you have completed a number of individual chapters each of a good standard, that is no guarantee of a good grade. It is how the chapters link together as a holistic piece of work that is important. Thus, you may have a detailed and well-written methodology chapter, but if your chosen methodology is not appropriate to the research objectives developed from your review of literature, then the worth of the chapter is significantly reduced. Remember that all work that you hand to your tutor should be word processed.

Q. *Will my tutor tell me what to do if I have a problem with my project?*

A. Your tutor will help you solve the problem, but do not expect them to solve the problem for you. Problem solving is part of your work. Your tutor may suggest materials to read, refer you to someone else who may be able to give advice, or give you some ideas on how to solve the problem.

You should, whatever happens, make the most of your tutor – remember, they are there to help you! Conflict can, and does, happen however between tutor and student, often as a result of differing expectations. Phillips and Pugh (1994) provide a useful list that is informative for both students and tutors. They suggest that tutors expect students to:

- Be more independent than the student expects.
- Produce regular written work.
- Seek help from others, not just the tutor.
- Organise and attend meetings regularly at their own initiative.
- Follow advice given in those meetings.
- Report progress honestly.
- Be enthusiastic!

For their part, students expect their tutors to:

- Actively supervise them.
- Have a good knowledge of the subject area.
- Be friendly, open and supportive.
- Read and understand written work provided by the student.
- Be constructive in their criticisms.
- Recommend appropriate reading.

Thus the student–tutor relationship is clearly a two-way process, and you should approach it as such. However, you need to remember that overall responsibility for the completion of the research project lies with the student!

COMMON FAULTS IN STUDENT RESEARCH

It is a good idea at this stage to alert you to some of the most common faults that are found in research projects, so that you may be aware of them before you commence, rather than reading about them when your research is almost complete! Although by no means an exhaustive list, these are the sorts of issues that you should consider, and hopefully avoid!

- *Time management.* Often the time required to complete a piece of research is underestimated. Although the written research report may often be relatively short, the time required for the entire research process is disproportionate. It is simply not possible to leave a research project until the last minute and complete it successfully.
- *The research question is too broad.* If the topic is too broad, then it is difficult to cover it in sufficient depth. You must be focused, and be realistic in terms of what you can achieve. Often students are concerned that a focused question is unlikely to be able to provide them with the ten thousand or so words required by their institution. In reality, this is rarely a problem!
- *The research is too descriptive.* Often there is insufficient theoretical content to allow you to analyse and explain your findings. What theories are you using to inform your research? If you are unsure, then it is likely that your research will be descriptive rather than analytical.
- *Not acknowledging the research process.* There should be clear links between each section, and the research should follow a logical process, as highlighted in Chapter 3. The final written report should not read as a collection of unrelated chapters, but as an integrated piece of work.

student issues

- *Coming to conclusions that are not based upon the evidence.* Remember that research adds to knowledge through considering evidence gathered with the purpose of answering your research question.
- *Limited sources.* Good research shows evidence of wider reading. Do not simply use sport-related books as your main source of information. You should also be using texts from your theoretical discipline, e.g. sociology or marketing, and also a wide range of journal articles.
- *Lack of objectivity.* The research can be based too much on personal opinion, anecdotal evidence, and a lack of detachment. Often, the conclusions may not be based upon the evidence that is presented, rather they are selected to highlight a particular opinion of the author.
- *Poor presentation.* This is often a problem with rushed reports! The research report has to be acceptable in terms of spelling, grammar, punctuation, layout and overall appearance. If the report is being undertaken for a particular body or institution, ensure that you have adhered to its particular requirements, e.g. word limits, referencing format and so on.

SUMMARY

1   You can undertake research as a student for a number of purposes. A research project may be carried out to complete your study at undergraduate level and for most masters degrees. Alternatively, the research may form the basis of the entire degree, such as for some masters and most doctoral degrees.

2   As a student, there are a number of key issues that you must consider about your research. Is it feasible given your time scale? Do you have the necessary resources to complete the research?

3   One key issue is that of gaining collaboration. This is an important task, and must be carried out carefully and thoughtfully. You need to be realistic in terms of your chosen partners.

4   Use your tutor or supervisor appropriately. They are not there to do the research for you – but they can ensure that you are on the right track and give useful advice.

Once you have been allocated your tutor or supervisor, you should ensure that you clarify each other's expectations at an early stage. What do you want from your tutor? What does your tutor expect from you? Doing this at an early stage can help prevent misunderstandings later on! If possible, write down each other's expectations for reference throughout the project.

FURTHER READING

Phillips, E. and Pugh, D. (1994). *How to get a PhD*, Buckinghamshire: Open University Press. Although aimed at PhD students, there is a lot of valuable information of use to the undergraduate researcher, especially at the beginning of a research project.

GLOSSARY

The following is a brief, and not exhaustive, glossary of some of the key terms used in the text.

Analysis of Variance (ANOVA) A statistical procedure to determine whether mean scores obtained from two or more groups are statistically different.

Annotated bibliography An annotated bibliography is an organised list of sources, each of which is followed by a brief note or 'annotation'.

Bias The misrepresentation of facts through distortion in their measurement.

Case One particular instance or unit of the phenomenon under investigation.

Causality The concept whereby one event brings about another event, that is that X causes Y.

Census Data collection from an entire population, as opposed to a sample.

Chi-squared test A non-parametric statistical procedure used to measure differences between groups.

Confirmation bias Data that confirms the researcher's hypothesis is selectively used at the expense of data that refutes it, thus providing false support for the hypothesis.

Content analysis The collection of information from communications such as newspapers, films and so on.

Convenience sample A sample that is chosen because it is easy or available to access.

Correlation A measure of the direction and magnitude of the relationship between two variables.

Dependent variable The variable that is affected by another variable (the independent variable); for example level of performance may be a dependent variable.

Descriptive research Research that measures the characteristics of a sample, with no reference to issues of causality.

Descriptive statistics   Statistical techniques for the organisation and display of data.

Determinism   Associated with the positivist paradigm, determinism suggests that all events have a cause, and the link between cause and effect can be identified through research.

Emic perspective   Taking the perspective of the research participants, rather than the researcher.

Empirical evidence   Evidence based on data.

Epistemology   The branch of philosophy that deals with the nature of knowledge, and how such knowledge is acquired.

Ethnography   The study of a group or culture through immersion within the group, often using a variety of methods and a flexible and extended approach to data collection.

Etic perspective   Taking the perspective of the researcher, rather than the sample under investigation.

Experimental method   A research design whereby the researcher assigns subjects randomly to groups. The independent variable is manipulated while other variables are controlled, allowing the effect of the independent variable to be assessed.

External reliability   The degree to which a measure is constant over time.

Extraneous variable   see *Moderating variable*.

Focus group   An interview involving several participants who are free to interact with each other as well as the researcher.

Grounded theory   A methodological approach whereby theory is developed directly from data collection.

Hypertext   Words or points in an Internet document providing links with other related documents.

Hypothesis   The predicted, testable relationship between two variables, for example X will cause Y.

Independent variable   The variable that affects the dependent variable; for example experience may be an independent variable if it affects levels of self-efficacy.

Informed consent   The procedure whereby the researcher is ethically required to inform subjects as to the nature of the research, the data to be collected, and the outcomes of the data collection as far as is possible.

Internal reliability   The extent to which all the elements of a measure are measuring the same construct.

Interview schedule   The guidelines for the researcher conducting an interview, indicating which questions are to be asked and in which order.

Laboratory research   Research where the external environment is controlled.

Likert scale   A scale that asks respondents to indicate the extent to which they agree or disagree with a given statement.

Longitudinal research   A research design involving the measurement of the same variables with the same sample group over an extended period of time.

Methodology   The overall framework within which the research is conducted.

Methods   The tools used to collect data, such as a questionnaire survey.

Moderating variable   A variable that affects the relationship between the independent and dependent variables.

Multiple regression   A statistical procedure to determine the extent of the relationship between two or more independent variables and a dependent variable.

Narrative analysis   The analysis of secondary data in the form of narratives such as anecdotes, stories, etc.

Non-parametric test   A statistical test which makes no assumptions about the normal distribution of data.

Null hypothesis   A prediction that there will be no relationship between two groups.

Objective tests   Tests that provide the participant with the possible responses for each item.

Operationalisation   Determining how a variable is to be measured.

Outlier   A score that differs considerably from the other scores of the sample.

Parametric test   A statistical test that makes assumptions regarding the normal distribution of data.

Parsimony   The view that phenomena should be explained in the simplest and most economic manner, avoiding undue complexity, generally associated with the positivist paradigm.

Pilot study   A small scale, preliminary procedure to test the methods to be used in the main research study.

Population   All of the potential subjects for a study, from which a sample is drawn.

Positivism   The doctrine that reality is unbiased, measurable, and follows the laws of the natural sciences.

Qualitative research   Research that assumes that reality is subjective, and uncovers these subjective meanings, experiences and attitudes through words and rich description, rather than measurement and statistical analysis.

Quantitative research   Research that describes and explains using the measurement and statistical analysis of observable behaviour.

Questionnaire   A series of questions in a standardised format.

Random sample   A sample that has been chosen by a method whereby all members of the population had an equal chance of selection.

Reactivity The effect on participants caused by their awareness that they are being studied.

Reductionism The belief that human behaviour can be reduced to component parts, each of which can be explained, then put back together to understand the working of the whole.

Reflexivity The act of the researcher focusing upon their role in the social world of the participants, and how they affect that world.

Reliability The extent to which findings would be similar if the research were to be repeated, with all other things equal.

Research design The overall blueprint that guides the researcher in the data collection stages in terms of what data to collect, from whom, and when.

Sample A selected set of units or cases drawn from the population under investigation.

Sampling error The extent to which a measurement from the sample differs from the same measurement if taken from the entire population.

Sampling frame The 'list' of the population from which the sample is drawn.

Semantic differential A question format that asks respondents to rate their place on a scale between two bipolar adjectives, for example happy/sad.

Semi-structured interview An interview following a series of predetermined questions, but with the option of developing additional questions during the interview depending upon the responses given.

Significance A statement of the level at which the researcher is prepared to accept that their findings are representative of the population.

Snowballing A sampling method whereby the initial sample is asked to recommend further participants, who are then asked to recommend further participants themselves and so on, until the desired sample size is reached.

SPSS for Windows – Statistical Package for the Social Sciences A software package for the manipulation, analysis and presentation of data.

Standard deviation The extent to which the range of scores obtained deviates from the mean of the scores.

Standardisation Having a consistent procedure for the administration of data collection methods and analysis of the data.

Structured interview An interview with a set of standardised questions.

Subjective test A test where the participants respond to each item in their own words.

T-test A statistical test to determine whether two sample mean scores come from different populations.

Theory A set of concepts that explain and predict a phenomenon.

Time series design A research design where data is collected from a single sample at several instances, with the treatment being administered in one of the intervals between measurement.

Triangulation   The use of multiple methods, sources of data, theories or researchers to enhance the validity of research.

Type I error   Rejecting the null hypothesis when it is true, that is finding a significant relationship where, in reality, none exists.

Type II error   Accepting the null hypothesis when it is false, that is not finding a significant relationship where one does exist.

Unstructured interview   A form of interview where the researcher does not use a predetermined schedule, but develops the interview as it progresses depending upon the responses given.

Validity   The extent to which measurements actually reflect the phenomena being studied.

Variable   A construct that can be measured.

BIBLIOGRAPHY

Albert, E. (1999) 'Dealing with Danger', *International Review for the Sociology of Sport* 34 (2), 157–71.

Atkinson, P. and Hammersley, M. (1994) 'Ethnography and Participant Observation', in Denzin, N. and Lincoln, Y. (eds) *Handbook of Qualitative Research*, London: Sage, pp. 248–61.

Baker, T. (1994) *Doing Social Research*, New York: McGraw-Hill.

Bandura, A. (1977) *Social Learning Theory*, Englewood Cliffs, NJ: Prentice-Hall.

Biddle, S., Markland, D., Gilbourne, D., Chatzisarantis, N. and Sparkes, A. (2001) 'Research Methods in Sport and Exercise Psychology: Quantitative and Qualitative Issues', *Journal of Sport Sciences* 19, 777–809.

Birrell, S. and Loy, J. (1979) 'Media Sport: Hot and Cool', *International Review of Sport Sociology* 14, 5–19.

Bloor, M. (1997) 'Techniques of Validation in Qualitative Research: A Critical Commentary', in Miller, G. and Dingwall, R. (eds) *Context and Method in Qualitative Research,* London: Sage, pp. 37–50.

Brackenridge, C. (1999) 'Managing Myself', *International Review for the Sociology of Sport* 34 (4), 399–410.

Bray, S., Martin, K. and Widemeyer, W. (2000) 'The Relationship Between Evaluative Concerns and Sport Competition State Anxiety Among Youth Skiers', *Journal of Sport Sciences* 18, 353–61.

Brewer, J. (2000) *Ethnography*, Buckingham: Open University Press.

Carey, D., Smith, G., Smith, D., Shepherd, J., Skriver, J., Ord, L. and Rutland, A. (2001) 'Footedness in World Soccer: An Analysis of France '98', *Journal of Sport Sciences* 19, 855–64.

Chelladurai, P. (1990) 'Leadership in Sports: A Review', *International Journal of Sport Psychology* 21, 328–54.

Chelladurai, P. and Saleh, S. (1980) 'Dimensions of Leader Behaviour in Sports: Development of a Leadership Scale', *Journal of Sport Psychology* 2, 34–45.

Cialdini, R., Borden, R., Thorne, A., Walker, M., Freeman, S. and Sloan, L. (1976) 'Basking in Reflected Glory: Three (Football) Field Studies', *Journal of Personality and Social Psychology* 34 (3), 366–75.

Clarke, G. and Humberstone, B. (1997) *Researching Women and Sport*, London: Macmillan.

Clarke, M., Riley, M., Wilkie, E. and Wood, R. (1998) *Researching and Writing Dissertations in Hospitality and Tourism*, London: Thomson Business Press.

Coakley, J. (1998) *Sport in Society: Issues and Controversies*, Boston: McGraw-Hill.

Coakley, J. and Dunning, E. (eds) (2000) *Handbook of Sport Studies*, London: Sage.

Cooper, D. and Schindler, P. (1998) *Business Research Methods* (6th edition), Boston: McGraw-Hill.

Creswell, J. (1994) *Research Design: Qualitative and Quantitative Approaches*, Thousand Oaks: Sage.

Dean, R. and Whyte, W. (1978) 'How do you Know if the Informant is Telling the Truth?' in Bynner, J. and Stribley, K. (eds) *Social Research: Principles and Procedures*, Harlow: Longman, pp. 179–88.

Dennis, P. and Carron, A. (1999) 'Strategic Decisions of Ice Hockey Coaches as a Function of Game Location', *Journal of Sport Sciences* 17, 263–8.

Denzin, N. and Lincoln, Y. (eds) (1994) *Handbook of Qualitative Research*, London: Sage.

De Vaus, D. (2001) *Research Design in Social Research*, London: Sage.

Dey, I. (1993) *Creating Categories: Qualitative Data Analysis*, London: Routledge.

Dingwall, R. (1997) 'Accounts, Interviews and Observations', in Miller, G. and Dingwall, R. (eds) *Context and Method in Qualitative Research*, London: Sage, pp. 51–65.

Donnelly, P. and Young, K. (1988) 'The Construction and Confirmation of Identity in Sport Subcultures', *Sociology of Sport* 5, 223–40.

Eichler, M. (1988) *Nonsexist Research Methods,* London: Routledge.

Elias, N. (1986) 'Introduction' in Elias, N. and Dunning, E. *Quest for Excitement*, Oxford: Basil Blackwell, pp. 19–62.

Finn, M., Elliott-White, M. and Walton, M. (2000) *Tourism and Leisure Research Methods: Data Collection, Analysis and Interpretation*, Harlow: Longman.

Fishwick, L. and Leach, K. (1998) 'Game, Set and Match: Gender Bias in Television Coverage of Wimbledon 1994', in Scraton, S. and Watson, R. (eds) *Sport, Leisure Identities and Gendered Spaces*, Eastbourne: Leisure Studies Association, pp. 31–44.

Fontana, A. and Frey, J. (1998) 'Interviewing: The Art of Science', in Denzin, N. and Lincoln, Y. (eds) *Collecting and Interpreting Qualitative Materials*, Thousand Oaks: Sage, pp. 47–78.

Frankfort-Nachimas, C. and Nachimas, D. (1996) *Research Methods in the Social Sciences* (5th edition), London: Arnold.

Gall, M., Borg, W. and Gall, J. (1996) *Educational Research: An Introduction* (6th edition), White Plains, NY: Longman.

Gallmeier, C. (1988) 'Methodological Issues in Qualitative Sport Research: Participant Observation among Hockey Players', *Sociological Spectrum* 8, 213–35.

Gill, F. and Johnson, P. (1997) *Research Methods for Managers* (2nd edition), London: Paul Chapman.

Giulianotti, R. (1995) 'Participant Observation and Research into Football Hooliganism: Reflections on the Problems of Entrée and Everyday Risks', *Sociology of Sport* 12, 1–20.

Glancy, M. (1986) 'Participant Observation in the Recreation Setting', *Journal of Leisure Research* 18 (2), 59–80.

Grills, S. (1998) 'An Invitation to the Field: Fieldwork and the Pragmatists' Lesson', in Grills, S. (ed.) *Doing Ethnographic Research: Fieldwork Settings,* Thousand Oaks: Sage, pp. 3–18.

Gruneau, R. (1989) 'Making Spectacle: A Case Study in Television Sports Production', in Wenner, L. (ed.) *Media, Sports and Society*, Newbury Park, CA: Sage, pp. 134–54.

Hammersley, M. and Atkinson, P. (1995) *Ethnography: Principles in Practice* (2nd edition), London: Routledge.

Hannabus, S. (1996) 'Research Interviews', *New Library World* 97 (1129), 22–30.

Hardin, B. (1999) 'Expertise in Teaching and Coaching: A Qualitative Study of Physical Educators and Athletic Coaches', *Sociology of Sport Online* (online journal) 2 (1), available at http://physed.otago.ac.nz/sosol/v2i1/v2i1a2.htm.

Henderson, K., Ainsworth, B., Stolarzcyk, L., Hootman, J. and Levin, S. (1999) 'Notes on Linking Qualitative and Quantitative Data: The Cross Cultural Physical Activity Participation Study', *Leisure Sciences* 21, 247–55.

Hoffman, S. (1992) (ed.) *Sport and Religion*, Champaign, Ill: Human Kinetics.

Holmes, R. (1998) *Fieldwork With Children*, Thousand Oaks: Sage.

Holt, N. and Sparkes, A. (2001) 'An Ethnographic Study of Cohesiveness in a College Team Over a Season', *The Sport Psychologist* 15, 237–59.

Holt, R. (1989) *Sport and the British*, Blackwell: Oxford.

Hussey, J. and Hussey, R. (1997) *Business Research*, Basingstoke: Macmillan.

Ingham, A. and Donnelly, P. (1992) 'Whose Knowledge Counts?', in Yiannakis, A. and Greendorfer, S. (eds) *Applied Sociology of Sport*, Champaign, Ill: Human Kinetics, pp. 247–55.

Jankowicz, A. (1995) *Business Research Projects* (2nd edition), London: Chapman-Hall.

—— (2000) *Business Research Projects* (3rd edition), London: Thomson.

Jayaratne, T. (1993) 'Quantitative Methodology and Feminist Research', in Hammersley, M. (ed.) *Social Research: Philosophy, Politics and Practice*, London: Sage, pp. 109–23.

Jones, I. (1997) Mixing Qualitative and Quantitative Methods in Sports Fan Research, *The Qualitative Report* (online serial) 3 (4), available at http://www.nova.edu/ssss/QR/QR3-4/jones.html.

Jones, I. (2002) *Final Year Dissertation Handbook*, Department of Tourism and Leisure, Luton Business School, University of Luton.

Jones, R., Murrell, A. and Jackson, J. (1999) 'Pretty versus Powerful in the Sports Pages', *Journal of Sport and Social Issues* 23 (2), 183–92.

Kellehear, A. (1993) *The Unobtrusive Researcher*, St Leonards: Allen and Unwin.

Krane, V., Anderson, M. and Stean, W. (1997) 'Issues of Qualitative Research Methods and Presentation', *Journal of Sport and Exercise Psychology* 19, 213–18.

Kvale, S. (1996) *Interviews: An Introduction to Qualitative Research Interviewing*, London: Sage.

Lee, R. and Fielding, N. (1996) Qualitative Data Analysis: Representations of Technology: A Comment on Coffey, Holbrook and Atkinson. Sociological Research Online 1 (4), available at http://www.socresonline.org.uk/socresonline/1/4/lf.html.

Leedy, P. (1985) *Practical Research: Planning and Design*, New York: Macmillan.

Leonard, W. (1998) *A Sociological Perspective of Sport* (5th edition), Boston: Allyn and Bacon.

Lincoln, Y. and Guba, E. (1985) *Naturalistic Inquiry*, Newbury Park, CA: Sage.

Lucas, S. (2000) 'Nike's Commercial Solution', *International Review for the Sociology of Sport* 35 (2), 149–64.

MacClancy, J. (1996) 'Nationalism at Play', in MacClancy, J. (ed.) *Sport, Identity and Ethnicity*, Oxford: Berg, pp. 1–19.

Madrigal, R. (1995) 'Cognitive and Affective Determinants of Fan Satisfaction with Sporting Event Attendance', *Journal of Leisure Research* 27 (3), 205–27.

Maguire, J. and Poulton, E. (1999) 'European Identity Politics in Euro 96: Invented Traditions and National Habitus Codes', *International Review for the Sociology of Sport* 34 (1), 17–29.

Malcolm, D., Jones, I. and Waddington, I. (2000) 'The Peoples Game? Football Spectatorship and Demographic Change', *Soccer and Society* 1 (1), 129–43.

Miles, M. and Huberman, A. (1994) *Qualitative Data Analysis,* Thousand Oaks: Sage.

Nau, D. (1995) 'Mixing Methodologies: Can Bimodal Research be a Viable Post-Positivist Tool?', *The Qualitative Report* (online serial) 2 (3), available at http://www.nova.edu/ssss/QR/QR2-3/nau.html.

Neuman, W. (2000) *Social Research Methods: Qualitative and Quantitative Approaches* (4th edition), Boston: Allyn and Bacon.

Nixon, H. and Frey, J. (1996) *A Sociology of Sport*, Belmont: Wadsworth.

Ntoumanis, M. (2001) *A Step-by-Step Guide to SPSS for Sport and Exercise Studies*, London: Routledge.

Oppenheim, A. (1992) *Questionnaire Design, Interviewing and Attitude Measurement*, London: Pinter.

Palmer, C. (2000) 'Spin Doctors and Sportsbrokers: Researching Elites in Contemporary Sport – A Research Note on the Tour de France', *International Review for the Sociology of Sport* 35 (3), 364–77.

Phillips, E. and Pugh, D. (1994) *How to get a PhD*, Buckinghamshire: Open University Press.

Pol, L. and Pak, S. (1994) 'The Use of a Two Stage Survey Design for Gathering Data from People who Attend Sporting Events', *Sport Marketing Quarterly* 3 (3), 9–12.

Reber, A. (1995) *Penguin Dictionary of Psychology*, London: Penguin.

Roberts, J., Jones, R., Harwood, C. and Mitchell, S. (2001) 'Human Perceptions of Sports Equipment Under Playing Conditions', *Journal of Sport Sciences* 19, 485–97.

Rosenthal, R. and Jacobsen, L. (1968) *Pygmalion in the Classroom,* New York: Rinehart and Winston.

Sands, R. (2002) *Sport Ethnography*, Champaign, Ill.: Human Kinetics.

Saunders, M., Lewis, P. and Thornhill, A. (2000) *Research Methods for Business Students* (2nd edition), Harlow: Prentice-Hall.

Scanlan, T., Stein, G. and Ravizza, K. (1991) 'Sources of Stress in Elite Figure Skaters', *Journal of Sport and Exercise Psychology* 13, 103–20.

Seidman, I. (1991). *Interviewing as Qualitative Research*, New York: Teachers College Press.

Smith, A. and Stewart, B. (2001) 'Beyond Number Crunching: Applying Qualitative Techniques in Sport Marketing Research', *The Qualitative Report* (online serial) 6 (2), available at http://www.nova.edu/ssss/QR/QR6-2/Smith.html.

SNCCFR (1996, 1997, 1998, 1999, 2000) *FA Carling Premiership Survey*, Leicester: Sir Norman Chester Centre for Football Research, University of Leicester.

Sparkes, A. (2000) 'Illness, Premature Career-Termination, and the Loss of Self', in Jones, R. and Armour, K. (eds) *Sociology of Sport: Theory and Practice*, Harlow: Longman, pp. 13–28.

Sport England (2002) 'What We Do – Evaluating the Regional Economic Impact of Sport (2002–03)', available at http://www.sportengland.org/whatwedo/research/strategic/evaulating_regional.htm.

Sugden, J. (1996) *Boxing and Society*, Manchester: Manchester University Press.

Sugden, J. and Tomlinson, A. (1999) 'Digging the Dirt and Staying Clean: Retrieving the Investigative Tradition for a Critical Sociology of Sport', *International Review for the Sociology of Sport* 34 (4), 385–97.

Theobald, W. and Dunsmore, H. (2000) *Internet Resources for Leisure and Tourism*, Oxford: Butterworth-Heinemann.

Thomas, J. and Nelson, J. (2001) *Research Methods in Physical Activity* (4th edition), Champaign, Ill.: Human Kinetics.

UK Sport (1999) *Major Events, The Economics: A Guide*, London: UK Sport.

Veal, A. (1997) *Research Methods for Leisure and Tourism* (2nd edition), London: Pitman.

Vincent, W. (1995) *Statistics in Kinesiology*, Champaign, Ill.: Human Kinetics.

Wakefield, K. and Sloan, H. (1995) 'The Effects of Team Loyalty and Selected Stadium Factors on Spectator Attendance', *Journal of Sport Management* 9, 153–72.

Walliman, N. (2001) *Doing your Research Project*, London: Sage.

Wann, D. (1994) 'Biased Evaluations of Highly Identified Sports Spectators: A Response to Hirt and Ryalls (1994)', *Perceptual and Motor Skills* 79, 105–6.

—— (1997) *Sports Psychology*, New Jersey: Prentice-Hall.

—— and Branscombe, N. (1993) 'Sports Fans: Measuring Degree of Identification with their Team', *International Journal of Sports Psychology* 24, 1–17.

Watson, B. and Scraton, S. (2001) 'Confronting Whiteness? Researching the Leisure Lives of South Asian Mothers', *Journal of Gender Studies* 10 (3), 265–75.

West, A., Green, E., Brackenridge, C. and Woodward, D. (2001) 'Leading the Way: Women's Experiences as Sports Coaches', *Women in Management Review* 16 (2), 85–92.

Witz, A. (1990) 'Patriarchy and Professions: The Gendered Politics of Occupational Closure', *Sociology* 24 (4), 675–90.

Worsley, P. (1992) *The New Introducing Sociology*, London: Penguin.

Yiannakis, A. (1992) 'Toward an Applied Sociology of Sport: The Next Generation', in Yiannakis, A. and Greendorfer, S. (eds) *Applied Sociology of Sport*, Champaign, Ill.: Human Kinetics, pp. 3–21.

—— (2000) 'The Relationship of Theory to Application in the Sociology of Sport', in Jones, R. and Armour, K. (eds) *Sociology of Sport: Theory and Practice*, Harlow: Longman, pp. 114–33.

Yin, R. (1994) *Case Study Research: Design and Methods*, London: Sage.

Zajonc, R. (1965) 'Social Facilitation', *Science* 149, 269–74.

JOURNALS PUBLISHING SPORTS-RELATED RESEARCH

The following is a list of journals publishing sports-related articles. The list is not exhaustive, and you should not limit yourself to these journals. We have not included those from a purely sport science perspective. However, we have included science-oriented journals that publish articles from a social studies perspective. You should also investigate more generic journals that publish sports-related research, such as *Sociological Review*, for example.

Adapted Physical Activity Quarterly
Annals of Leisure Research
British Journal of the History of Sport
British Journal of Physical Education
Bulletin of Physical Education
Canadian Journal of the History of Sport
Cyber Journal of Sports Marketing
European Journal of Physical Education
European Journal of Sport Management
European Physical Education Review
European Sports History Review
Football Studies
Health and Fitness
Healthy Lifestyles Journal
International Journal of Sport Psychology
International Review for the Sociology of Sport
Journal of Applied Sport Psychology
Journal of Human Movement Studies
Journal of Leisure Research
Journal of the Philosophy of Sport
Journal of Sport Behavior

Journal of Sport Economics
Journal of Sport and Exercise Psychology
Journal of Sport History
Journal of Sport Management
Journal of Sport and Social Issues
Leisure Sciences
Leisure and Society
Leisure Studies
Managing Leisure
Olympic Review
Play and Culture
Research Quarterly for Exercise and Sport
Soccer and Society
Sociology of Sport Journal
Sociology of Sport Online (Internet-based journal)
Sport, Culture and Society
Sport, Education and Society
Sport and Place
Sport Psychologist
Sporting Traditions
Sports Law Bulletin

INDEX

Note: page numbers in **bold** refer to boxes and figures

283

286